Weird New York

Weird
NEW YORK

Your Travel Guide to New York's Local Legends and Best Kept Secrets

by CHRIS GETHARD
Mark Moran and Mark Sceurman, Executive Editors

WEiRD NEW YORK

STERLING and the distinctive Sterling logo are registered trademarks of Sterling Publishing Co., Inc.

Published by Sterling Publishing Co., Inc.
387 Park Avenue South, New York, NY 10016
© 2005 Mark Moran and Mark Sceurman
Paperback edition published in 2010.
Distributed in Canada by Sterling Publishing
c/o Canadian Manda Group, 165 Dufferin Street
Toronto, Ontario, Canada M6K 3H6
Distributed in the United Kingdom by GMC Distribution Services
Castle Place, 166 High Street, Lewes, East Sussex, England BN7 1XU
Distributed in Australia by Capricorn Link (Australia) Pty. Ltd.
P. O. Box 704, Windsor, NSW 2756, Australia

10 9 8 7 6 5 4 3 2 1

Photography and illustration credits are found on page 271 and constitute an extension of this copyright page.

Sterling ISBN 978-1-4027-3383-3 (hardcover)
            978-1-4027-7840-7 (paperback)

For information about custom editions, special sales, premium and corporate purchases, please contact Sterling Special Sales Department at 800-805-5489 or specialsales@sterlingpublishing.com.

Design: Richard J. Berenson
        Berenson Design & Books, LLC, New York, NY

DEDiCATiON

I'd like to dedicate this book to my brother Gregg, without whom I wouldn't be nearly as weird as I am today. Franny G., you're okay too.
—*Chris Gethard*

CONTENTS

A Note from the Marks

Our weird journey began a long, long time ago in a far-off land called New Jersey. Once a year or so, we'd compile a homespun newsletter called *Weird N.J.*, then pass it on to our friends. The pamphlet was a collection of odd news clippings, bizarre facts, little-known historical anecdotes, and anomalous encounters from our home state. The newsletter also included the kinds of localized legends that were often whispered around a particular town but seldom heard outside the boundaries of the community where they originated.

We had started *Weird N.J.* on the simple theory that every town in the state had at least one good tale to tell. The publication soon became a full-fledged magazine, and we made the decision to actually do our own investigating to see if we could track down where all of these seemingly unbelievable stories were coming from. Was there, we wondered, any factual basis for the fantastic local legends people were telling us about? Armed with not much more than a camera and a notepad, we set off on a mystical journey of discovery. Much to our surprise and amazement, a lot of what we had initially presumed to be nothing more than urban legends turned out to be real—or at least to contain a grain of truth, which had sparked the lore to begin with.

After a dozen years of documenting the bizarre, we were asked to write a book about our adventures, and so *Weird N.J.: Your Travel Guide to New Jersey's Local Legends and Best Kept Secrets* was published in

2003. Soon people from all over the country began writing to us, telling us strange tales from their home state. As it turned out, what we had perceived to be something of very local interest was actually just a small part of a larger and more universal phenomenon.

When our publisher asked us what we wanted to do next, the answer was simple: "We'd like to do a book called *Weird U.S.*, in which we could document the local legends and strangest stories from all over the country," we replied. So for the next twelve months, we set out in search of weirdness wherever it might be found in the fifty states. And indeed, we found plenty of it!

After *Weird U.S.* was published, we came to the conclusion that this country had more great tales than could be contained in just one book. Everywhere we looked, we found unwritten folklore, creepy cemeteries, cursed locations, and outlandish roadside oddities. With this in mind, we told our publisher that we wanted to document it ALL and to do it in a series of books, each focusing on the peculiarities of a particular state.

But what states would we start with? New York seemed one obvious choice. For several years we had been writing about New Jersey's neighbor in our magazine's "Fringe" section. Soon we realized that we were gaining a following in the Empire State. Letters started pouring in from New Yorkers eager to fill us in on all the bizarreness found in their state. We began investigating some of these things for ourselves and jealously wished we could have claimed them as New Jersey's.

When it came time to decide which author we wanted to be our New York eyes and ears, we were fortunate to have a ready cohort. Chris Gethard started working at *Weird N.J.* while he was still a student at Rutgers University and continued on full-time after his graduation. His contributions over the years showed us that Chris had a keenly developed "Weird Eye."

The Weird Eye is what is needed to search out the sort of stories we were looking for. It requires one to see the world in a different way, with a renewed sense of wonder. And once you have it, there is no going back—you'll never see things the same way again. All of a sudden you begin to reexamine your own environs, noticing your everyday surroundings as if for the first time. And you begin to ask yourself questions like, "What the heck is that thing all about, anyway?" and "Doesn't anybody else think that's kind of weird?" These are the kinds of questions that Chris asked every day for the five years or so that he was employed at *Weird N.J.*

Alas, though, if Chris has any drawback it is undoubtedly that he is too talented to be confined to just one creative outlet. In addition to writing for us, he was also acting on television and in improv theater and writing for Comedy Central. He decided to pursue his fortunes in the Big Apple. But happily, he promised that once he'd moved to New York he'd set about discovering all the weirdness the state had to offer and write a book about it.

So come with us now and let Chris take you on a tour of the state that has become his adopted home. With all of its cultural quirks, strange sites, and oddball characters, it is a state of mind we like to call *Weird New York*.

—*Mark Moran and Mark Sceurman*

What is it about human nature that makes us so fascinated by weirdness? Why are we so enthralled by tales of vindictive ghosts, cursed roads, and creatures that lurk in the dead of the night? And what is it that makes us get out there on the highways and byways seeking to experience these terrifying things for ourselves? After all, if these were just good stories, we'd be content simply hearing them, wouldn't we? So to go out there looking for them for ourselves speaks to the idea that on some level, we hope for them to be true. But if we do think that they are true, isn't it dangerous to look for such things?

It is dangerous—and that's exactly why we do it. Because part of the nature of being an American is to know the urge to rush headlong into harm, with no real care to the consequences of our actions. On some level, to be an American is to be an adventurer.

Let's not forget that the very first Europeans to set foot on American soil were setting out into a great unknown. The precedent was established from day one that we as a people would find fulfillment and enjoyment from heading into wild, uncharted places. This trend has continued throughout American history. Much of our collective canon of folklore is based upon this idea—we are taught as youngsters to idolize adventurers, such as those who set out on the western frontier and those who landed on the moon. We are, as a people, obsessed with going to places that are thought of as impossible to reach.

For the average American, this is a hard tradition to uphold. There aren't many places in the world that someone hasn't set foot upon. The majority of us won't ever visit the moon. And the western frontier was proclaimed closed before the turn of the twentieth century. When it was, historian Frederick Jackson Turner talked about its significance to the American psyche and referred to the frontier as "the meeting point between savagery and civilization."

Participating in our shared local legends is an attempt by people today to find their own "meeting point between savagery and civilization." Most aspects of our daily lives are pretty routine. We have jobs, bills to pay, schedules to live by. We buy the same products from the same stores and watch the same shows

Chris Gethard *standing in front of the Ralph Kramden statue at New York's Port Authority*

New York is crammed full of places of intrigue, mystery, and wonder. From the artists putting forth their bizarre visions in densely packed city neighborhoods to remote lone graves in isolated mountainous areas, this state truly has a grasp on what it means to be weird.

When many people think of New York State, they see it as a vast, disconnected place, a handful of metropolitan areas separated by huge expanses of mountainous and rural regions. In a sense, this is certainly true. Yet despite the disconnected nature of many of the regions, there is one thing that binds every corner of the state together. The same quiet sense of majesty can be found no matter where you are in the Empire State. In a way, the endless vineyards of the Finger Lakes region inspire the same sense of awe as Manhattan's skyscrapers. Standing on the shores of the St. Lawrence River to the west is a humbling experience similar to staring at the outline of the Adirondacks from the shores of Lake George in the east of the state. From mountains to lakes, from natural to manmade, there is something impressive and breathtaking around every corner in New York. Another facet of the state shared by all areas is that wherever you go in this great land, you are never far away from something or somebody truly weird.

This book is a compendium of stories that have been told by and to New Yorkers for many years. These stories have survived because they are important to us. They fulfill that desire in all of us to set out there on the roads less traveled to see life for ourselves, no matter how strange that journey may be.

—Chris Gethard

with the same commercials telling us which of those products to buy. This style of living is comfortable, but it takes away our ability to find our way, to be those explorers landing on unknown shores, to round up our own wagons at the pass.

So instead of setting outward, we have chosen to set out inward. We look for adventures in our own lives. We seek out the unknowns that lie in our own backyards. We manage to find hidden frontiers in our cities, our suburbs, down our country roads. Even (or especially) if it means facing dangerous moments, we look for situations that are uncontrolled to remind us that the world is still thriving and unpredictable, even if our daily routines convince us otherwise.

Local Legends and Lore

"Legends die hard. They survive as truth rarely does." —Helen Hayes, Actress

New York has many faces. In some places, the Empire State is citified and bustling. In others, it's as natural and pristine as it was centuries ago. It would seem that there isn't much to bond people from such different landscapes together. But all New Yorkers have at least one thing in common. No matter where they go in this vast, expansive state, they will come across incredible tales that have somehow sprung up and taken root in our collective imaginations.

We are a society where even the news, supposedly a true account of our daily lives, is increasingly prepackaged info-tainment. Our local legends, on the other hand, are often violent, horrific, and tap into our most primal fears and darkest desires. You won't find the *Legend of Sleepy Hollow* in these pages. Instead, we will explore some of the lesser known locations that inspire our modern mythology today. These are sites that, for one reason or another, possess the rare power to strike fear and dread in the hearts of those who dare venture to them—even in our increasingly jaded times. These stories come from our pasts and will extend in some form or another far into our futures. To know them is to realize that there is more to our land than the thin stuff we find in our newspapers and on TV.

Devil's Hole

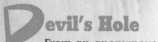

From an anonymous correspondent comes this tidbit:

Once considered the Honeymoon Capital of the World, Niagara Falls is more than just motels filled with starry-eyed newlyweds. It is also the site of the infamous Devil's Hole. Just beneath the famous hauntings of Clet Castle, a long, crumbling stairwell leads those who dare down to the Devil's Hole.

Littered with graffiti, the Devil's Hole—a cave carved into the side of the rocky cliff—is a popular teenage party spot. The cave is several yards long and wide, and has a unique design caused by water action from the nearby falls. The Seneca Indians referred to it as the Cave of the Evil Spirit and thought it to be the entryway into hell. Supposedly, bad luck followed any who visited the dark, dank orifice. It is well known to locals as being cursed or haunted, and it has a host of unhappy incidents that justify its reputation.

In early 1763, in the Bloody Run incident, a convoy of British soldiers was ambushed by the Seneca Indians. After being scalped, the bodies of the soldiers were thrown off the cliff into the ravine below the cave. The only survivor was a young boy who fell from an overturned wagon and hid in a patch of bushes.

Hours before his assassination in Buffalo, President McKinley visited the cave as part of a tour of Niagara Falls.

And lastly, because of the ravine, bodies from the Niagara River often wash ashore right beneath the cave.

The Lady of Lake Ronkonkoma

Lake Ronkonkoma is Long Island's largest freshwater lake and a popular summer destination. But any man who goes there had better beware. This body of water is said to be the home of a vengeful spirit that claims one male life per year.

Supposedly, Ronkonkoma was the name of an Indian princess who fell in love with a white settler who lived near the lake. Of course, their union was forbidden by her father, who didn't want his daughter fooling around with any treacherous European. Every night the couple would sneak out to send messages of love to each other. Ronkonkoma would paddle her canoe out to the middle of the lake, where she would then float a message the rest of the way to her lover, who was waiting on the opposite shore. This continued for years until one day the princess was no longer able to deal with this arrangement and snapped. She wrote a final farewell note to her lover and floated it out onto the lake. He received it on the shore, and minutes later her canoe washed up in front of him as well. Inside it was the princess's body. She had committed suicide in the middle of the lake. Crazed with grief, her lover also took his life.

Since that day, Ronkonkoma has haunted these waters, becoming known to many as the Lady of the Lake. It has been said that she now drags one man into the lake each year, angered because she was not allowed the fullness of her love in life. Many others have reported being drawn by some unseen force out to the center of the lake, as if something was trying to drag them under. These souls have been able to resist the pull of the Lady of the Lake and have lived to report the existence of this strange phenomenon.

Another myth of Lake Ronkonkoma is that it is bottomless and its depths are dotted with caverns and subterranean passageways. Many of the bodies lost to

Ronkonkoma never surface on the lake's shores, but are sucked into these underground tunnels and later turn up in Long Island Sound, on the shores of the East River, and even as far away as Connecticut. In some cases, bodies have disappeared for as long as three months before being discovered miles away from the spot where the unfortunate victim vanished.

Lake Ronkonkoma is a site of anguish, lost love, and vengeance. Be mindful while walking its shores. The Lady of the Lake is forever looking for a new lover to keep her company.

Castle of the White Lady

In the small town of Irondequoit, outside Rochester, is Durand-Eastman Park. It's a verdant place, frequented by many hikers and nature enthusiasts who spend their days exploring its vast area. But there are others who travel to this park for very different reasons. They come from far and wide to make their way to the crumbling remains of a structure that sits near Lake Ontario along Lake Shore Boulevard, the mysterious White Lady's Castle.

Before this area became Durand-Eastman Park, it was the home of a reclusive woman and her teenage daughter. The daughter was very beautiful and was pursued by many young male suitors. Her protective mother, however, insisted that she ignore the seductive charms of these boys and spend her time at home on their isolated estate. These boys had nothing but unsavory intentions, her mother warned. Her daughter was respectful of her mother's wishes, but still secretly longed for the company of a young man.

One night the young woman left their home to take a walk down to the shores of the lake. Her mother waited up all night for her, but her daughter never returned. The mother convinced herself that her daughter had met a young man and must have run off with him. But some people think that the young woman was far too devoted to her mother to have run away, and they believe the girl was murdered that evening.

As time went on, the mother became somewhat unhinged and took to wandering the desolate area every night with her two white dogs, looking for her daughter or the young man she had run off with. People would see the grief-stricken old woman, wearing a white dress, out on her solitary walk every night. After years of nightly vigils, she died alone and heartbroken.

Her house fell into disrepair, until eventually nothing was left but a foundation. Inevitably, teenagers began using the quiet, private area as a lovers' lane. It's ironic that a woman so suspicious of young love wound up providing a haven for parking teens.

Anyway, reports began to spread of some unusual events at the site. Many of these young couples were scared away from their amorous activities after seeing a white apparition, followed by two ghostly dogs, coming toward their car. Some reported seeing the specter rising out of the waters of the lake, always flanked by two dogs. Most witnesses say they are Dobermans, which are good ghostly dogs.

The tragic story of the mother and daughter has been passed down from one generation to the next for years. The foundations of the former home have come to be called White Lady Castle, and she is known to all in the area as the White Lady. Today Durand-Eastman Park is frequented by many curious locals and ghost hunters, who spend their evenings in the vicinity of the castle, hoping for a glimpse of this enigmatic entity.

White Lady's Revenge

My friends had heard that kids from different high schools congregated by the White Lady's Castle, so we made our way down there, hoping to join the party. When we got there, it seemed unimpressive. Just an old foundation tucked away in the park. But the locals filled us in on the real deal of the place, told us all about the lady who showed up looking for her daughter. We were told that she was particularly aggressive toward men, especially ones who were disrespectful of women.

One story they told us was of a real wannabe tough guy. You know the type—high school jock jerk. The type of guy whom people despise, but who for some reason runs the show and gets the girl in those teenage years. Well, he had this girl in high school, and everyone knew he was cursing her out, all sorts of awful things. So one day he brought her to the park to make out in their car, and she did something wrong—spilled a soda on him

As time went on, the mother became somewhat unhinged and took to wandering the desolate area every night with her two white dogs, looking for her daughter or the young man she had run off with.

White Lady's Down by the Lake

My friends and I have seen the White Lady many times. She's kind of a guardian of these parts. She lost her daughter many years ago; now her ghost walks around looking for her daughter's killer. My friends and I (all girls) always agreed that she seemed very peaceful, yet extremely sad. She appears as a sort of mist or fog that is shaped vaguely like a woman, and moves around very slowly. We've seen her down near the lake, never near the castle. *–Felicia*

She Didn't See the White Lady, and She's Glad

The supposed residence of the White Lady is actually the base of a demolished hotel that was built in the 1800s. One summer afternoon, in broad daylight, my friends and I went to check it out. Everything was very overgrown, and you could see that other kids had been there—probably to party and to spook themselves. I found a place to stand and then sit. I remember the woods were very quiet, and you couldn't hear the traffic anymore from the street. It wasn't exactly unpleasant, but I was relieved when we all decided to head back to the car. I have heard that the White Lady is visible mostly at night during a full moon. *–Janet*

or something trivial like that—and he went nuts. He started yelling at her, calling her stupid, and even shook her up a little bit physically. Well the next thing anyone knows, there was this white flash outside the car and the sound of something banging against the door. He turned around, freaked out, thinking someone's messing with him. Being a testosterone-ridden jock, he gets out looking for a fight, only to come face to face with the White Lady. No one knows exactly what he saw or what happened, but the girl told everyone that when he got in the car his face was all scratched and he wouldn't speak. He was never the same. He barely graduated from high school and became totally antisocial. Nowadays he still lives with his parents and never leaves his house. He just sits in his room all day, watching TV.

Now I don't know that this story is true. But to be standing at the White Lady's Castle, hearing about how the White Lady hates men, knowing you came out looking for trouble—well, that will put a little bit of fear in you!
–Ray Jay, Rochester

Devil Worship on Long Island

When I was growing up in Long Island, there was this house in North Massapequa that was known for devil worshipping. They painted their sidewalks black, and the house had an old-fashioned coffin carriage in the front yard. The windows on the house had velvet curtains. It was pretty dark. There also was another house in the upper Brookville area that painted their sidewalks black and had an upside-down cross painted on their tree. This was all twenty years ago when Long Island was known to have devil-worshipping activity.–*Karen R.*

Devil Worshippers Leave a Light Burning for You

I remember the devil-worshipping house well. Supposedly, the devil worshippers kept a candle burning every night in one of their windows. If you were to drive by one time, you would see this lone candle. But if you went for a second lap past the house in your car, the number of candles would be adjusted to match the number of people in your car—instead of one, there would be two, three, four, or five, depending on how large the crew was that you brought with you on that particular night. We tested the legend, and it turned out to be true. When we went by for our second lap, the number of candles had indeed changed according to our carload. This was incredibly frightening—it meant that the devil worshippers were watching you!–*Todd*

Devil Worshippers Are Counting on You

I went to the devil-worship house maybe three times. There'd be four of us in a car, and we'd drive pretty slowly past the house. It looked pretty normal, but for a few things. There was the black sidewalk, the hearse in the driveway, and the red electric candle in the front window. We'd slowly cruise past, then go around the corner so we could see the back of the house. Invariably, we'd see four red electric candles in the window. I remember it working each time. Pretty freaky.–*Flynn Barrison*

Sidewalks Run Red at Satan House

There's a house on Long Island in Massapequa that looks just like the Addams Family house. They have big metal gates and red velvet curtains throughout. On most nights, you can see and hear them chanting through the windows. They burn candles and have pentagrams all over the windows. They even have a red sidewalk (I don't know how the town allows that).

Rumor has it that they are a satanist cult and that Anton LaVey, who is kind of like the god of the satanist cult, has actually been inside this house and has done lectures and sermons there. I have seen the people who live in the house, and they are very scary-looking. They dress in black and are very gothic-looking with their black makeup and the black clothes.–*Jennifer*

Untermeyer Park

I wanted to let you in on a little not-so-secret location around where I live called Untermeyer Park, in Yonkers. Back in the '70s, the Son of Sam (who lived not too far away) and his Satan-worshipping friends hung out there and sacrificed animals. That story accounts for only half of its spookiness, though, as the park is designed to look like ancient Greece. There are tons of scary pillars, steps, caves, as well as a stone house that looks like a church with no roof, doors, or windows. It is one of the scariest and coolest places I've been to.–*Matt*

The Devil Waits for Mary Oxford

Every year when I was younger, my church used to take a fall retreat to a place called Camp Quinipet, on Shelter Island, the little island between Long Island's two forks. Quinipet is a colony of old mansions that was bought by the Methodist Church for use by retreat groups. There was one particular old house up on a hill, called Oxford House, and it was said to be haunted. The first time I heard anything about it was when I was about seven and some teenagers from my church told me the legend.

It was said that a rich family lived there back in the 1800s and had one little kid. One night they went out and left the kid with the babysitter, Mary Oxford. Late at night as Mary was doing her homework in the back wing of the house, she suddenly heard the kid crying uncontrollably and then silence. Frightened and alarmed, she slowly climbed the stairs, and when she got to the top, she saw the child splattered all over the place. Before she could scream, legend says she saw the shadow of a man with a hatchet cast on the wall by the oil lamp, and all was over.

Later, when the parents came home, they found the child's body and the decapitated head of Mary Oxford hanging from the third of three windows in the attic. The story scared the living daylights out of me, and my parents made the teenagers tell me it was fake. But I know that the legend is an old one in the area and that there is possibly some truth to it.

Years later, when I was about eleven, a friend and I asked the old caretaker, a creepy bearded guy named Carl, if we could have the key to go explore Oxford House. I will never forget, his eyes turned to fire, and he shouted, "Oxford is closed! It's condemned!" There never seemed to be any good structural reason for its condemnation.

There was, finally, something that I personally experienced in relation to the place. I had also been told, by a separate source, an alternate version of the plight of Mary Oxford. It was said that there was a fire that fateful night, and, trapped in the attic, she looked down and saw the devil, who offered to catch her if she would become his. They never said what her decision was, but . . .

My dad and I went up the hill to look at the house one year as we always did when we went to Quinipet, and I swear to you, as heaven is my witness, there were hoofprints burned into the side porch, under the attic. There were three crescent-shaped prints leading up to the door. I know this sounds as incredible as Bigfoot or any other yarn, but take it from a twenty-four-year-old naval officer with a very good education and a pair of good eyes.

Unfortunately, I can offer no photos of Oxford House, as it was indeed torn down—leveled and carted off, every last piece of red-painted wood. That year Carl disappeared as caretaker as well.—*A.M. Moir, Ensign, USNR*

A Very Evil Place

There is a place, a very evil place. It was the scariest place I have ever been to in my life. At the top of Clausland Mountain in Orangeburg there are tunnels originally built as an army base during World War I in case of invasion. They were also used for drills and training. There are miles of these tunnels throughout the mountain. Visible concrete walls run through the woods. Each tunnel also has another tunnel under it. There are many secret caverns and rooms throughout the passageways. Some are collapsing, and you must crawl through a rotted tree to get into one tunnel. There are also bomb-shelter rooms and rooms under rooms, called hellholes.

I've heard that dead bodies are often found in this area. Suicides are common, as are dumped homicide victims. The police never go there. Most people say the whole place is haunted.

On the brighter side, if you visit the tunnels, there is much great graffiti from crews like NVSP, 076, DMS, First Crew, and ABK. Other local writers such as Domain and Rook also have pieces there.

There are runs on top of the cliffs with the Hudson River underneath. You have to look for two painted rocks. Between the rocks runs a trail. Follow this trail downward for less than a quarter mile, and you will come to the tunnels of Satan's Lair.

My experience there was ridiculously terrifying. My friends and I were exploring the tunnels in the middle of the night one summer. These tunnels are completely pitch-dark. We had two flashlights for the five of us. Each time a light would hit the ceiling of a tunnel, I would see huge spiders and other giant bugs. Finally, we reached a room with a big noose tied to the ceiling. It was pure evil.

We finally made our way out of the tunnel unharmed, just a little grimy. The whole time there we didn't hear any noise in the quiet night air. All of a sudden from within the trees we heard the loudest, most morbid sound ever. You had to be there to understand the intensity of this shrill scream. I swear it wasn't human. We heard it moving through the woods toward us. We all took off through the forest. It was pitch-dark, and I remember running into trees and trying to follow the person's sound in front of me.

Finally we made it back to my car. I peeled out a quick U-turn, and we headed back down the mountain, breathing fast. As we got into town there was a ton of cop cars and ambulances. As we drove past, I saw the worst car accident I think I will ever see in my life. There was tons of blood everywhere. After this sight of morbid reality, we agreed that the screams we had heard were of some poor person's soul elevating through the mountains and up toward the heavens. *–Ralph Sinisi*

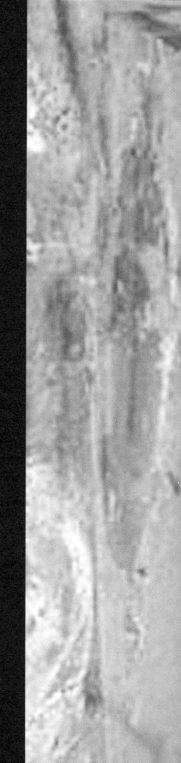

I've heard
that dead bodies
are often found
in this area. Suicides
are common, as are
dumped homicide victims.
The police never go there.
Most people say the
whole place is haunted.

Not Just Evil, but Also Dangerous

The reason why the police don't like to go in "there" is because there was and still is a practicing satanic cult who use Clausland Mountain for their rituals. There have been many bodies found up there, most of whom have died in a sacrificial manner. The cult members are referred to as the Omega Men. Their names are the only ones scribbled down the farther tunnels and all around the opening of the first with threats and the like.

Anyway, I believe the one tunnel, the one where you have to crawl through a rotting tree to get in, has something very evil about it. A little way down that tunnel, there is something like a wormhole or portal. This is not something physical, but metaphysical. When you stand beside it, you can feel a wind blowing straight out of the side of the wall. There is no hole, nor is there a feasible scientific explanation. I myself am a bit of a cynic due to having a scientific mind, but I am still a believer. You can feel the presences pouring out from that spot.

Another thing about this spot is that before you go into any tunnel, there are three buildings on the left. In the first one of these, before the first tunnel, there resides an apparition. The story as to who he was has always been unclear, but there are two versions of the tale: He was a soldier who went insane and killed many in his platoon, or he was killed by an insane bunkmate.

This apparition has some weird events surrounding him also. When his presence is felt, there is always a feeling of absolute anger. I have some friends who feel he is responsible for some of the suicides that have happened up there. They, all being Wiccans, decided for the better of the people to exorcise him. One of them began to try and then weakened. The apparition became enraged, and they decided to leave quickly before matters got worse. As they speedily walked away, the apparition hurled two of them a couple of yards. One's walking stick flew out of his hand and continued to fly for ten feet. The two who were trying the most to get rid of the apparition were the only ones attacked. After that they never really came back, except during daylight hours.

All the things I have told you are true whether you choose to believe them or not.–*Mark Miljko*

Tweed Is a Very Evil Place Indeed

As young and stupid teens, my friends and I left our comfortable homes in NJ and went to the mountains in Orangeburg to party in the woods. For some reason, we nicknamed this place Tweed. It was very easy to become scared out of your wits there even during the day, but words cannot describe how terrifying it was at night.

There was one trip that stands out in my mind. Eight of us trekked through the woods to the first open area that had a tunnel entrance. As we walked into the pitch blackness, we couldn't even see our hands in front of our faces. Every so often someone would light a lighter in an effort to feel better. This was always the wrong thing to do. The light in the tunnel only showed the reality of the grotesque bugs stuck to the walls or the creatures whose remains were left on the floor. Nevertheless, the group of us, one dumber than the next, continued down the tunnel. When we finally reached the end, there was a platform you could get on—and then, with a little crafty climbing, you could get out of the tunnel, back into the fresh air. We had to watch our step while doing this. The other side of the wall was about a fifty-foot drop-off.

When we finally reached the platform at the end of the tunnel, most of us were scared out of our minds, but it wasn't until someone yelled, "There is a light coming down the tunnel!" that things got significantly out of control. After accounting for everyone in our group, we nearly all jumped out of our skin as the "light" continued to draw closer to us. In a mad frenzy of fear, everyone leaped onto the platform in hopes of getting out of the tunnel quicker than the light was approaching.

Two people successfully reached the top of the tunnel and climbed out, helping others to climb out as well. It was just then, as six of us were still stuck inside the tunnel, that the platform collapsed! All you could hear was the echoing of the wood crumbling and breaking. I remember thinking that our poor families would never know what happened to all of us.

Our only hopes of getting out of the tunnel now was to shimmy up on a very old, narrow, and shaky metal beam until someone on top could reach in and pull you up the rest of the way. Everyone quickly shimmied up the metal beam and successfully reached the top of the tunnel.

We were all ready to leave now, but no one was going to go back down into that tunnel. There was a wall on top you could walk on, but it could be treacherous, especially at night. There were areas that would be only a foot or so wide, forcing you to carefully balance or fall off one of the sides (anywhere from a five- to fifty-foot drop-off). Just as we began to go back along the top, we saw a lone stranger, stumbling and chanting something as he surfaced from the tunnel.

I didn't get a good look at his face, but my friend said that it seemed that he was all mauled up and bloody. Everyone stepped back and let him continue to stumble around. It wasn't long before we saw him fall over the edge of the wall. There was no yelling or cries for help. He landed with a thud. By this point, no one had a single nerve left, so we literally ran, boys and girls alike, in single file on top of the tunnel and carefully scaled the areas with high drop-offs. We silently loaded back into the cars and drove home. I don't know what happened to that strange man, and I'll never go to Tweed again.–*T. Sarubbi*

Grave Matters and Misdeeds at Tweed

There is a site a few minutes outside the NJ border in Orangetown, NY, on the cliffs overlooking the Tappan Zee Bridge, very close to the Nike missile base. The name that it is referred to by is Tweed, because the easiest way to get there is off a winding road through the woods called Tweed Boulevard.

Even after all the time I've spent there, to this day it still has the power to completely frighten me. There was one incident in particular that stays fresh in my head. We ventured down into what we call the hole (an underground system that extends along the first wall). Once down there, we noticed what seemed to be a perfect grave-size hole in the ground filled with water. In front of it was a stone wall that seemed to be someone's attempt to cover up what was behind it. Underneath the wall was another grave-size hole. Once we saw the ripped pieces of clothing, it just got way too disturbing to be underground with what seemed to be some sort of burial ground. This is one of the scarier occurrences that have happened while I have been exploring Tweed. There is a world of mystery and evil there.–*Philip Buccellato*

Warlock of Mink Hollow

About ten years ago some friends of mine and I had a weird experience in the area collectively known as Brookfield. Brookfield is, or was, a bunch of little hamlets spread over a large area of probably ten square miles. Many of the towns are gone now; there are just one or two houses on a bend in some road, and an abandoned house or two here and there. Part of this area is used for horse-riding trails, which is what we were doing there at the time.

We were on our way down this abandoned logging road, and we came to a small valley, at the bottom of which was a cemetery of maybe ten or twelve stones. There was a strange smell in the air that none of us could quite place. Just then our horses FREAKED! They were pawing at the dirt, snorting, eyes bugging out, rearing up. They would go no farther, so we turned around and found another route to get to where we were going.

Skip ahead several years, and I find a book about the area written by Roy Gallinger, a local author. I was reading through it and found a chapter titled, "Faud Yantis–Warlock of Mink Hollow."

My mouth hit the floor. Mink Hollow was where the occurrence with our horses happened. Yantis is buried in that little cemetery, with his grave facing west to signify his practice of the black arts (all graves traditionally face east). This is a quote from Gallinger's book: "And on moonlit nights, there is a strong smell of sulfur in the air around the little cemetery of Mink Hollow." That was exactly what we all agreed later that we smelled—sulfur!–*Rich Klingman*

Unsolved Mysteries and Unexplained Phenomena

"Mystery creates wonder, and wonder is the basis of man's desire to understand."
—Neil Armstrong, Astronaut

Events happen every day that the average person can never hope to explain. Call them mysteries or call them miracles, these things force us to consider the world around us as something more than a collection of things we can see and feel. The world is a place full of intrigue, the unknown, and the inexplicable.

The idea that there are things in our society that science can't explain is both terrifying and hopeful. Terrifying because what we don't understand can be very frightening. Hopeful because things beyond our comprehension also offer limitless possibilities—for good or evil. Many of the events in this chapter are mere rumors, whispers of things that may or may not have happened, in places that may or may not exist. Others are well documented, but their meanings may not be known. They may be encounters with some alien beings, ancient rock formations whose purpose has been lost to time, or tiles with cryptic messages embedded in the ground by someone unknown. They may be tales rooted in New York's storied history, mysterious disappearances, and weird objects falling from the sky out of nowhere. All are some of the strangest things we will ever encounter.

It is not our place to seek out logical explanations for what's reported here. Not only would explanations take all the fun out of it but having them would do no good. Whether rumor or documented fact, these things exist as they are. It is up to us to experience them and draw our own conclusions.

The UFO Capital of New York

To the casual observer, Pine Bush is just like any of the other towns in northern Orange County. It's small, filled with local flavor, and is being encroached on by chain stores and condos, which are slowly replacing the rural life old-timers are accustomed to. Yes, on the surface, Pine Bush faces the same problems as all the other suburbs of the area.

But Pine Bush is far from a normal, quiet suburb. If it were, flocks of outsiders would not have consistently swarmed the town at night for the past quarter century, racking up trespassing fines and clogging local roads. If Pine Bush were normal in any way, it wouldn't be known to conspiracy theorists the world over, and it certainly wouldn't be the subject of endless discussion in Internet chat rooms. Locals wouldn't linger in the checkout line at the supermarkets, telling tales of their strange encounters, and they wouldn't make incredible claims about alien abductions and nefarious experiments conducted on the unsuspecting townsfolk.

No, Pine Bush is no normal Orange County suburb. Pine Bush is the UFO capital of the East Coast.

The Hudson Valley of New York has long been home to some truly weird occurrences. Ghost lights are seen in the woods regularly. Ghosts themselves run rampant throughout the entire area. And most famously, the Hudson Valley has long been known to attract strange vessels and beings from outer space. Pine Bush has come to be known worldwide as the primary destination for these extraterrestrial visitors in the area.

Some Pine Bush locals have personal stories of alien sightings, abductions, and encounters dating as far back as the 1960s, but the town's reputation as a hotbed of UFO activity was cemented largely during an incredibly active flurry of strange sightings that occurred in the mid-1980s and continued into the 1990s. Throughout the early part of the '80s, a mysterious aircraft that has come to be referred to as the Westchester Boomerang was seen over two thousand times, including a handful of sightings in Pine Bush. As the craft's name suggests, however, most of the sightings occurred not in Orange but in Westchester County. Yet while the sensational Westchester Boomerang was occupying the attention of researchers, events that were curious, quieter, and just as strange were happening on a frighteningly regular basis in Pine Bush. And as the hype over the Westchester sightings died down, more and more people began to realize that truly odd things were occurring in this seemingly normal rural village.

Locals first began to speak to one another about the weird events they were noticing. Many of them had seen different types of otherworldly aircraft making regular sojourns in the skies above their homes. Looking up, they saw boomerang-shaped vessels, or pencil-thin hovering objects, or quickly moving balls and beams of light. People began whispering about strange strobe lights that were emanating from forests and wooded areas scattered about town. Unfamiliar noises and odd things were happening at the Jewish Cemetery on Route 52. Town officials were also confused by the recurring phenomenon at a small bridge in town. No matter how many times they would repaint the structure, the paint would quickly peel away for no apparent reason.

These stories were told privately, if at all, among confused and frightened locals. If they spoke openly of what was happening, they were afraid their neighbors would think they were crazy. They didn't realize that other people were having experiences similar to their own.

Attitudes started to slowly change in 1991, with the publication of *Silent Invasion: The Shocking Discoveries of a UFO Researcher* by Ellen Crystall. The author, a New Jersey resident, had been traveling to Pine Bush for eleven years,

researching stories of alien encounters there. She detailed UFO sightings and other related phenomena in her book and also included a series of controversial photos said to depict actual run-ins with alien craft. The book made only a very small splash, but it did lead to a series of appearances for Crystall on a number of talk shows. A few magazines and television programs visited Pine Bush to conduct their own investigations. Most important, the book touted the town as a focal point of UFO activity and made people much more comfortable about coming forward with their personal tales.

As locals began sharing stories with one another, they realized the astonishing number of incidents people had experienced in Pine Bush. Many of the stories were completely sensational, telling of groups of dozens of strange aircraft flying over the town at once. People began meeting at certain spots at night to keep a lookout for more UFOs. They became known as skywatchers or UFOers. Over time, more and more outsiders joined their ranks. The town's reputation grew as more sightings were reported. By the middle of the 1990s, Pine Bush was widely recognized as the most active hub of UFO activity on the East Coast of the United States. The town's reputation grew even larger when it was revealed that popular author Whitley Strieber had written two books reporting his own encounters with alien beings set in a small cabin he owned just outside the borders of Pine Bush.

Large crowds gathered nightly at a number of locations throughout the town. The most attended spot was West Searesville Road. Hundreds of people said they saw objects in the sky above this desolate street, and as the sightings grew in number, so did the crowds. Eventually, the number of people skywatching on West Searesville became so large that the town was forced to prohibit the activity. The crowds were disrupting traffic, and people were wandering off onto private property, hassling and waking up residents (who were probably so used to reports of UFO visits that they weren't even bothering to go out and look anymore). Police patrolled the road each night to make sure crowds were not forming.

Their efforts worked on some level, but smaller groups still hit the road looking for visitors from beyond. Others formed on South Searesville, at the Jewish Cemetery on Route 52 (which was also the location of strange rumbling sounds and even unidentified animal sightings), and at other spots around Pine Bush. Amazing photographs began to show up, and even videotapes appeared of bizarre objects flying in the sky. Local newspapers started reporting people's encounters, and some of them were truly incredible.

One *Times-Herald Record* article told of a sighting by Pine Bush resident John Lewis, who videotaped a thin black object flying in the sky. "Lewis watched the object move slowly downward at a 45-degree angle for about five minutes," the paper recounted. "Then he rushed for his video camera. The unidentified flying object was

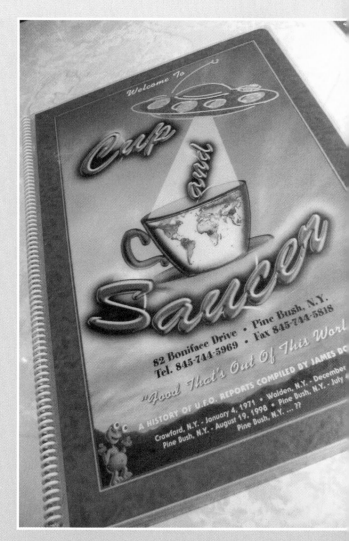

UFO enthusiasts flock to the diner . . . to share stories of experiences and tips on the best locations to sight UFOs, and to network with those who believe Pine Bush is a hub of extraterrestrial activity here on earth.

pencil-shaped and black with a long tail. There was not a glint of reflection from the sun.

"Maybe it is a missile, maybe an asteroid," [Lewis] says. "I don't know. It is beyond me. It's not a plane, not a cloud."

The *Poughkeepsie Journal* ran an article detailing the activities of the United Friends Observer Society (UFOS), a support group founded in Pine Bush in 1993 for people who'd had encounters with or were abducted by the aliens that seemed to be frequenting the town. Local Bill Wiand told the *Journal*'s reporter of his experiences.

"I did recently have an invasion and it terrified me," he said. "It started like it always does, with the noise in my ears, and it just kind of rumbles through. I couldn't move my body, but I could move my eyes, and I knew the room was filled with entities."

The article goes on to detail other people's abductions, including one researcher who claimed that "they immobilized me and undressed me and put this device on my genitals and took a sperm sample."

In another *Times-Herald Record* article, a number of people shared their stories of odd occurrences. Among them were the recollections of Jim Smith, a Pine Bush resident and a sergeant at the Woodbourne Correctional Facility. He told the paper, "I've seen so many of the beings, I know exactly how they move. They're different sizes, different shapes, but when you see them so much, you know they're not of this earth. Not long ago, I saw this figure about six foot six and dressed in all black standing beneath the traffic light in Pine Bush. I said to Hilda, my fiancée, 'What's that woman doing?'

"Hilda said, 'Oh my God, I thought I was the only one who saw the thing.'

"When she moved, it wasn't like walking. It wasn't in frames either, like most of them move. In frames, they're someplace and then they're suddenly in another place,

like time-lapse photography. But this one moved horizontally.

"In Pine Bush, you see things you don't expect. I've seen a cat with no head walking across the floor. It just had a piece of cardboard where the head should be. A lot of people in Pine Bush tell me they've seen that cat. But not everyone can see the cat or the beings. You have to be open to things like that."

These days, most people in Pine Bush are "open to things like that." UFO encounters and other unexplainable incidents have become a fact of life. People trade stories regularly—and a number of local businesses have embraced the town's strange reputation. Butch Hunt's barbershop on Main Street in Pine Bush features a UFO-themed sign hanging out front, and the interior is riddled with articles about sightings and photos said to capture images of unidentified flying objects.

A diner in town is named Cup and Saucer, and its sign proudly displays a cup and a flying saucer. Not surprisingly, UFO enthusiasts flock to the diner not just for food and drink, but to share stories of experiences and tips on the best locations to sight UFOs, and to otherwise network with those who believe Pine Bush is in fact a hub of extraterrestrial activity here on earth.

By all accounts, the UFO activity around Pine Bush has fallen off considerably since its glory days in the 1980s and '90s. Most attribute this to the real estate development that has occurred in the area. The past twenty years have seen condos fill in what used to be farmland, and as new construction has been completed, UFO sightings have decreased substantially. Other phenomena are still reported, though, including sightings of strange shadowy figures, weird noises permeating desolate areas, flashing lights, and more. UFOs are still seen in Pine Bush more often than in your average town, but not with the frightening frequency of the past two decades.

Mysterious Booms of Cayuga Lake

Since the days when Native Americans were the only humans to walk along their shores, Cayuga and Seneca lakes have been plagued by mysterious, loud percussive noises that no scientists have been able to explain. The sounds, most often described as like the pounding of drums or the firing of guns, are heard at random times. It is impossible to predict when they will occur.

The Seneca and Cayuga Indians who frequented the lakes created stories to explain the existence of the weird noises. They were drums played by the ghosts of deceased ancestors or the warnings of a Thunder God; they were signs that danger or evil was approaching the tribe.

Europeans noted the presence of the mysterious booms upon their arrival to the area centuries later. One myth from the early 1800s said the noises were produced by the spirit of a soldier from the Revolutionary War who was trying to find his way home.

The most oft-cited explanation today is that they are produced by gas escaping from the lake bottoms. This theory purports that the sounds are the results of a sort of massive belching up of gas that occurs from time to time. No studies have proved this hypothesis.

The next time you visit Cayuga Lake, kick back and experience a truly peaceful area. Its serene shores are welcoming to all. But be wary. At any given moment, one of the lake's infamous "booms" could knock you off your feet!

Math Formulas in the Sky

In late July 1973, radio station manager Bob Hill saw something very strange above the skies of North Greenbush. Thousands of feet above him, Hill witnessed numerous white objects floating toward the earth. "I'm certain the things must have been above 10,000 feet," Hill was quoted as saying in the 1978 book *Weird America.* "It took something like half an hour to forty-five minutes for the objects to land." When the objects finally did land, Hill was amazed to find that they were sheets of paper upon which were written hundreds of intricate mathematical equations. The source of the papers and the reason they were dropped from the sky have not been determined to this day.

Defying Gravity on Spook Hill

We have a strange road in the Finger Lakes region of New York State. It's in Italy Valley on the west side of Canandaigua Lake, and it's called Spook Hill.

If you look in your rearview mirror, it looks as if you're being dragged UP the hill when you're actually going DOWN the hill. It's very cool. I've never heard of any "ghost" stories associated with this road. It's just a very cool optical illusion.—*Tracy Smith*

Whispering Secrets

Manhattan's Grand Central Terminal is one of the most bustling hubs of transportation in the world. It is the last place you'd think of having a quiet conversation with someone standing clear across the room. But this is exactly what takes place there. Grand Central is home to a little-known Whispering Gallery.

Just outside the station's Oyster Bar restaurant is a domed area usually crowded with people. The noise is constant, and the thought that one could whisper across the room seems ludicrous. But if two people stand facing pillars that are diagonally across from each other, even the softest whisper into the wall will travel down the tiles of the room and can be heard quite clearly by the person on the receiving end.

The Whispering Gallery exists because of an architectural choice that must have been intentional. What is most puzzling about the space isn't how it works but why it was done. What purpose does it serve? Who thought it was necessary to be able to communicate through whispers in a loud, busy train station? It also seems strange that such a feature, in such a public place, is completely unpublicized.

New York is the city that never sleeps, a city of noise. Given the trains, the constant car horns, the music pouring out of clubs onto the street, it is difficult to have a quiet conversation. Whoever thought that the best place to go for a quiet little talk would be right in the middle of one of the world's busiest centers of transportation? Whoever is responsible, we applaud his attention to this weird little architectural detail. Stop by some day during rush hour and try it out for yourself!

Floating Rocks

The November 4, 1815, edition of the *Niles Weekly Register* told the story of a batch of floating rocks that amazed visitors at an otherwise ordinary cow pasture near Marbletown, outside Kingston. The rocks would float some three feet above the ground and then travel between thirty and sixty feet horizontally at a time. This mystery from the early nineteenth century remains completely unsolved.

Sonic Sand

Some of the shores of Lake Champlain have sand that produces sound. A beach in Plattsburgh, New York, is supposedly home to sand that, when placed in two bags that are then struck against each other, makes a sound resembling the barking of a dog. Most strangely of all, if the sand is removed from the beach, it stops producing the sounds. There is no explanation for this mysterious occurrence.

Better to Be Hit with Math Than a Rock . . .

The world's most famous researcher of the strange, Charles Fort, published a request for information in a 1924 issue of *The New York Times*. Mr. Fort was trying to solve the riddle of a peculiar rock that fell from the skies above Ulster County in the spring of 1883. When locals retrieved the rock after its landing, they were stunned to find that etched into its surface was a set of strange hieroglyphiclike writings. To our knowledge, Mr. Fort never discovered the answer to the curious riddle behind the existence of this strange stone. The whereabouts of the stone today is unknown.

The Frost Valley Petroglyph

The Frost Valley area of the Catskill Mountain range has long been considered one of the most remote sections of New York. Home to just a handful of farmers, it has remained largely undisturbed for centuries. This makes the presence of what has come to be known as the Frost Valley Petroglyph even more shocking to those who stumble across it.

Perched along the north bank of the Neversink River within the town of Denning, the petroglyph is a boulder with a distinct spiral pattern carved into it. The carving was discovered in 1995, but it's believed to have been made between one and two hundred years ago. Though its true meaning and significance are not completely understood, it's thought that the rock was carved for religious purposes by a Native American decades before Europeans ever found their way into Frost Valley.

The North Salem Dolmen

North Salem is the home of a truly impressive structure, one with an origin shrouded in intrigue and mystery. Located along a roadside in the quiet, tiny town is a ninety-ton boulder balanced on five smaller stones that have been driven deep into the earth. Some guess that the stones came to be in their current formation simply through chance, shifted and placed there by glacial movements. Most people, though, recognize that the odds of this happening are indeed very slim. They theorize that Native Americans set the structure up centuries ago to serve as a worship point. This has led to the site being referred to as the North Salem Dolmen. Dolmens are stone structures that were found scattered throughout the prehistoric world and are thought to have been used by ancient peoples as altars and markers of holy sites.

Balanced Rock

There is a dolmen—a huge boulder that is unbelievably balanced on smaller rocks—in North Salem. It was reputably built by ancient seafaring Celts who crossed over to the New World long before ol' Chris was a sparkle in Mr. Columbus's eye.

I must tell you some less enlightened scientists claim this to be simply an erratic leftover from the glacial retreat of many thousands of years ago. To that I say poppycock! I have done years of research on this and have concluded that only humans could have created such a monument. Only ancient drunken Irish or Scots would have wanted to.

Does it mark the solstice? Is it a huge grave? Did someone have a big party there some thousand years ago and get carried away? Who knows? But you can draw your own conclusions after you too see the dolmen in North Salem.—*Dr. Seymour O'Life*

Suicide Birds

In 1948, the world-famous Empire State Building was the site of an extremely curious incident. Inexplicably, hundreds upon hundreds of birds launched themselves straight into the building. The birds hit the building many stories up, then plummeted to their deaths on the street below. Dozens of different species were later identified among the fallen. Needless to say, this behavior is nearly unheard of. In an eerie coincidence, the date of this incident was September 11, 1948.

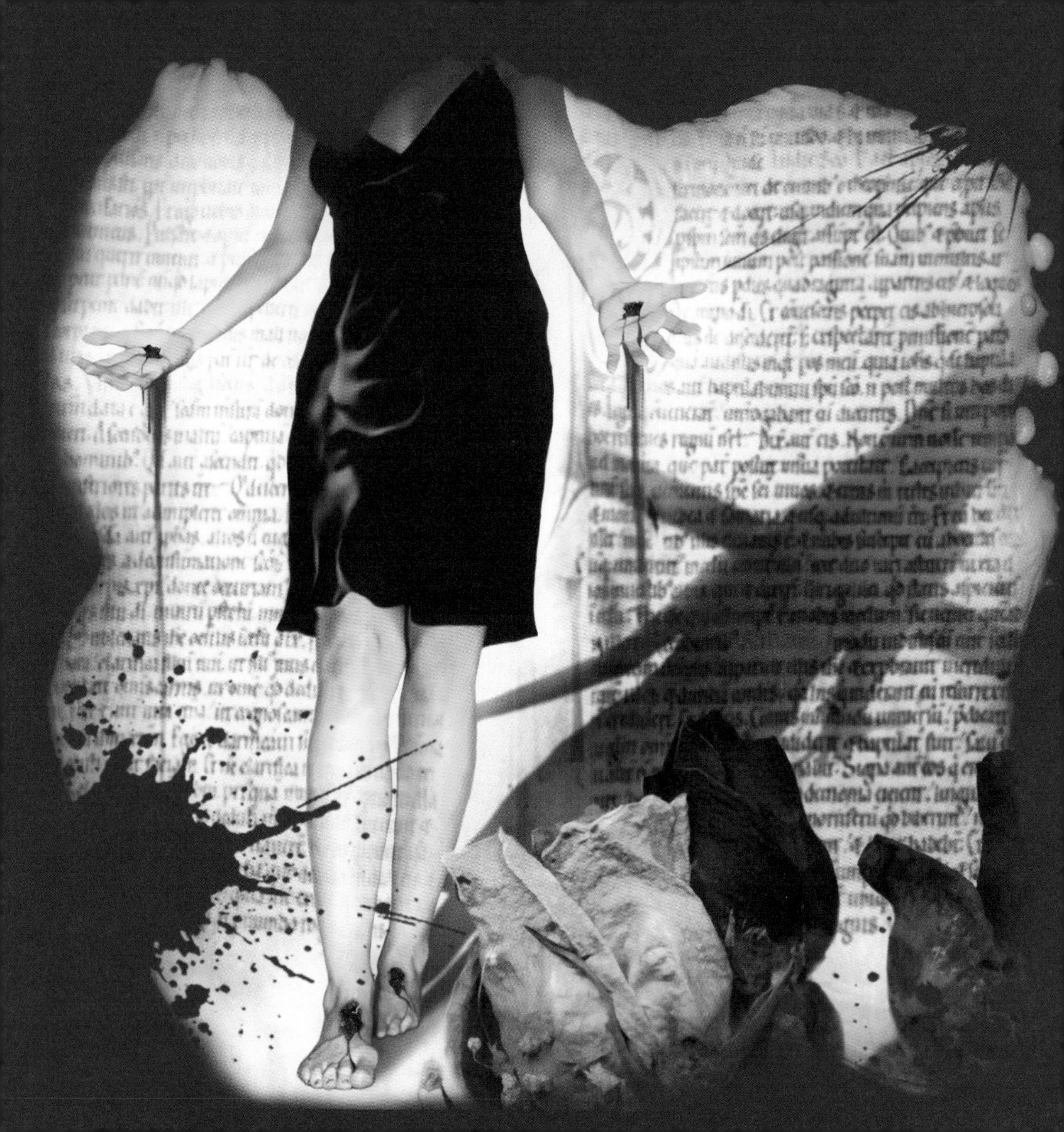

A New York Miracle?

In June 2003, the *Buffalo News* reported on a compelling public speaker who was touring western New York State, creating much discussion. Her name is Lilian Bernas, and she was visiting churches claiming to have experienced stigmata, a religious miracle in which an individual undergoes unprovoked bleeding consistent with Jesus' bleeding during his crucifixion.

Bernas, a convert to Catholicism, often displayed blood pouring from her palms, the backs of her hands, the tops of her feet, and occasionally her forehead. Sometimes drops of blood simply trickled from the sites. On other occasions, witnesses have been shocked to see blood spurt forth at an alarming rate. Bernas first experienced the phenomenon during the Easter season of 1992. Before that, she had made claims about seeing visions of Jesus, who would visit her and refer to her as "my suffering soul" and "my sweet petal."

The stigmata tours have attracted thousands of the faithful anxious to see a miracle in action. They have also attracted equal numbers of skeptics, who arrive hoping to prove that Bernas is nothing more than a hoaxster. Skeptics argue that she is inflicting the wounds on herself and that they have nothing to do with any sort of divine intervention. Others, including a photojournalist sent to document the phenomenon objectively, have reported that when the bleeding begins, Bernas is also surrounded by an intense smell of roses. She has a number of scars on her body and claims that the locations of her wounds cause her intense physical pain even when they are not bleeding.

Originally a native of Ottawa, Canada, Bernas was asked by church officials in that area not to speak publicly about her experiences. Historically, the Catholic Church has been hesitant to support the stories of those claiming to experience miracles.

Bernas has embraced her lot in life as a bearer of stigmata. Referring to its first appearance, the *Buffalo News* reported that she told a crowd in Tonawanda, "That was my Good Friday. Marvelous. Beautiful."

Disappearing Act

Although the identities of those involved and the time period in question remain shrouded in mystery, Internet conspiracy theorists have often said that the Lincoln Tunnel, which connects New Jersey and Manhattan, was the site of a mysterious incident that was immediately covered up by the powers that be.

While driving during a sudden and severe winter snowstorm, one couple stopped in the middle of the tunnel to remove snow from their windshield. What happens next has never been explained, say the theorists, and was quickly swept under the rug by government authorities. The couple disappeared without a trace. Their car remained behind, but its two passengers were never seen or heard from again.

Is this just a mere rumor? Or is it a sign that one of the most traveled tunnels in the world is a window into something mysterious and perhaps even sinister? The answer may never be known.

Time Travel in Times Square

An incredibly strange story about New York has attracted much attention in Europe, of all places. While most Americans have never heard this odd tale, it has made the rounds of magazines in Spain, France, Italy, Norway, and Sweden. It details the mystifying journey of a man named Rudolph Fentz, a man many believe was a time traveler.

On a June night in 1950, everything seemed normal in the Times Square area of Manhattan. By eleven fifteen, the area was filled with the regular foot and automobile traffic one would expect as theaters let out in the busy district. Nothing seemed unusual about the evening until a strange man appeared—literally out of thin air.

The man materialized in the middle of the street, amid traffic. He was about thirty years old. His facial hair and clothes were outdated. He looked frightened as he spun around, taking in his surroundings. In a fit of panic, the man attempted to run away from the cars making their way down the street, when he was struck by a taxi and killed instantly.

The story only gets stranger from there. When police rushed to the man's body, they found on his person a number of curious items. His wallet was full of antique money. He had business papers and cards with the name Rudolph Fentz listed on them. And most inexplicable of all, he was carrying a letter addressed to the same name, postmarked 1876.

In seeking out the man's family, police kept hitting dead ends. The addresses on his business papers and letters led nowhere; no one at any of the addresses had ever heard the name Rudolph Fentz. He was not listed in any current telephone directories, although one officer named Hubert Vihm found a Rudolph Fentz, Jr., listed in a phone book from 1939.

Officer Vihm called the number and spoke to a woman who said that she was the widow of the son of the man who had died in Times Square. According to this woman, her father-in-law had vanished in 1876. He left under usual circumstances, telling his family he was going out for a smoke. He wasn't seen again until he materialized in New York City seventy-four years later and was killed.

This piece of information led police to a missing persons report filed in 1876. The mystery of Rudolph Fentz, his disappearance, and his reappearance decades later has never been solved. Many believers point to his case as evidence of time travel in action.

Missingest Man in New York

No disappearance in the history of New York has left the public more baffled than that of New York State Supreme Court Associate Justice Joseph F. Crater. The mystery surrounding his whereabouts and the dozens of reported sightings of the judge in following years have perplexed people for decades. The mystery has led to Crater's nickname, the Missingest Man in New York.

Crater was last seen on August 6, 1930, climbing into a taxi after leaving a restaurant in Manhattan. He was never seen again. It seems impossible that someone as prominent as a State Supreme Court judge could disappear into thin air, but that is exactly what happened. Speculation swirled; had the judge been killed? Had he taken off in fear of someone? Or was he wandering the streets of some remote area, afflicted with amnesia? Nobody knows.

Crater grew up in Pennsylvania and came to New York to study at Columbia Law School. After he started practicing law in New York in 1913, he quickly became involved in the workings of the local Democratic Party. He excelled at the political game, in no small part because of the connections he developed with the infamously corrupt Tammany Hall political machine. Tammany helped him secure his post on the Supreme Court, allegedly at a cost to the judge of $20,000. He also was involved in a number of real estate deals and became a very wealthy man. Some say this too had to do with his close ties to Tammany. By 1930, Judge Joseph F. Crater was professionally successful, privately wealthy, and had a happy marriage. This made it all the more sensational when he disappeared without a trace.

Crater and his wife had been vacationing in Maine during the summer of 1930. Late that July, the judge received a mysterious phone call and told his wife he had to return to New York. All he said of the trip was that he had to "straighten those fellows out."

Upon arriving in New York, Crater began a period of

JUSTICE JOSEPH F. CRATER,
Who Vanished on Aug. 6 After
Drawing $5,100 From Banks.

secretive behavior. First, he and a call girl took a trip to Atlantic City. Upon his return, he had his assistant cash more than $5,000 worth of checks. On the same day, he had the same assistant help him carry two locked briefcases to his apartment. He never said what was inside them. When the briefcases were delivered to his home, he gave his assistant the rest of the day off.

That night, Crater attended a Broadway show and had dinner with some friends afterward. His friends—a lawyer and his date—said that during this meal Crater seemed upbeat and happy. There didn't seem to be anything wrong. After the meal, Judge Joseph F. Crater went outside, hailed a taxi, and was never seen or heard from again.

Crater's disappearance didn't become news for some time. His wife assumed he was tending to business and didn't think his lack of communication was odd until ten days had passed. And colleagues didn't think his absence was strange until he missed the opening day of New York State Supreme Court.

The disappearance of Judge Crater became instantaneous front-page news. Had he been killed? Or had he taken off to avoid one of his shady business partners? Whatever, his disappearing act became so well known that anyone who slipped away in those days, for any reason, was said to be "pulling a Crater."

Investigators became even more puzzled when they realized that the judge's safe had been cleared out and the two briefcases he and his assistant had carried to his apartment were also missing.

Crater's wife, Stella, believed that he had been murdered because of some political back-door dealings that had gone wrong. Many others thought Crater had taken off on his own to avoid such a fate. For decades, Judge Crater sightings were reported around the country. None of them ever paid off.

Mrs. Stella Crater, *the wife of the judge, reads a letter she received from a Mrs. Atwell who said that she had seen Judge Crater*

New developments in the Judge Crater case came out recently, in August 2005. An elderly woman, who died of natural causes, left behind a letter that her family found in a safe deposit box. The letter was marked "Do not open until my death." It told of the woman's personal knowledge of the Judge Crater case and claimed that his body was buried in Coney Island, somewhere near the present location of the New York Aquarium. In the letter, the woman claims her husband was at a bar where he learned that a cop, his cabdriver brother, and a few others had kidnapped and killed Judge Crater.

Police are looking into the location for bodies and are checking records to see if any were unearthed during the construction of the aquarium in the 1950s. While it is considered a major break in the case, New York police are unwilling to proclaim the Judge Crater mystery solved.

The Heiress Who Never Came Home

Dorothy Arnold had it all. She was young, beautiful, came from a wealthy family, and had a bright future ahead of her. That future was cut short on December 12, 1910, when she disappeared from a busy New York City street without a trace.

Dorothy left her house that December morning to go dress shopping. Her sister was having a coming-out party and the holiday season was just ahead, so the young lady wanted to make sure she had fashionable clothes for the various events. She made her way to Fifth Avenue and Twenty-seventh Street, which was then a fancy shopping area. While in the neighborhood, she visited stores where she was known by the owners and ran into a number of acquaintances on the street. Everyone who saw her said that she seemed cheerful and untroubled. She gave no signs of depression and spoke of no unusual plans for the future. These people would be the last to see her. Dorothy Arnold never made it home that night, and she was never heard from again.

The times being what they were, Dorothy's family didn't contact the police. Their social prominence and wealth made them feel that private investigation was the more prudent course of action. The family hired the famous Pinkertons, as well as a close family friend, to investigate the case. The Pinkertons came up with nothing. The family friend, who had a sincere interest in Dorothy's well-being, since he had often escorted her to social affairs, spent years scouring morgues, hospitals, and prisons up and down the East Coast. Despite his best efforts, he never found a clue to the girl's whereabouts.

After six weeks of fruitless investigation, the Arnold family finally turned to the police and to the press. They acknowledged her disappearance and made known their theory that Dorothy was already dead. Many people thought this hopelessness was macabre, but the family believed it to be true. The only other option that occurred to them was that Dorothy had run away with a man. And they would rather she be dead than with the man they had in mind.

George Griscom, Jr., was an overweight forty-year-old who lived with his parents in Philadelphia. The summer before her disappearance, Dorothy had lied to her family in order to arrange a rendezvous with him. She told the family she was going to Boston to meet up with a classmate from Bryn Mawr. Instead, they learned later, she met Griscom. For weeks, the two spent time in Boston having a secret relationship. Even though they stayed in separate hotels, Dorothy was apparently smitten with the man.

Her parents learned of her true whereabouts only after she pawned some jewelry for money to extend her trip. She returned home shortly after but maintained a correspondence with Griscom. Her parents were incensed and determined that their socialite daughter would never be allowed to wind up with this man.

Griscom was tracked down in Naples, Italy, shortly after the press learned of his relationship with Dorothy Arnold. The Arnold family secretly sent representatives to Italy to confront the man. They roughed up Griscom, trying to get him to reveal the girl's whereabouts, but he insisted that he knew nothing about it. He did say that her letters to him showed that she was suffering from severe depression. He maintained that it was because her writing career, which she had been hoping to launch, was not getting off to the start she had anticipated. Her family and friends maintained that she was depressed because her relationship with Griscom had fallen apart.

The most popular theory as to the fate of Dorothy Arnold did involve Griscom. Many people suggested that during her affair with the man, she had accidentally gotten pregnant. A botched abortion followed, and Dorothy's remains were buried in secret. While this theory was never proved, it did gain some credibility years later, when an imprisoned man in Rhode Island came forward to the press. He claimed that he had been paid a small sum to dig a grave for a girl he believed to be Dorothy Arnold. While he never asked the name of the man who hired him to do it, the description he gave fit the general appearance of George Griscom. The convict said he had buried the body in the cellar of a home near West Point. Many homes were excavated, but no body was ever found.

Sightings of Dorothy Arnold were reported for decades after her disappearance. Her family spent hundreds of thousands of dollars following leads, attempting to find her. George Griscom himself spent many thousands of dollars on newspaper ads, reading "Dorothy Come Home." Some said this proved he was genuine in his affection for the girl and his wish to find her. Others said his efforts were nothing more than a way to divert suspicion away from him.

Either way, the case of the missing heiress is one of New York City's oldest unsolved mysteries and still perplexes to this day.

The Toynbee Tiles

A strange message is embedded in the streets of dozens of cities across the world, and New York is no exception. The message is contained on the surface of some tiles, which have come to be referred to as Toynbee Tiles because of their numerous references to the famous historian Arnold J. Toynbee. No one is certain who created the tiles, why this person has traveled to so many places with them, or what their message is supposed to mean.

Toynbee Tiles made their first appearance in Philadelphia, then quickly began to turn up in cities across America and abroad. There are more than fifty of them in Manhattan alone. The large majority feature the same message: "Toynbee Idea in Movie 2001—Resurrect Dead on Planet Jupiter." Some are more elaborate and feature strange political theories and ideologies.

It is believed that the author of the tiles was influenced by a Ray Bradbury science fiction story, "The Toynbee Convector." This short story speaks of the need for humanity to look to the future for ways to survive. Ideas in Stanley Kubrick's classic movie *2001: A Space Odyssey* speak of colonizing Jupiter. While the message on the tiles is vague, at the very least it reveals that their maker enjoys a good sci-fi story as much as anyone.

Since the majority of the 130 tiles known to exist have been found in Philadelphia, and because a tile found in Santiago, Chile, lists a Philadelphia address, it is widely believed that the inventor of the tiles resides in the City of Brotherly Love. The most likely suspect is a Philadelphia social worker named James Morasco, who died in 2003. In the early '80s, Morasco had written a number of letters to Philadelphia newspapers that included language similar to that found on many of the tiles. He died, however, without

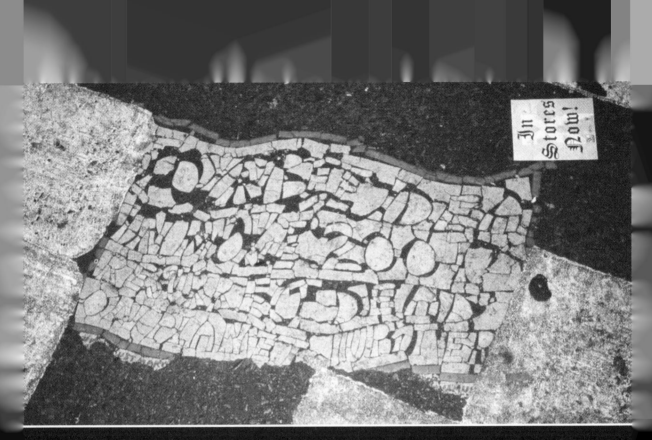

ever admitting responsibility for them. Curiously, new tiles have continued to appear in the years since his death, only heightening the mystery.

The tiles are affixed to asphalt in a rather ingenious way. They are wrapped in tar paper and coated in glue. Then the tiles are placed in the middle of busy intersections. As cars drive over the streets, the tiles are pressed into the asphalt. As the glue dries, they stay in place. As cars continue to pass over them, the tar paper slowly degrades until it has completely peeled away, revealing the messages below. Cities generally don't spend money removing the curious plaques, as their messages contain no vulgarity or profanity. Many of the tiles, however, have been destroyed by road construction.

After so many years of mysterious appearances, the Toynbee Tiles have become a cult phenomenon. Dozens of websites chronicle their locations and search for answers as to the identity of their creator and the reason for their existence. No one has come up with any concre facts yet. The Toynbee Tiles may remain a mystery forever.

The large majority of Manhattan's Toynbee Tiles can be found in Midtown, starting around Thirty-sixth Street and appearing frequently all the way up to Fifty-seventh Street. While some have been painted over through the years, more than thirty have appeared in this twenty-block stretch. Still others are scattered throughout the ci but the Midtown group is one of the highest concentrations of Toynbee Tiles in the entire world.

What Happened on the *Mary Celeste?*

One of the greatest maritime mysteries in history involves a ship that set sail out of New York. This ship's strange tale has been retold thousands of times, most famously in a fictionalized account by the author of the Sherlock Holmes series, Sir Arthur Conan Doyle. Over the years, many different retellings and theories have added even more layers of mystery to the story. No matter the embellishments, one thing is certain—when the *Mary Celeste* sailed out of New York on November 7, 1872, it carried the captain, his wife and daughter, and seven crew members. When the ship was found floating aimlessly at sea, in perfectly fine condition, none of these people were present. Their whereabouts and fate have never been determined.

The *Mary Celeste* seemed, in many ways, to be a cursed ship, suffering disasters before and after the mysterious disappearance of its crew and passengers. Originally a Canadian vessel known as the *Amazon*, it was bought, refitted, and moved to New York after an accidental grounding in 1868. The ship was under the command of Captain Benjamin Spooner Briggs, who was regarded by all who knew him as capable, competent, and fair. His crew was reportedly dedicated to him. The ship had been contracted to carry a large quantity of liquor to Europe, and hundreds of barrels were loaded onto the vessel. It sailed out of New York in November under normal circumstances.

The *Mary Celeste* was to be followed by another ship known as the *Dei Gratia*. The *Dei Gratia* followed the exact path of the *Mary Celeste* from a few hundred miles back. Everything seemed fine during the first few weeks of the journey. The *Mary Celeste* sailed into a number of ports along the route, signing in properly and noting nothing unusual on board. Then, on December 4, 1872, the truly inexplicable happened.

As the crew members of the *Dei Gratia* approached Gibraltar, they were shocked to see their lead ship sailing out of control. They were six hundred miles offshore and had no idea what had occurred. The ship itself seemed to be in perfect condition, with no sign of an accident or foul play. A decision was quickly made to board the *Mary Celeste* to determine what was going on.

Upon boarding, crew members of the *Dei Gratia* were baffled to discover that the people supposedly on board the *Mary Celeste* had vanished without a trace. The ship's chronometer and the captain's log were missing. Besides these indisputable facts, most of the details of what the *Dei Gratia*'s crew discovered on the *Mary Celeste* differ, having been tainted by folklore and word-of-mouth rumors over time.

Most agree that a clock had been strangely mounted upside down. Some say that there were bloodstains on the ship's sails and a bloody sword was found lying on the deck. Most report that the ship's lone lifeboat was missing, although some accounts say that the boat strangely remained behind. Legend has it that those on board evacuated so suddenly that their meals were left behind, still on plates, half eaten. Other accounts say the ship's deck and private quarters were in disarray.

The crew of the *Dei Gratia* split in two, and one half sailed the *Mary Celeste* into the port of Gibraltar. From there, it was left to the courts and insurance companies to determine who would claim the *Mary Celeste*'s cargo and the ship herself. These matters were relatively simple. Finding out what happened to the ship's crew and passengers on the high seas was another matter entirely.

Most people naturally assumed that pirates had attacked the ship and done away with all those on board, which was a common occurrence in the area at the time. But a quick glance at the circumstances of the ship's

away. This seems unlikely as well. Winds had been blowing strong for the seven or eight days before the discovery of the *Mary Celeste,* according to the crew of the *Dei Gratia.* But the ship's pristine condition makes it doubtful that everyone was swept away in some sort of storm. More damage would have been done to the vessel in such a situation.

Some have theorized that the ship was set upon by those sailing behind them on the *Dei Gratia.* These theorists paint the members of the sister ship not as valiant heroes boarding the drifting vessel in an effort to help, but as jealous, greedy scoundrels who wanted to take the *Mary Celeste*'s cargo as their own. In this scenario, the *Dei Gratia* would have paid off members of the *Mary Celeste*'s crew to betray their captain and hold the ship's passengers and the rest of the crew captive, ultimately disposing of them. The *Dei Gratia* crew could then board the ship and would legally have a right to the profits made in the delivery of the *Mary Celeste*'s cargo. This is a feasible scenario, but no investigations ever yielded any proof that a situation like this came close to occurring.

As decades have passed, many have offered up other ideas as to what happened on the *Mary Celeste.* Some have gone so far as to say that alien abductors swept down upon the ship, removed the passengers and crew onto spaceships, then took off into the cosmos. After almost a century and a half of theorizing, it appears that what really happened on board the *Mary Celeste* on that November journey will never be known.

The ship itself remained in use for a number of years after the disappearances, although it quickly gained legendary status for being cursed and was avoided by most sailors. It sailed on for another decade, continuing its legacy of bad luck. An end finally came to her mysterious story after she crashed on the shores of Haiti in 1884.

discovery proved this was definitely not the case. A number of valuables were still on the *Mary Celeste,* most notably her cargo of liquor. While nine barrels had been emptied, hundreds remained undisturbed. Clearly, pirates would have stolen any cargo on a ship they boarded, especially hundreds of barrels of liquor and wine. That's what pirates do.

Another theory is that a large wave washed everyone

Fabled People and Places

*S*omewhere deep inside all of us lies a desire to see, if only for a moment, those mythical things we have heard whispered about, perhaps in some far-off land, perhaps right here at home. It's part of the human process to search after the fabled and fantastic, whether it be something as high minded as the Holy Grail, which medieval knights traveled across the world to find, or something really practical, like the Fountain of Youth that Spanish explorers thrashed through the swamps of Florida to locate.

New York is a downright bastion of truly incredible fabled people and places. All are somehow hidden from us—some intentionally, because individuals crave privacy, and some not intentionally, because they exist only in people's imaginations. Whether it's the military's covering up of Top Secret activities or dark enclaves of funny-looking people, there's a hidden underside to the state of New York. It's up to all of us to find these things that lie out there, somewhere between fiction and fact. We are the modern-day conquistadors, traveling the back roads of our neighborhoods, looking for the fountains of youth that may bubble somewhere just beyond the borders of our hometowns.

CLOSED TO PUBLIC
DO NOT ENTER BUILDING

Military Mayhem in Montauk

World War II saw the advent of many top-secret projects aimed at developing new forms of weaponry and technology. Obviously, the most famous of these was the Manhattan Project (named for New York, interestingly, but actually housed in New Mexico), which yielded the atomic bombs that helped end the war with Japan. Other World War II projects have either been forgotten or were covered up because of their dangerous implications and unexpected results. Several of these darker experiments, according to some, did take place right here in New York, in the town of Montauk on Long Island's eastern end, where their effects, some say, are still going on.

The events on Long Island have come to be known as the Montauk Project, which refers to a series of top secret experiments in mind control, time travel, psychotronics, and the creation of black holes. The experiments were carried on in an old air force radar station or, more accurately, in a vast complex hidden in the earth beneath this station.

How could this be? How could such radical experiments be hidden beneath a town not all that far from the largest city in the world? The story of the Montauk Project begins in 1943, not on Long Island but in Philadelphia.

The Philadelphia Experiment was the informal name of the Rainbow Project, which was an attempt by the United States military to create technology that would allow vessels to achieve radar invisibility. In other words, this was early research into what we now call stealth technology. These experiments came to be focused on the U.S.S. *Eldridge,* a navy destroyer based in the Philadelphia Naval Yard. According to legend, the ship was bombarded with electromagnetic energy and did in fact become radar-invisible. Much to everyone's surprise, it also became literally invisible, vanishing from sight. Then, for a few scant seconds, the ship materialized off the coast of

Norfolk, Virginia, disappeared again, then reappeared miles away in Philadelphia. When it reappeared, the ship seemed fine. Things didn't go so well for the rematerialized people on board.

A number of members of the *Eldridge*'s crew had died horrible deaths in the process of the teleportation. Some were literally fused to the metal parts of the ship. Those who didn't die were driven to insanity by the terrible ordeal they had undergone. Government officials and military brass were horrified by the results of their experiments. Official funding was quickly pulled from the Philadelphia Experiment, and the Manhattan Project became the focus of secret military weapons spending.

But there were some, both scientists and military officials, who wanted to continue exploring the possibilities they'd seen in the experiments at the Philadelphia Naval Yard. True, the dangers were great, but the potential for new types of superweaponry was even greater. These scientists and military men went over the heads of Congress and somehow got their funding.

It was decided that a secret military installation would be created where experiments on the new technologies could be conducted away from prying eyes. An old air force facility in the beach town of Montauk, on the eastern tip of Long Island, was chosen as the perfect site. Known by the code name of Camp Hero, the station had recently been decommissioned because new satellite technologies made its radar capabilities obsolete. Montauk, a quiet and, at that time, sparsely populated spot, was considered the perfect location. It was remote, but still fairly close to New York City.

Construction began on a huge subterranean complex that would house the newly formed alliance of scientific and military minds known as the Montauk Project. This base went into operation sometime in the early 1960s. By

It was decided that a secret military installation would be created where experiments on the new technologies could be conducted away from prying eyes.

the 1970s, the experiments being conducted under the surface of the sleepy Long Island town had reached epic proportions. If the stories are true, the work going on there seemed more like the stuff of a science fiction novel than military reality.

The focus of the Montauk Project was primarily on mind control. Young males with psychic sensitivity were identified and brought to the lab. There they were seated in a chair specially developed to enhance their latent psychic abilities. This chair was blasted with energy waves that allowed the researchers to control their young subjects' minds. Amazingly, it was discovered that the most adept of these young psychics were able to focus on imagined objects so intensely that the objects would momentarily physically materialize. Legend says that the most noteworthy wielder of this power was a young man named Duncan Cameron.

Experiments on the powerful Mr. Cameron led scientists to realize that their efforts could allow them to manipulate reality not just spatially but temporally as well. In other words, they had become masters not just of physical space but also of time.

At around this time, many involved in the Montauk Project began to feel that it was reeling out of control. Scientists were creating wormholes on the base that could then be used to further test time travel. The more conservative researchers regarded this as maniacal and dangerous. The base itself was growing extensively; by now, its subterranean layers had snaked out until they lay directly beneath the center of Montauk. Time was being tampered with, and civilians were being endangered. Many thought the project would meet with a disastrous end. In August 1983, they were proved correct.

At some point in the experiments, it was decided that those involved in the current project would travel exactly forty years into the past to establish contact with their predecessors aboard the U.S.S. *Eldridge* in the Philadelphia Experiment. Those who wished to end the

project saw their chance. They got Duncan Cameron to envision a large, angry, powerful Sasquatch-like creature at the exact moment the two experiments came together in time. This beast materialized at Montauk and began destroying the base in a rage. It utterly trashed the place, disconnecting the project from the past and destroying the equipment that harnessed people's psychic power. As soon as this was accomplished, the beast disappeared and the time tunnels maintained by the scientists collapsed upon themselves. The project was over. The base was closed and abandoned.

Many of the participants were brainwashed into forgetting what they had witnessed. Others swore oaths of secrecy, vowing never to reveal what they had seen out on the eastern tip of Long Island. Some say minimal activity still occurs there and is tied to the activities of nearby institutions such as Brookhaven Labs. Some conspiracy theorists have claimed that these ongoing experiments helped, inadvertently, to cause the tragic crash of TWA flight 800 off the coast of Long Island in 1996.

These days the surface of the supposed site of the Montauk Project, where the old radar station is located, is officially a state park. However, the United States military still owns all the property underneath the park. And police and military officials have been said to patrol the entire area, even the part that, on paper, is listed as publicly accessible. Tales are told from time to time of suburban families, looking for a little experience with nature, being chased off the grounds of the former Camp Hero by gun-toting military men who offer little explanation for their actions.

Who knows if the Montauk Project is still ongoing? Who knows how deep these cavernous laboratories stretch? Who knows what vast secrets they hold? The world may never know the full truth of what has happened beneath the sandy soil of Montauk.

Does Montauk Live On in Rome?

Internet speculation swirls that a project connected to the experiments conducted in Montauk still exists beneath the Rome National Air Base in Rome, New York. Apparently, scientists in an underground facility there are in possession of a "Montauk Chair" that achieves psychic effects similar to the equipment at the Long Island facility. An even smaller facility exists nearby, beneath the city of Rochester. Apparently, the two are connected by a tunnel beneath Rochester's Andrews Street Bridge.

Montauk Project Keeps Us Wondering

I live in New Jersey, but work on Long Island. I recently became aware of an old military base at the easternmost tip of Long Island in Montauk. The base is all the way at the end of the island if you follow Route 27 to the end. During World War II, it was used for coastal defense and had some large guns and bunkers. After World War II was over, it became known as Montauk Air Force Station. Reportedly, it was used as a radar station during the Cold War.

The area is now a New York state park, but the buildings are intact and radar equipment remains standing. Also, from what I learned, what is really strange is that while the government gave the land to the state, it still owns the land beneath the base.

Apparently, there are many levels beneath ground that were used for research, and the base was really a cover-up. Some people say that it is absolutely documented that beneath the base there is a subterranean city that is still being used today by secret branches of the military. People say that the radar equipment was built as a cover-up so that the military could conduct experiments in time travel and mind control and this is what all the electronics equipment was for. Apparently, this base was also in cooperation with Mitchell Air Force Base on Long Island.

There are a lot of really weird stories about this place. The base and the Montauk Project were said to have something to do with the Philadelphia Experiment and the Rainbow Project. These may all be related.–*Derden*

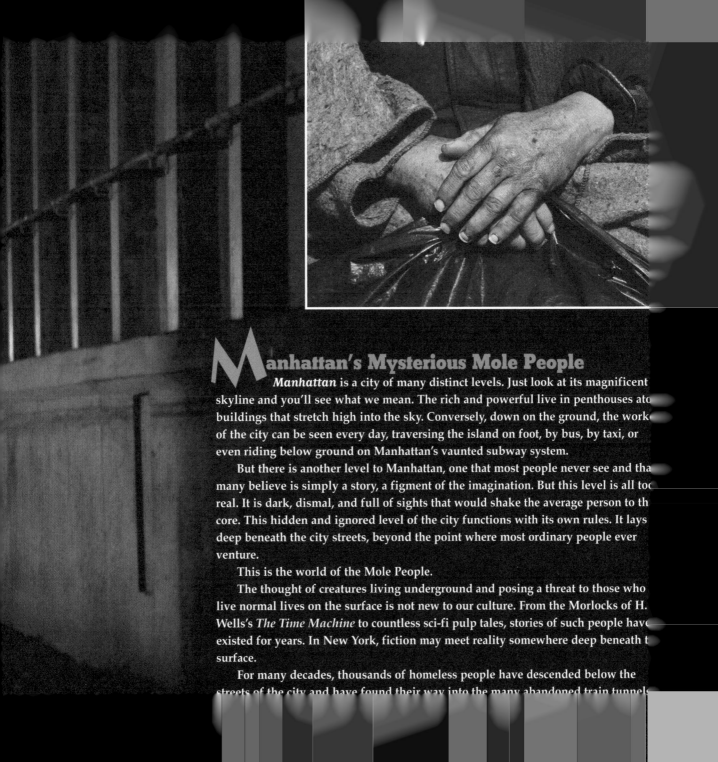

Manhattan's Mysterious Mole People

Manhattan is a city of many distinct levels. Just look at its magnificent skyline and you'll see what we mean. The rich and powerful live in penthouses atop buildings that stretch high into the sky. Conversely, down on the ground, the worke of the city can be seen every day, traversing the island on foot, by bus, by taxi, or even riding below ground on Manhattan's vaunted subway system.

But there is another level to Manhattan, one that most people never see and tha many believe is simply a story, a figment of the imagination. But this level is all too real. It is dark, dismal, and full of sights that would shake the average person to th core. This hidden and ignored level of the city functions with its own rules. It lays deep beneath the city streets, beyond the point where most ordinary people ever venture.

This is the world of the Mole People.

The thought of creatures living underground and posing a threat to those who live normal lives on the surface is not new to our culture. From the Morlocks of H. Wells's *The Time Machine* to countless sci-fi pulp tales, stories of such people have existed for years. In New York, fiction may meet reality somewhere deep beneath t surface.

For many decades, thousands of homeless people have descended below the streets of the city and have found their way into the many abandoned train tunnels that lay buried and forgotten beneath the always evolving metropolis. Here the destitute, the addicted, and the otherwise forgotten have gathered, simultaneously shunning the street-level society that rejected them while forming societies of their own. They build homes, steal electricity, tap into water pipes, and create dwellings that are far more habitable than anything they could put together on the streets.

The myths concerning these people grew more elaborate over the years. It was said that some never emerged from underground and that years without sunlight had affected their physical appearance to the point that they looked more like bug-eyed monsters than men or women. It was whispered that children had been born into these underground societies and that some of these kids lived their entire lives in subterranean cities, never once coming up to the surface. The Mole People were rumored to hate "surface dwellers," as they called them, with a fiery passion, and would kill any who dared enter their dwellings. More audacious versions of this legend claim that the Mole People didn't simply kill surface dwellers, but ate them as well. Just as terrifying was the rumor that people had been kidnapped by vindictive Mole People and taken underground, never to be seen or heard from again.

Most New Yorkers dismissed the stories without a second thought. They were just tall tales, like the stories of alligators in urban sewers. However, in the early 1990s it was discovered that the Mole People, who seemed far too outlandish to be real, were actually an all too real, and all too grim, part of life in Manhattan.

In 1993, journalist Jennifer Toth released her landmark book *The Mole People: Life in the Tunnels Beneath New York City.* Toth had heard the sensational rumors regarding these people and decided to track down the truth of the existence, or nonexistence, of these legendary folk. She spent a year networking with the city's homeless and exploring the tunnels beneath Manhattan. Her findings are truly shocking, illuminating an aspect of the homeless problem in New York that many had denied or thought of as fiction.

Toth didn't happen upon any mutated beings or inhuman creatures during her forays into New York's abandoned rail tunnels. She did, however, find that there were close to five thousand people living in dwellings built in these tunnels. Some were loners—mentally ill, drug-addicted, alcoholic, or those who shunned human contact for whatever reason. Incredibly, there were also organized groups who banded together to form cohesive societal units, some with a membership of over two hundred people. Toth encountered many different types of Mole People gathered together in the tunnels: loose-knit groups who stayed close to each other for safety, others that lived communally and treated each other as family. Most lived in tunnels beneath Grand Central Terminal, one of the busiest commuter junctions in all of New York.

Many of these people had their own social structures in place. For example, some groups had designated runners, whose responsibility it was to go to the surface to forage for food and medicines. Several groups had created intricate systems of tapping on pipes to communicate with each other over distances in the darkness of the underground. There were those who were violent and hoarded weapons, while others were gentle souls who wanted only to be left in peace. Most didn't trust New York City's shelter system; they thought that the violence and thievery that happened there made the shelters worse places to reside than the tunnels.

Not all of those Toth encountered were looking for makeshift families or solitary peace. Her book also chronicles run-ins with criminal gangs who made their headquarters in the tunnels, graffiti artists who made the

tunnels their canvas, and perhaps most chillingly, a charismatic Mole Person referred to as Satan or the Dark Angel by other Mole People, who feared him and his supposed supernatural powers.

Toth's work exposed the reality of the Mole People's lives. Once the issue was brought to the surface, attempts were made to bring the people to the surface as well. Most reports say that today there are far fewer Mole People than the five thousand estimated in the late 1980s and early 1990s. However, a substantial number of the homeless still live in enclaves buried beneath the surface of Manhattan.

Margaret Morton's book *The Tunnel,* published in 1995, combined words and stunning photographs to chronicle the lives of these people. Marc Singer's shocking 2000 documentary, *Dark Days,* follows the daily lives of a group of tunnel dwellers in an abandoned Amtrak tunnel.

Not only were the subterranean residents the subjects of the documentary, they were the crew. Singer lived in the tunnel beneath Penn Station for close to two years, filming his tunnel mates, who also built equipment for the shoot, helped route electricity to the tunnel, and served as cameramen, lighting technicians, and sound operators. The film won accolades at the Sundance Film Festival and brought attention to the horrid living conditions of New York's homeless. It also showed the sense of community they are able to develop in spite of it all.

The Mole People are legendary, but they are no urban legend. They are a group of people living in unthinkable circumstances for a variety of extreme, unfortunate reasons. The next time you visit Manhattan and walk its streets, think of the unseen, the unheard, and the unknown residents living their lives in the dark recesses below you.

More Manhattan Mysteries Underground

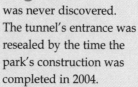

Conspiracy theorists speak of tunnels beneath Manhattan that house secrets far more sinister than enclaves of homeless people. And the groups behind these secret tunnels and their nefarious purposes are two favorites of the conspiracy crowd: the federal government and that not-so-secret society the Masons. The Masons are a fraternal organization with branches throughout the world, and many believe that their most powerful upper-level members are also involved in a number of covert conspiracies.

In an issue of *Shavertron* magazine published in the fall of 1981, an author named R. L. Blain-Sanders claimed to know the location of an enormous triangular set of tunnels set hundreds of feet below the surface of Manhattan. The author contended that this was a deeply secret meeting ground used by a Masonic lodge to plan its most shadowy operations. The author's claim has become famous among conspiracy theorists, although it has never been verified or followed up on.

Other strange caverns have been discovered or are rumored to exist beneath New York City. During the reconstruction of East River Park, where Houston Street meets the FDR Drive, Con Ed had to halt construction after drilling into a two-hundred-foot-deep tunnel below the north end of the park. The reason for the existence of this tunnel was never discovered. The tunnel's entrance was resealed by the time the park's construction was completed in 2004.

A number of well-known Manhattan landmarks are also rumored to house tunnel entrances. The Episcopal Church of St. John the Divine, at 110th Street and Amsterdam Avenue, is said to be one such place. Supposedly, the church's basement contains an entrance to a vast system of interconnected tunnels that are used by an occult group for some dark purpose. Whether this is the same system of tunnels purportedly used by the Masons is unknown.

There are also rumors that a number of subbasements exist beneath the Empire State Building. These are supposed to be the homes of hidden federal government offices. Apparently, they go deep below the surface to connect with a set of subterranean tunnels that allow those in the know to travel throughout the city without ever appearing aboveground.

While many stories of secret tunnels seem far-fetched, there have been some discoveries over the years that support them. During an excavation, the remnants of the wall for which Wall Street was named were discovered many layers underground. And keep in mind that the first subway was a pneumatic tube built completely in secrecy by one Alfred Beach. (He was attempting to demonstrate the practicality of "pneumatic dispatch.") This is a city that has a long-held tradition of doing secret things underground, out of sight of the surface dwellers going about their business above.

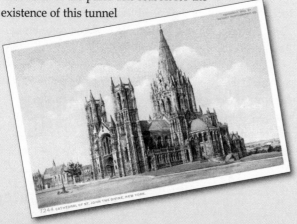

The Clawfoot People

The Zoar Valley is a small area near Gowanda in the northwest portion of the state. Its history has long been associated with tales of the strange and bizarre. Perhaps the strangest tale of all to come out of the valley is that of the Clawfoot People.

In the late nineteenth and early twentieth centuries, many of the inhabitants of the Zoar Valley were descendants of the same woman, an English prostitute who had settled in the area in the early 1800s. There were over two hundred relatives of this apparently very fertile woman, and all were known for their strange appearance. These were the Clawfoot People.

Because of an exposure to syphilis, the prostitute was said to have passed on to all her male offspring a genetic abnormality that caused their hands and feet to be deformed into clawlike extremities. As the family grew and the abnormality appeared among more and more of the town's residents, the Clawfoot People became legendary in the area. They were shunned—social outcasts, with no place in "normal" society.

Not surprisingly, this had severe psychological effects on members of the family. One man, in a fit of despair, used an axe to remove his fused fingers. Another well-remembered tale tells of a man who was miraculously not afflicted with the condition. He tried to live a normal life, and he married, choosing not to tell his wife that he was a member of the infamous clan of the Clawfoots. However, he was soon outed. When their first son was born, he clearly had the deformity. The wife abandoned both husband and child. The curse of the Clawfoot People had struck again.

In the 1920s, the Clawfoot People took action in one of the most tragic scenarios imaginable. Every member of the family, male and female, assembled and made a secret pact. In an effort to stop the grotesque deformity from being passed on, no member of the group would marry or have children. In other words, the Clawfoot People chose to exterminate themselves.

The unhappy people held true to their pact. One by one, they grew old and died off. Today no member of their tragically afflicted lineage remains alive. What is now a condition easily corrected by surgery caused this entire family to choose mass death over continued life.
—John Stoneman contributed to this story.

The Curious Tale of the Jackson Whites

Since the Revolutionary War, legends have circulated about a motley group of social outcasts living in the Ramapo Mountains in the southern New York State towns of Hillburn and Suffern. The tales tell of a group now inbred to the point of mutation, descended from renegade Indians, escaped slaves, Hessian mercenary deserters, and refugee prostitutes. They are known as the Jackson Whites. But the story of these peoples has been confused by less-than-scholarly historical texts that present local legends as authenticated fact.

Probably the earliest written reference to this group is in an article entitled "A Community of Outcasts" in *Appleton's Journal of Literature, Science and Art*, dated March 23, 1872. The relevant passage reads:

> In relation to this particular people, there are half a dozen legends current, all possessing more or less romance and attractiveness; but the most favored one is, for a rarity, the most reasonable.
>
> The people will tell you that this stain upon their fair country was first put there by fugitive slaves, more than a hundred years ago.
>
> There was gradually added to these fugitive slaves, fugitives of other descriptions, and the general antagonism to the world made each individual endure the others. They buried themselves deep in the fastnesses and gorges of the mountains, and reared children, wilder and more savage than themselves.

An early written reference to the Ramapo people as Jackson Whites dates back to 1900, in J. M. Van Valen's *History of Bergen County,* which states:

> The Ramapo Indians sometimes visited the settlements in the township of Franklin. They were known

formerly as the Hackensack Indians, but are more properly described as the Jackson Whites. They bear little resemblance to the Indians, yet as tradition gives it they are descendants of Hessians, Indians, and Negroes, but know nothing of their ancestry, so ignorant have they become.

Arthur S. Tompkins's 1902 *History of Rockland County, New York* told the saga of the Jackson Whites this way:

> The Jackson Whites originated when the Indians were yet living in the lowlands along the Ramapo Mountains. The first race came by a union between the

Indians and half breeds on one side, and colored laborers brought from the lower part of the county to work in the Ramapo factories on the other side. The colored people were either freed slaves or their children grown up, and many of the names today may be traced as identified with some of the old Holland pioneers of Orangetown, for the slaves in old times bore the surnames of their masters. Inter-marriage among these people has caused them to degenerate intellectually if not physically.

In 1906–07, the New Jersey historical society's annual report contains this passage explaining the Jackson Whites' curious lineage:

> The Secretary wrote that his understanding had been that they [the Jackson Whites] were a people of mixed Indian and Negro blood. . . . They are supposed to be the offspring of former Negro slaves, runaways, and free Negroes, who sought refuge in the mountains where they could eke out a living by cutting hoop-poles and wood for charcoal, in the days of charcoal iron furnaces. They have been regarded as outcasts, and hence have been allowed to sink into a degraded state. . . .

In 1911, the Jackson Whites' story took on a pseudo-scientific authority when a University of Pennsylvania anthropologist named Frank Speck published an article that claimed that the Jackson Whites were

> Algonquian Indians, probably Minisinks of the Delaware, with some of the Tuscarora who lingered for a rest in the Ramapo Valley on their way from Carolina in 1714 to join their colleagues, the Iroquois, in New York State. To this small nucleus became

added from time to time runaway Negro slaves and perhaps freed men from the Dutch colonial plantations in the adjoining counties in New Jersey. Vagabond white men of all sorts also contributed a share to the community from the early days until now. The Jackson Whites may be regarded, therefore, as a type of triple race mixture.

Also written that same year was an even less well-researched study by the head of New Jersey's Vineland Training School, Henry Herbert Goddard, entitled *The Jackson Whites: A Study in Racial Degeneracy*. Taking his liberties with history, Goddard gave his own slant to the Ramapo people's lineage.

> The Indian blood found in the Jackson Whites, whether it came down through individuals held as slaves or through isolated free Indians who intermarried with the emancipated Negroes, is supposed to have belonged to a remnant of the Algonquin Tribe— to the Minsi, or Wolf Clan, who were natives of the Upper Delaware Valley in Pennsylvania, New Jersey, and New York. . . . There were also a few families of the Tuscarora Indians who remained in the Ramapo mountains after their tribe had made there a three years sojourn, from 1710 to 1713, on its way to join the five nations in New York State.

The document that solidified the Jackson Whites' legend was a 1936 book self-published by John C. Storms, a small-town newspaper editor. *The Origins of the Jackson Whites of the Ramapo Mountains* contended that the first ingredient in the Jackson Whites' racial stew was a group of Tuscarora Indians who had fled North Carolina between 1711 and 1713. Storms drew upon the day's prevailing mythology more than on any personal investigation, and he had a well-known penchant for embellishment and romanticism. According to Storms:

> Originally the Ramapo Mountain region was a favorite resort of the Hagingashackie (Hackensack) Indians, part of the Leni Lenape family of the Iroquois [in fact, they were part of the Algonquin language group, not the Iroquois]. . . . These aborigines had practically all disappeared by the end of the seventeenth century. However, a few remained together with a scattered population that had sought the security of the mountains to evade their brother white man, his laws and customs. Thus it was a sort of No Man's Land.
>
> The first real influx of a permanent population in the Ramapo Mountains was in 1714. This was a remnant of the Tuscarora Indians . . . perhaps it was because there were to be found congenial spirits among the remaining Hagingashackies and the wild renegades who were hiding there. But the ultimate object was to unite theirs with the powerful Five Nations that ruled the country to the northward. . . .

The second strain in the Jackson Whites' bloodline, according to Storms, came from Hessian mercenaries fighting for the British during America's Revolutionary War.

> Reaching America under duress, placed in the forefront at every important battle in which they were engaged, beaten by their officers with the broadside of swords if they attempted to retreat, made to do the menial labor of their British companions, their fate was a particularly cruel one. With no interest in the outcome of the military struggle . . . they proved unfaithful, and deserted the army at every opportunity.
>
> In the fighting that took place in the vicinity of

New York City, from the camps scattered throughout this region, and at the marches across New Jersey, these men, known by the general name of Hessians, fled to the nearest place of safety—the Ramapo Mountains. There was no possibility of escape, no opportunity to return to their native land, so they made for themselves homes in their retreat, mated with those they found already there, and reared families.

The third genetic element in the Jackson Whites' lineage, according to Storms, derived from English and West Indian women brought to New York to serve as concubines for British soldiers.

> The British War Office had a problem on its hands—

keeping New York City loyal to the Crown as a Tory city, while keeping thousands of its soldiers in the military camp that General Clinton had established there. . . .

But there was a way out of the difficulty, a way that had long been in vogue by warring European nations, in fact, by England herself. A little judicious questioning and a man was found who would accept the undertaking. The man's name was Jackson — history has not preserved for us anything more about him than this, not even his given name.

A contract was entered into that Jackson was to secure thirty-five-hundred young women whom England felt it could very well dispense with, and transport them to America to become the intimate property of the army quartered in New York City. . . .

Jackson set his agents at the task of recruiting from the inmates of brothels of London, Liverpool, Southampton and other English cities along the sea coast. . . . If a young woman or matron chanced to be on her way home from her occupation, or on the street on an honest mission she fared the same fate as the inmates of the houses of ill fame, and many a respectable working girl or young housewife was shanghaied, and carried off to a life of shame across the sea. Lispenard's Meadows [a low, swampy, salt meadow on the west side of Manhattan near the present entrance to the Holland Tunnel] had been secured as quarters for the anticipated "guests," and was being duly prepared. . . .

In 1783, when New York was repatriated by American army forces, the stockade of women was evacuated and the prisoners beat a hasty retreat along with British soldiers and Tories.

By far the larger portion of the human stream that flowed out of Lispenard's Meadows on that eventful Evacuation Day of 1783, by some unknown means, reached the western shore of the Hudson. . . . The horde has been estimated at about three thousand or slightly more. . . . To the company was added a few soldiers who preferred to cast in their lot with the refugees, having formed a quasi-attachment for some member of it. Tories, too, who had been unable to secure passage to the Canadian ports considered their bodily safety rather than their social standing. . . . Then, too, the confusion of departure afforded an added opportunity for a number of Hessians to make their escape. . . . Then followed another memorable trek. Across the Hackensack Meadows, up the Saddle River valley, these derelicts made their way on foot. . . . Pillaging of orchards and deliberate raids on fields and

gardens provoked the farmers, who drove the wanderers on with hard words and often with harder blows, all of which was retaliated. No one wanted these unfortunates. . . .

At last, with Oakland past, the crowd entered the Ramapo Pass and soon found itself in a country that, while wild and inhospitable in character, yet offered the boon of peace; there was no one to drive them away. Here the colony scattered, finding shelters in the woods and among the rocks. Here the individual members found companionship of peaceful Indians, escaped outlaws, Hessians, runaway slaves—there was ample companionship and it was readily accepted.

Storms cites a New York Tory newspaper, known as *Rivington's Loyal Gazette,* as the first publication to coin the name Jackson Whites and adds that escaped slaves would contribute the final piece to their ancestral puzzle.

The Dutch settlers kept these bondsmen as servants principally, and the bondage was not particularly hard in most cases. Still, it frequently happened that these escaped slaves would seek their own freedom, and the most accessible place and most secure was the fastness of the Ramapos. . . . These people carried with them names of former masters, white acquaintances, or those that they had adopted. Thus we sometimes find family names among them that are borne by prominent and socially acceptable white persons.

How much of Storms's account of the Ramapo Mountain people's origins is historically accurate and how much was merely transcribed from oral folktales is unclear. It is certain, however, that his "evidence" influenced people's perceptions of the Jackson Whites and tainted supposedly scholarly works and subsequent literary references to them, which reinforced the mythology.

The Ramapo Mountain people themselves will tell you a variety of stories to explain their ancestry, intertwining elements of the Dutch, Hessian, and Tuscarora Indian sagas. Most insist that they are really a tribe of Indians called the Ramapough, though they bear little physical resemblance to Native Americans (most appear to be light-skinned African Americans). They have been petitioning the federal government for twenty years to be recognized as a legitimate American Indian tribe. The state governments of New York and New Jersey have recognized them as such, but the federal Bureau of Indian Affairs has denied their petitions. Such recognition is considered crucial because it brings certain federal benefits, such as housing and health-care assistance and the right to operate a casino.

According to the bureau, though, the Ramapoughs are not a tribe at all but rather descendants of settlers with African and Dutch blood who, beginning in the late 1600s, moved to the area from Manhattan in search of farmland. The bureau asserts that they have failed to show that they are descendants of a historic Indian tribe and cannot prove that they have led a continuous existence as a separate band of people since the time of their first contact with Europeans.

In the end, there is not much historical evidence to support any version of the Jackson Whites' legend. It is almost certain that many tales were originally told to create a derogatory stereotype of the mountain people among their white neighbors. While the Ramapough show a fierce pride in their unique identity, you would be hard-pressed to find a person in Suffern or Hillburn who would call him- or herself a Jackson White. "Those people," it would seem, are always to be found just over the next mountain.

Defending the Jackson Whites

I went to school with these people. They work at the reservoirs, drive our school buses, were our lunch aides in our elementary schools, and are overall a big part of our community. If you don't bother them, they aren't gonna bother you. How would all of you people like it if your home and family were known as freaks of nature?

A couple of interesting facts I learned from talking to my Jackson White schoolmates in high school was that they do in fact inbreed, or have done so in the past, but usually only with cousins. Also the police only go up there if someone is dead because they will be attacked under other conditions.

Most of them never finish high school, but two out of the five with whom I grew up, and who were in my grade, finished high school and one of those two is now in college! Anyway, it has really bothered me to hear that people are traveling up there and bothering them. I mean they're human too. Oh, and about that electricity, they have phones and cable. Which is more than I have. I have a phone and electricity, but no cable!—Liz

The Incest Butterflies

A popular legend at Colgate University says that Oriskany Falls, a tiny quaint village near the university, with a population of less than eight hundred people, is actually the home of a secret cult whose members are all united by familial bonds and the practice of incest. The cult is well known on campus because its members supposedly hate the nearby university and its students and faculty. Students warn each other not to set foot in the town, lest they face the wrath of the cult's members, who do not want to be gawked at by the prying eyes of local college students. They prefer that their strange customs remain secret. To ensure this, they mark their territory to identify themselves and warn outsiders that they are on dangerous grounds.

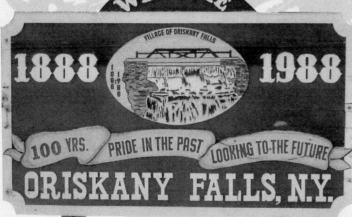

The student newspaper of Colgate University, the *Colgate Maroon News*, explored the story in an article published on February 21, 1997. The paper first laid out the legend, mentioning the ornamentation that members of the cult place on their homes: "Oriskany Falls is the incest capital of the world and the butterflies on many of the houses represent membership in a secret incestuous cult. . . . This rumor is one of the oldest at Colgate. . . . We, the writers of the article, did not go to Oriskany Falls and question any of the town's residents for various reasons, mainly because we were afraid."

When traveling through Oriskany Falls, beware—secrets lurk beneath the surface of this seemingly peaceful town. Be on the lookout for butterflies, because it is said that the incestuous cult members are never far behind.

Tinker Town

America is riddled with stories of neighborhoods built by and for little people. There are dozens of supposed Midgetvilles, Midget Towns, and Hobbitvilles spread across the country. New York is no different. In the following passages, readers tell us their tales of a mythical neighborhood in Long Island said to be the home of a group of reclusive (and diminutive) residents. Most people have only heard of this fantastic place, as is the case with most Midgetvilles. We have yet to meet anyone who can actually tell us how to get there!

Remembering Merrick's Tinker Town

I was recently speaking with many of my friends who grew up with me on Long Island. We remembered a place called Tinker Town, which I believe is somewhere in Merrick.

It is a small geographic area of several streets where everything is built in miniature! There are small houses and such, as little people live there. If you haven't already heard about it, it might be something to investigate.–*Jan Moran*

Tall Tales of a Tiny Town

I first heard about Midgetville in high school, right around the time everyone started being able to drive. My friends frequented a few diners, one of which was the Seaford Palace. I heard that near the Palace was a neighborhood of little people called Midgetville. No one knew exactly where it was, but we all had a general idea. I don't recall anyone I know actually going there, but someone always knew someone who went.

It was purported to be a community of small houses, about half the size of "normal" houses. The street signs were lower to the ground (which of course makes no sense when you consider that cars are the same height no matter who is driving them). I remember hearing that there were not only many NO TRESPASSING signs around, but sinister ones like TRESPASSERS WILL BE SHOT ON SIGHT. I heard about Midgetville residents running out of their homes with shotguns, trying to scare curious gawkers away.

Sometimes late at night, after the diner run, we'd go looking for Midgetville. I was a wimp, so the shotgun stories worked on me. We'd drive around the neighborhood we thought it was located in, but usually gave up after about twenty to thirty minutes.

We never called it Tinker Town. We knew the place as Midgetville. We were always told that it was in Seaford, LI, south of Merrick Road, somewhere near the bay.–*Flynn Barrison*

For Scares and Intrigue, Nothing Beats Tinker Town!

Growing up, Tinker Town was unbeatable. My friends and I had been in our fair share of abandoned buildings—even asylums. We had gone looking for ghosts and had explored more sewer tunnels than most Con Ed workers. But nothing scared us and intrigued us more than the idea of an entire town full of angry midgets just waiting to lash out at normal-sized people like ourselves.

We often got drunk and went looking for the midget section of town. I only remember finding it once, and we were so hammered that we never managed to find our way back there again. The houses were shorter than usual, I remember that. We didn't see any low street signs or cameras set up, though.

We got out of there fast, because something happened that completely freaked us out. As we drove past each house, the lights would come on inside. These weren't motion detectors, either. These lights were inside the house. And it was well after two in the morning. The idea that people were up and waiting for people like us made us get out of there fast. In our minds, the light on meant that all the rumors we had heard about the midgets murdering outsiders and torturing people who came to laugh at them were entirely true.

That was many, many years ago, and we never went back. But I still think that growing up on Long Island, Tinker Town was easily the craziest local legend. And that's saying a lot, considering all of the strange things that happen out there every day.–*Shane Figg*

Did Giants Once Roam Cardiff?

In October 1869, workmen digging a new well on a farm in Cardiff made a startling and peculiar discovery—a man, but a giant of a man! Stonelike, it was called petrified by some local scientists of the day. Word spread like wildfire, and a tent was erected over the giant. People came from hundreds of miles to see what the religious scholars of the day called a Giant from the Ancient Bible.

But this discovery, which at the time must have seemed like a great archaeological find, is actually the story of one of the greatest hoaxes ever perpetrated on the people of New York. It all started back in 1866, when a fellow by the name of George Hull, an avowed atheist, decided to play a little prank on local folks for what he believed were their gullible beliefs in stories from the Bible, religion, and the church in general. He and a partner, H. B. Martin, commissioned a block of gypsum to be cut from a quarry in Iowa and then sent to sculptors in Chicago. In the Windy City, the artists cut the stone into the image of a giant man, almost twelve feet tall. Acid was used to make the stone look petrified, and small needles were even used to emulate skin pores. Then the finished "giant" was secretly shipped to the farm of one Stub Newell, near Cardiff, buried some five feet below ground, and left for a few years.

After his giant was discovered by the well diggers, Hull erected a tent over it and charged local townsfolk fifty cents to take a peek. So much media attention was paid to the Cardiff Giant that it was shipped to Syracuse to be put on display. More cash rolled in. P. T. Barnum offered thousands for it, but Hull refused. So Barnum created his own giant instead.

Over the ensuing months, much debate raged over the giant, which had now gone on tour. Even after it was generally considered a fake, the Cardiff Giant still drew the attention of onlookers willing to part with their cash for a glimpse. Today you'll pay a few bucks to take a look at America's greatest hoax. I know I happily shelled out for it!

The Cardiff Giant can be seen at the Farmer's Museum, Lake Road, Cooperstown. —*Dr. Seymour O'Life*

Learning Family Values with the Klan

Mannsville, just a few miles south of Watertown, is a rural and peaceful little town. It's easy to see why a group of people planning to build an orphanage saw it as a perfect setting. What better place to house and teach unfortunate children than somewhere so quaint and tranquil?

Yet, when you know the history of the people who built their orphanage here in Mannsville, the thought is ironic. This group was far from quaint or peaceful. Known as the Klan Haven Home, the institution was founded and run by members of the Ku Klux Klan. It served as home to up to thirty children at a time, all of them children of deceased members of the famously racist organization.

The Klan Haven Home, a large farmhouse, was situated upon three hundred acres of land. Boys living here were trained in agriculture, and girls were given lessons on activities of a domestic nature, cooking, sewing, and so on. One wonders what else was taught to these impressionable youngsters, considering the notorious reputation of the organization that sponsored the institution.

The Ku Klux Klan had a strong presence in New York State (and most other states) in the early part of the twentieth century, when the organization was at the height of its popularity and influence. As time went on, its membership in the Empire State waned and its presence became less and less. The Klan Haven Home has been closed for many years now, but residents of Mannsville still remember the unusual orphanage.

LILY DALE ASSEMBLY
THE CITY OF LIGHT
Lily Dale ASSEMBLY
WORLDS LARGEST CENTER
FOR
THE RELIGION OF SPIRITUALISM
EXIT ONLY

The Most Spirited Town in the State

Looking for a clairvoyant to predict your future? Hoping to have one last conversation with that deceased relative you want to settle an old score with? Interested in mystical healing for those aches and pains that won't go away? No need to travel far and wide, from town to town, looking for the best in these psychic services. Just drop by Lily Dale, a village of colorful Victorian gingerbread houses on small, placid Cassadaga Lake, just a few hours south of Buffalo. Lily Dale, home to about one hundred year-round residents, is the place to go for all spiritualist needs and has been for well over a century.

The year 2004 marked the 125th anniversary of Lily Dale, which easily qualifies as one of the most unusual towns in America. The town was founded in 1879 by the Laona Free Thinkers Association at the height of America's fascination with the concept of Spiritualism, which is a loosely defined philosophy that incorporates a number of different beliefs and practices. Central to its core is the belief that the human spirit lives on after a person's death. What Vatican City in Rome is to the Catholic religion, Lily Dale is to followers of the spiritual movement.

Spiritualism and the state of New York have long been linked together. In the mid-nineteenth century, the Fox sisters of Hydesville first popularized Spiritualism after staging a series of séances, "communicating" with the dead through mysterious raps and knockings. (See the chapter on Local Heroes and Villains for more about the Fox girls.) For some reason, Americans were eager to talk to their dead at the time and Spiritualism became a sensation. Lily Dale was established as something of a spiritualist colony. Mediums registered their abilities with the town, and those seeking psychic advice of all kinds began flocking there. Spiritualism was considered chic among society's elite, and many famous Americans visited Lily Dale to sample the available services. Susan B. Anthony, Harry Houdini, and Mae West all experienced Lily Dale in its heyday. (But Houdini, a famous trickster in his own right, rejected Spiritualism's supposedly spectral conversations as fakes.)

People still make sabbaticals to Lily Dale today. There are over

thirty registered mediums in the small hamlet, operating in an atmosphere that is part religious commune, part ghostly summer camp, and all business. Calling themselves by different names—mediums, clairvoyants, telepaths—the practitioners peddle their services out of private homes selling half-hour- or hour-long sessions for up to $75 a pop. Free public services are also held during the summer. Twice daily, at one p.m. and five thirty p.m., visitors to the local pet cemetery are treated to spiritualist readings. Also, local "temples" offer free services. Public group healings are held twice a day at one temple, where dozens of visitors gather to attempt to rid themselves of various maladies.

While some may dress in the stereotypical mystic garb of flowing robes and turbans, you won't see any tarot cards, crystal balls, or Ouija boards here. The mediums of Lily Dale frown upon the use of such cliché props and say that they need no such devices to communicate with the dead. After all, they are serious professionals.

How serious are they? Well, to become a registered medium in the community, aspiring clairvoyants must pass tests including forty public readings, three private readings, and a reading before the town's board of directors. Potential candidates are then judged on their mystical merits. Only the best of the best pass; about one out of every twelve applicants is allowed to hang a shingle and set up shop in Lily Dale.

Lily Dale is a place to go in the summer. (Cold weather apparently chills the medium's visions.) Visitors pay $7 for each day they spend in the village. A number of local lodges and bed and breakfasts, most of them situated on Cassadaga Lake, have sprung up to accommodate the tourists. For more information on the most psychic town in the state of New York, visit www.lilydaleassembly.com.

The Oracle Sees All (and Tells Some) in Brooklyn

The Pintchik Oracle, located in the Flatbush neighborhood of Brooklyn, doles out the wisdom of the ages to all seekers of knowledge who pass by. The oracle is a black billboard located on the side of Pintchik's Hardware on Flatbush Avenue. Across the street from the store is an old-fashioned phone mounted on a wood box. Passersby are invited to pick up the phone and ask the oracle a question. The billboard will display personalized answers.

The oracle is actually an unseen man, known only to be a writer from Brooklyn, who sits inside Pintchik's Hardware manning an answering machine. He has a laptop computer to compose the sayings on the billboard. From his vantage point, he can see what people look like and what they are wearing, and incorporates that into his prophecies.

Just trying to track down information on the oracle is a difficult task. When we called Pintchik's Hardware, a young woman picked up the phone.

"Pintchik's Hardware, how may I help you?" She sounded cheerful enough.

"Is this the hardware store with the oracle?" I asked.

"Yes, it is . . . the oracle makes appearances from time to time," she said, her voice lowering in volume and pitch.

"There's no telling when the next appearance will be?" I asked. There was a long, drawn-out, melodramatic pause.

"Hold on. Let me see if the oracle has announced the next date," she said, and put me on hold for a good three minutes. Was the girl heading through some hidden doorway at just that moment, moving a book on a bookshelf in order to rotate a bookcase that disguised a secret hallway leading to the oracle's residence? While I contemplated the possibility, a man's voice suddenly appeared on the phone.

"This is the oracle's representative," the man said without any sense of facetiousness. "How may I help you?"

"I was just wondering if the oracle is currently in operation," I responded.

"No, it's not, but it will be back in July. Why?"

"Well, I'm a writer. I write about weird things and . . ."

When the man heard I was a writer, his voice perked up. "Oh," he said. He then began rattling off a number of facts about the oracle. He told me that people have called Pintchik's from as far away as Michigan, asking the oracle for sports scores and betting odds. He let me know that the oracle was taking a break so the hardware behind it could be upgraded. When it comes back, he explained, there is going to be an oracle dating service.

"I would tell you more . . . but I don't want to anger the oracle," the man told me with a tinge of regret in his voice. I should call back when the oracle returned and was fully functioning.

I hung up feeling genuinely bewildered. The Pintchik Oracle is a very strange phenomenon. Who knows if it is good, evil, a sociological experiment, or simply some bored guy looking for a way to mess with people?

In ancient times, Greeks headed to Delphi to ask their oracle questions. These days, New Yorkers can just head to Flatbush Avenue.

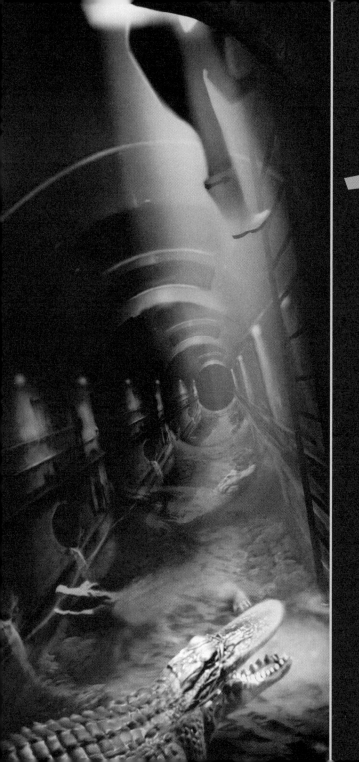

Bizarre Beasts

Today most people have to go out of their way to experience nature. We live in cities or suburbs, among other people, separate from the woods and waterways and wild things that our ancestors took for granted. On top of that, we live in a so-called age of reason, where every fact must be analyzed and explained, where everything must be summed up by an equation, a principle, or at the very least a theory. Unlike our ancestors, who looked to the stars and seasons as sources of guidance, wonder, and magic, we look inward, to our minds.

Perhaps this is why nature is such a constant source of intrigue in our mythology. We're not sure what lurks deep in those forests of which we see only the edges or in the bodies of water whose surfaces we only skim. These are places that lie beyond what we know firsthand and therefore beyond what we can explain. It is in these unknown places that New York's most bizarre beasts lurk.

Some swear these creatures are real. Others say they are simply scary stories, like the boogeyman. Have we merely dreamed them up to account for aspects of our natural world that defy explanation and classification? Or do they really roam the dark forests and swim through the murky waters of this state, living their secretive existences, not caring whether we believe in them or not?

Monsters of the Lake

New York is the home of an unusual number of monsters that lurk on the muddy bottoms of our lakes. What is it about this fair state that seems to breed long-necked, serpentine creatures that terrorize innocent swimmers and boaters?

The most famous lake monster in New York, and perhaps the most famous in the world except for Scotland's Loch Ness Monster, is found in Lake Champlain; over the centuries, it has affectionately come to be known as Champ. No discussion of bizarre beasts in the state of New York should begin with anything but stories of this aquatic titan of cryptozoology, that ever-fascinating study of unexplained animals.

Champ

Is this mysterious monster some water-dwelling version of a dinosaur? Or is it a bottom-dwelling sturgeon? Perhaps it's nothing more than a pile of floating debris playing tricks on the eyes. What exactly is—or isn't—it that lurks deep beneath the placid surface of Lake Champlain? While specific descriptions may vary, hundreds of eyewitness accounts and a world-famous photograph all agree: Something extraordinarily unusual calls America's sixth largest freshwater lake home. Rumors of an enormous creature living in Lake Champlain are ancient, predating even the European arrival on this continent. Legends of the lake monster were whispered among Native American tribes of the area. The Abenaki spoke of a creature, known as the Tatoskok, that periodically showed itself to hunters and fishing parties in the vicinity of Lake Champlain.

The first recorded report of a Champ sighting by a European dates from 1609, by the man who "discovered" the lake itself: Samuel de Champlain. In a log of his travels he mentions seeing in the lake a large, strange creature, some twenty feet long and as thick as a barrel. While he was the first European to see Champ, he was far from the last. Literally hundreds of people have claimed to have spotted the beast over the centuries.

In the summer of 1819, a newspaper in nearby Plattsburgh told of one ship captain's sighting of the infamous monster. He saw the beast rise out of the water roughly two hundred yards away from his vessel. He estimated that it was just under two hundred feet in length, stuck its neck almost twenty feet above the water, and was dark black in color. Incredibly, the captain provided a number of very specific details about Champ's appearance, stating that the monster had red markings on his neck, only three teeth, and a star on his forehead. Many say that the extreme specificity of this article points to its being a hoax, although this has never been officially proved one way or the other.

A large number of newspaper accounts of Champ sightings occurred in the 1870s. Fantastic stories were told of a large serpentine monster emerging along Lake Champlain's shore, frightening work crews who were building there. Another tale told of a steamship that was nearly capsized when something slammed into its underside. Minutes after impact, passengers of the ship witnessed the creature emerge from the lake about a hundred feet away from them. Soon reports were pouring in; most described Champ as resembling a serpent somewhere between twenty-five and thirty-five feet long, although one group of picnickers reported him as being over seventy-five feet in length. The Champ sensation was growing quickly, and his reputation soon extended beyond the shores of the lake. Champ became a nationally known phenomenon, so famous that showman P. T. Barnum offered a $50,000 reward for the capture of the monster fish, if fish it was. Barnum hoped to display its carcass in his New York City museum. Newspaper accounts of Champ sightings, which previously had been seen only in small local papers, were now showing up in *The New York Times.* In 1873, the newspaper of record chronicled the sighting of Champ by a railroad crew, who described the monster as being silver and poking its head out of the lake to watch them at work. They quickly left their job behind, opting to make their way back to a less desolate (and less monster-ridden) area.

Champ unmasked?

Eddie Green of Cumberland Head displays a six-foot piece of driftwood that bears a striking resemblance to artists' conceptions of Lake Champlain's legendary monster, Champ. Although the creature was reportedly seen 24 times during 1983, Green has more than a fleeting glimpse; he has a replica carved by nature. Or, if sightings suddenly stop, who knows? Maybe the Champ he's found is the real one. (P-R staff photo by Bruce Rowland)

Sightings continued into the twentieth century. Every few years someone would report witnessing the sea creature from shore or would claim to have had his boat terrorized by the beast. Most people said they encountered the creature right around dusk, leading to the belief that Champ was nocturnal. But as the years rolled by, Champ seems to have gotten less lively and reports of sightings became few and far between. Then, a century after the first wave of Champ-mania, some truly astonishing photographs brought the eyes of the world back onto the peaceful waters of Lake Champlain once again.

The year was 1977, and the Mansi family was enjoying a vacation along the lakeshore, as so many others have over the years. What started out as a routine day of swimming and picnicking ended as one of the most talked-about incidents in the history of cryptozoology. When Anthony Mansi made his way back to the family's car, his wife, Sandra, was keeping an extra-close eye on their children, who were swimming and playing in the lake. Sandra noticed an odd patch of water in the distance beyond her children and focused on it. Then, much to her surprise, a large serpentine beast rose from the water. It had a tiny head mounted on an incredibly long neck that led down to a series of humps protruding from the water's surface. Anthony returned to the lake to help hurry the children out of the now very dangerous waters. Sandra quickly grabbed her camera and began taking a series of photographs that may very well prove that what many thought was nothing more than old wives' tales is actually true.

Sandra Mansi's photographs, while taken from a considerable distance, clearly show what appears to be a green-colored serpentine creature sticking its long neck out above the waters of Lake Champlain. Its humped back is visible, and it appears to be twisting its head around, as if looking in all directions.

One of Sandra Mansi's photographs

These pictures are shocking upon first view, but not everyone buys into the story they seem to tell. Those who believe in the existence of a monster in Lake Champlain point to them as proof that something very weird does indeed live in the lake. Naysayers claim that the photos were staged or altered. However, tests have proved that the photos are authentic. Regardless of what they depict, the photos themselves have not been doctored in any way.

Once the Mansi photographs came to light, many people came forward, telling of their encounters with Champ. Efforts to find out more about the creature and to gain acceptance for his existence were spearheaded largely by social studies teacher Joseph Zarzynski, who throughout the 1970s and '80s investigated hundreds of claims with the Lake Champlain Phenomena Investigation, an organization he founded. Today many websites and monster hunters continue the quest to legitimize Champ, most notably Dennis Hall of the Champ Quest website.

By the early '80s, Champ had become a local treasure, attracting the curious around the world and, incidentally, contributing mightily to the tourist industry in Plattsburgh. In 1981, the town discouraged any Barnum-like bounty hunting by declaring their waters a safe haven for the beast. In 1982, the state of Vermont, which also borders Lake Champlain, followed suit, passing a resolution granting Champ protection.

Skeptics have many theories as to what Champ actually is. Most say it is probably a large fish, perhaps a garfish, a member of the sturgeon family that spends most of its time close to the lake's bottom. This would keep him pretty far out of sight, since in some spots Lake Champlain reaches four hundred feet in depth. This imposing creature is quite large and, if encountered at night, could be mistaken for something much more sinister. Others have said that Champ may actually be a plesiosaur, a species of aquatic dinosaur thought to have gone extinct in the Cretaceous period. These theorists say that during glacial movements, plesiosaurs may have found themselves deposited in newly created lakes, where they managed to survive while their ocean-dwelling ancestors died out. This, the theory goes, accounts for Champ and the infamous Loch Ness monster, as well as other elusive sea creatures found around the globe. They are all related! Others say that Champ is nothing more than wave formations, mistaken for a monster, and that submerged timber making its way back to the surface appears to be the strange creature's neck and head.

Whether there is some unidentified animal species living in Lake Champlain or not, four centuries of folklore have sprung out of the belief that a monster lives among us. From the Native Americans who hunted along Champlain's shores to the modern Americans who vacation there, belief in Champ is alive and well.

Fondly Remembers Vacations with the Monster

My older brother and sister loved taking me down to the shores of Lake Champlain at night and telling me about how the serpent was known to capsize boats and eat all the people it knocked overboard. They said that kids who would go into the lake for a swim by themselves at night often wouldn't come back. It would be said in the official records that their bodies were never recovered—but that this was just a code to note that they had become a late-night snack for the evil snakelike beast. I never saw any monsters in Lake Champlain for myself. My memories of it are of it being an absolutely beautiful, history laden, fun getaway. I wonder if there ever was anything in that lake.—*Kristy Fordman*

Seeing Champ Is Believing Champ!

Champ is real and should not be thought of as just a myth or story. He is to be respected and even feared. How am I so sure that he exists? Because I am one of the lucky ones who has seen him with my own eyes. During the summer of 1988 (I believe), I fell in with a group of fishing buddies who would meet at a regular spot very early each morning. We'd try to get in before all the tourists were out in the lake, generally scaring all the fish away. Well one August morning, I had just gotten to our spot, and there were already three or four guys out. They were wide-eyed, yelling for me to get over there, really going nuts. I ran over and looked out and my jaw dropped. About a hundred yards out, through the morning fog, I could make out what looked sort of, and I'm embarrassed to say this, but sort of like a dragon, sticking its head out of the lake. About ten seconds after I got there, it submerged and didn't come back up. I will admit, it was hard to make out, but all of us saw the exact same thing. Its neck was about eight feet long, in our estimation, and its head was really small.—*Gil O.*

The Reptile of Cayuga Lake

Since 1826, visitors to Cayuga Lake in Ithaca have reported encounters with an enormous reptilian creature that lives in the lake's waters. Believed to be some sort of sea serpent, the undulating monster is said to be somewhere in the range of twelve to fifteen feet long. Many theories abound regarding the existence of this strange creature. Some believe that there are a number of primitive beasts residing in the depths of the lake. Some think that the monsters are simply tricks of the eye or figments of the imagination. But many eyewitnesses swear that they have spied something mind-boggling from the shores of Cayuga Lake—something out of this world, something unbelievable.

An 1897 article in the *Ithaca Journal* commemorated the sixty-ninth anniversary of one of the earliest Cayuga Lake monster sightings on record. The article remembered that in the fury of the original sighting, reporters from the paper feared going down to the lake's shores due to the many reports of the frightening creature. The article then spoke of a number of subsequent sightings. A 1929 article theorized that the creature, or more likely creatures, found their way into the lake through a subterranean tunnel that connected Cayuga to Seneca Lake, which was thought to be the home of an entire family of strange sea animals. And a recent *Journal* article interviewed one Jack Marshall, who claims to have seen the beast in 1979.

Many residents of the Ithaca area enjoy Cayuga Lake for fishing, recreation, and its beauty. Who knows when one of these unsuspecting naturists will once again come face to face with the giant reptile or a whole wiggling school of them that call this lake home?

Capture of the Seneca Lake Monster

The entire Finger Lakes region is picturesque, serene, and peaceful. Yet something dangerous seems to hide just beneath its surface. For centuries, stories have been told of a mysterious monster that occasionally makes its presence known at Seneca Lake, the longest of the Finger Lakes.

Like its brothers—or sisters—Seneca Lake's monster has made appearances dating back to the times of the Native Americans. These original inhabitants of the area found the lake a mysterious place on many levels. Rumors were that it was bottomless, and it was widely believed that the monster that lived in its depths was a force not to be trifled with. When Europeans first encountered the natives of this area, they brushed off the stories as the superstitions of a primitive people. The early settlers had to swallow those words, however, when they began seeing the monster for themselves.

An early written account appeared in an 1899 edition of the *New York Sun*, which told of a paddleboat sailing the lake out of Geneva. The captain was cautious in making his way around what he thought was an overturned boat. His crew and passengers gathered on deck to observe the foundering vessel, and all were shocked to realize that it was no boat at all, but a living creature. As their own vessel came within one hundred yards of the object, the observers were stunned when the thing swam away.

Gallantly, the paddleboat's captain ordered full steam ahead, and the vessel took off in hot pursuit of the creature. The beast turned toward the boat, reared its head upward, and revealed to those watching a forbidding set of sharp white teeth. Undeterred, the captain ordered the crew to ram the creature in an attempt to kill it. They spent some time chasing the beast, which would emerge from the lake's surface, only to duck back under just in time to avoid the speeding boat. The newspaper reported that, miraculously, the captain was successful in striking and killing the mysterious beast.

The monster was examined by a local doctor, who described it as around twenty-five feet long, with a tapered tail and triangular head. It had round eyes, and its body was covered in a series of hard casings resembling turtle shells.

It is unknown what happened to the carcass of this great beast, but apparently it was not the only one of its species inhabiting Seneca Lake. Even today, occasional reports are filed stating that mysterious creatures have been spotted by people in the vicinity of the lake.

The Ford Street Beast

Ford Street, in Kent, is a small road no longer than a football field. But the tiny street is not as normal as it seems: It is plagued by a violent and ill-tempered creature. People from different religions, beliefs, and corners of the state all speak of this beast that stalks its victims in the woods of Orleans County. They all describe the creature as being around six to seven feet tall, having dark fur and a doglike face that seems to sit directly on its shoulders as if it has no neck at all. One person stated that it ran out in front of his car. It has the ability to run fast on all four legs much like a large feline, and when it feels threatened, it stands on its hind legs. People say they usually see it only at night, and when they do, it sometimes disappears in a cloud of vapor or dust.—*Tim Davis*

Wildman of Winsted

Around the turn of the twentieth century, the rural town of Winsted was overrun by reporters and curiosity-seekers from far and wide hoping to catch a glimpse of a creature that created a veritable firestorm of rumor and gossip. A large, hairy man was terrorizing area residents, and by 1895 he'd turned into a local phenomenon and become known as the Winsted Wildman.

The creature was first spotted by a politician named Riley Smith on Lowsaw Road in what was then referred to as the Indian Meadow. Smith was picking berries when he noticed his dog throwing a fit, snarling and cowering by his side. A moment later a huge feral man emerged from some nearby brush. The man was extremely tall and muscular, completely naked, and coated from head to toe in coarse thick hair. The Wildman let out a series of terrifying shrieks and screams while making his way into a patch of woods at superhuman speed.

Riley Smith was understandably rattled as he told his tale to the townspeople of Winsted. They were taken aback, especially at seeing Smith so visibly shaken, since he was considered to be a tough man, as well as an upstanding member of the community.

After Smith came forward, other Winsted residents began telling their own tales of encounters with this terrifying beast. As news of the creature spread, reporters from New York City and Boston made their way to Winsted hoping to see the Wildman for themselves. Theories were put forth as to what the feral creature was; some figured that it was a Bigfoot-type creature, while others assumed that it was an escapee from a nearby mental hospital. Some showed up hoping not just to see the beast, but to capture the Wildman of Winsted outright and whisk him off to a larger city for display.

No one was so lucky. No reporters ever had personal encounters with the Wildman, and as time passed, fewer and fewer locals had any either. Throughout the twentieth century, sightings were so scarce that many people forgot about the strange humanoid creature altogether. But every now and then a footprint is found or a strange cry is heard in the dead of night that reminds old-timers from this area that something may still be lurking out there, calling the woods of Winsted home.

The Seafaring Pachyderm of Staten Island

Sometimes a beast falls under the banner of "bizarre" not because of what it is, but where it is. For example, there's the truly weird incident that happened off the shores of New Dorp, Staten Island, in 1904.

Imagine yourself, if you will, in the shoes of Staten Island resident Frank Krissler. Frank met up with a friend at roughly four in the morning to break out the old rowboat for an early morning round of fishing off the Staten Island coast. Krissler and his friend had just situated themselves and their boat offshore and were setting up their lines when something terrifying happened.

An inhuman howl emanated from the water near the fishermen's boat. It shook the water and their boat, and was instantly followed by an even closer and more power-ful bellow. There was something huge in the water. It was making monstrous sounds. And it was heading right toward them. At first, they thought it was an attacking whale.

Rowing furiously, they set out for shore at a speed unlike anything the tiny boat had ever managed before, but the massive monster in the water kept up, staying right on their tail. Luckily, they made it to the safety of the beach.

Now, if you were Frank Krissler, you'd think that hitting that sand would mean safety, right? Imagine the horror you would experience, as he did, when you realized that this beast was able to follow you straight out of the ocean and onto the shore.

There was something huge in the water. It was making monstrous sounds. And it was heading right toward them.

Krissler and friend turned and, to their shock, saw a fully grown elephant lumbering out of the briny deep and onto the beach with them. The massive pachyderm might have seemed an ordinary beast in the jungles of Africa and India, or perhaps in a circus or zoo here in America. But climbing out of the waters of lower New York harbor? The fishermen were, to put it mildly, taken aback. Quickly, though, they realized the elephant was just as scared about its present situation as they were. It was not angry or aggressive. Instead, it seemed confused.

A few more fishermen arrived on the scene and, seeing the state of the giant beast, decided to help it. They tied rope around its tusks and led it through town to the police station, where the cops were just as surprised to see an elephant as the fishermen had been. It was placed in a stable, given hay and water, and hundreds of townsfolk gathered to see the miraculous seafaring animal.

By the end of that day, the mystery was solved. A representative from Luna Park in Brooklyn's Coney Island came forward, having heard about the appearance of the elephant. He explained that the renegade pachyderm had escaped from the park, made its getaway into the sea, and managed to swim some six miles from Coney Island to the New Dorp beaches. Incredibly, two other elephants had also made good their escapes along with him and swam in a different direction. They turned up in Long Island! The elephant was released into the Luna Park representative's custody, at which point he was walked through town to a waiting ferry that carried him back to Brooklyn. The next day *The New York Times* ran the story with the headline ELEPHANT LANDS IN JAIL FOR SWIMMING NARROWS.

An elephant may not by nature be a bizarre beast. But when it rises out of the ocean during an early morning calm, it takes that extra step into the unknown and turns into something truly strange.

Talking Fish of New Square

Workers in a fish market get pretty familiar with the various species they come in contact with during their daily gutting, scaling, skinning, and filleting chores. As you might imagine, after a while all fish probably tend to look alike.

Well, all fish might look the same, but they don't all sound the same. Just ask workers at the New Square Fish Market, where in February 2003 they came across a carp that could talk!

It was a typical day in New Square, and Luis Nivelo was working in the back of the market. He was in the process of gutting carp after carp. Just before he put his knife to one fish's belly, though, he was flabbergasted when the carp began speaking to him—in Hebrew! Nivelo, who is not of Jewish descent, ran to get some of his co-workers who spoke the language. New Square is populated almost entirely by Hasidic Jews, who founded the town in the 1950s.

The other workers claimed that the fish told them it was inhabited by the soul of a deceased Hasidic boy who had come back to earth to perform healing techniques on those in need. Stunned, one of the workers slipped and cut his finger on the knife he was carrying. The fish used the distraction as a chance to jump into a pile of other carp. Workers could not locate the miraculous fish, and he stopped talking and refused to identify himself. Hence, all of the carp were eventually sold as normal.

The story spread nationally, bringing much attention to the quiet town of New Square. Locals believed that the boy who inhabited the fish was a young Canadian Hasidim who had passed away the previous year, but we guess now we'll never know.

Bigfoot in Staten Island?

When you think of Bigfoot, if you do at all, the first images that probably come to mind are of remote wooded areas in the Pacific Northwest, where the creatures can live in isolation, avoiding human contact. Or maybe you think of Sasquatch up in the wilderness of Canada, where extreme cold and lack of development would allow the species to go undetected by the prying eyes of people. Or perhaps the Yeti come to mind, living atop the snowiest peaks of desolate mountain ranges.

Most likely you'd never think of Staten Island.

However, the suburban, densely populated borough of New York seems to be a surprisingly favorite stomping ground of a Bigfoot-like creature. In the mid-1970s, numerous sightings were reported in the vicinity of Historic Richmond Town. In December 1974, two Staten Islanders walking in a wooded area came face to face with a monstrous beast covered from head to toe in brown hair. Less than a month later, on January 21, 1975, a couple saw the same creature make its way across a church parking lot. And on that same night, a woman nearly crashed into the creature as it emerged from that same parking lot and darted across the road and into a garbage dump.

Since 1975, sightings have slowed down considerably, although they do happen every few years. Incidents have occurred as recently as 2002. It's thought that Bigfoot spends most of its time somewhere in the Greenbelt, a nature preserve consisting of 2,800 acres of dense forest. And while Historic Richmond Town is designed to display what life on Staten Island was like hundreds of years ago, it is also said to be a habitat of Bigfoot.

You'd think that with all the traffic, pollution, and Mafia activity, Staten Islanders would have enough to worry about without concerning themselves with big hairy beasts and ghosts wandering in their midst, but apparently not so. But then, they are New Yorkers!

Manhattan's Oldest Urban Legend Comes to Life

The rumor of alligators waddling around in the sewers of major American cities is a modern urban myth. Most people are familiar with the story, in large part because of Thomas Pynchon's 1963 novel, *V*, in which he wrote about cute little alligators, purchased as souvenirs from Florida and then discarded down toilets. Surviving the flush, the gators went on to grow and reproduce in the sewers of New York City.

Moving through the underground system, Pynchon told us, the alligators were big, blind, albino, and fed on rats and sewage. He envisioned an Alligator Patrol going into the depths of the sewer system, working in teams of two, with one man holding a flashlight while the other carried a 12-gauge repeating shotgun. As no one had before him, Thomas Pynchon wove the rumor of alligators in the sewers through the fabric of his fascinating work of fiction. But where does his fiction end and fact begin?

Who can say? Folklorist Richard M. Dorson repeated the oft-told tale that marijuana harvesters in pursuit of the elusive strain "New York White" (what did you think happened to all those seeds flushed down toilets by nervous potheads?) were experiencing difficulties because of the alligators swimming around in the sewer system scaring off the seed-seekers. The last word (supposedly) comes from the realm of science. The amphibian specialists Sherman and Madge Rutherford Minton, in their book *Giant Reptiles*, informed their readers that "one of the sillier folktales of the late 1960s was that the New York sewers were becoming infested with alligators. . . . We . . . would assure New Yorkers that alligators are not among their urban problems."

But believe it or not, finding actual records of alligators in the sewers is not a difficult task. Discoveries of out-of-place crocs date back more than a century and continue until the present. Though rare, findings of alligators slithering and slinking through the New York City sewer system prove to be more than baseless rumors. Newspapers in the city, in fact, have a long history of reported sightings of the crocodilians.

Surprisingly, the New York stories go back to the 1930s, not the 1960s—Pynchon simply stirred up the story. On June 28, 1932, "swarms" of alligators were seen in the Bronx River and a three-footer was found dead. On March 7, 1935, a three-foot alligator was caught alive in northern Yonkers, while at Grassy Sprain Reservoir a six-foot gator was found dead. A barge captain at Pier 9 on the East River captured an alligator four feet long on June 1, 1937. Five days later, at the Brooklyn Museum subway station, a New Yorker caught a toothy two-footer.

Probably the most exciting story of alligators in the sewers in the 1930s is the one told in a *New York Times* of 1935. Some teenagers living on East 123rd Street encountered and killed a seven-and-a-half-foot-long, one-hundred-and-twenty-pound gator. That sobering account gives one pause to consider the possibilities of the current urban gator population. The incident's no-nonsense retelling in a highly respected newspaper must have lent much credibility to the story. *The New York Times* of February 10, 1935, carried the following article, which is given here in its entirety:

ALLIGATOR FOUND IN UPTOWN SEWER

Youths Shoveling Snow Into Manhole See The Animal Churning In Icy Water.

SNARE IT AND DRAG IT OUT

Reptile Slain by Rescuers When It Gets Vicious — Whence It Came is Mystery.

SALVATORE CONDULUCCI, 16 years old, of 419 East 123rd Street, was assigned to the rim. His comrades would heap blackened slush near him, and he, carefully observing the sewer's capacity, would give the last fine flick to each mound.

Suddenly there were signs of clogging ten feet below, where the manhole drop merged with the dark conduit leading to the river. Salvatore yelled: "Hey, you guys, wait a minute," and got down on his knees to see what was the trouble.

What he saw, in the thickening dusk, almost caused him to topple into the icy cavern. For the jagged surface of the ice blockade below was moving; and something black was breaking through. Salvatore's eyes widened; then he managed to leap to his feet and call his friends.

"Honest, it's an alligator!" he exploded.

Others Look and Are Convinced.

There was a murmur of skepticism. Jimmy Mireno, 19, of 440 East 123rd Street, shouldered his way to the rim and stared.

"He's right," he said.

Frank Lonzo, 18, of 1743 Park Avenue, looked next. He also confirmed the spectre. Then there was a great crush about the opening in the middle of the street and heads were bent low around the aperture.

The animal apparently was threshing about in the ice, trying to get clear. When the first wave of awe had passed, the boys decided to help it out. A delegation was dispatched to the Lehigh Stove and Repair Shop at 441 East 123rd Street.

"We want some clothes-line," demanded the delegation, and got it.

Young Condolucci, an expert on Western movies, fashioned a slip knot. With the others watching breathlessly, he dangled the noose into the sewer, and after several tantalizing near-catches, looped it about the 'gator's neck. Then he pulled hard. There was a grating of rough leathery skin against jumbled ice. But the job was too much for one youth. The others grabbed the rope and all pulled.

Slowly, with its curving tail twisting weakly, the animal was dragged from the snow, ten feet through the dark cavern, and to the street, where it lay, non-committal; it was not in Florida, that was clear.

And therefore, when one of the boys sought to loosen the rope, the creature opened its jaws and snapped, not with the robust vigor of a healthy, well-sunned alligator, but with the fury of a sick, very badly treated one. The boys jumped back. Curiosity and sympathy turned to enmity.

"Let 'im have it!" the cry went up.

Rescuers Then Kill It.

So the shovels that had been used to pile snow on the alligator's head were now to rain upon it. The 'gator's tail swished about a few last times. Its jaws clashed weakly. But it was in no mood for a real struggle after its icy incarceration. It died on the spot.

Triumphantly, but not without the inevitable reaction of sorrow, the boys took their victim to the Lehigh Stove and Repair Shop. There it was found to weigh 125 pounds; they said it measured seven and a half or eight feet. It became at once the greatest attraction the store ever had had. The whole neighborhood milled about, and finally, a call for the police reached a nearby station.

But there was little for the hurrying policemen to do.

The strange visitor was quite dead; and no charge could be preferred against it or against its slayers. The neighbors were calmed with little trouble and speculation as to where the 'gator had come from was rife.

There are no pet shops in the vicinity; that theory was ruled out almost at once. Finally, the theories simmered down to that of a passing boat. Plainly, a steamer from the mysterious Everglades, or thereabouts, had been passing 123rd Street, and the alligator had fallen overboard.

Shunning the hatefully cold water, it had swum toward shore and found only the entrance to the conduit. Then after another 150 yards through a torrent of melting snow — and by that time it was half dead — it had arrived under the open man-hole.

Half-dead, yes, the neighborhood conceded. But still alive enough for a last splendid opening and snapping of its jaws. The boys were ready to swear to that.

At about 9 p.m., when tired mothers had succeeded in getting most of their alligator-conscious youngsters to bed, a Department of Sanitation truck rumbled up to the store and made off with the prize. Its destination was Barren Island and an incinerator.

But there is more evidence supporting the supposedly fanciful idea of alligators in urban sewers. Loren Coleman is a noted and respected cryptozoologist who has spent a lifetime tracking down and verifying, or debunking, accounts of strange, previously unidentified creatures. When Coleman's "Alligators-in-the-Sewers: A Journalistic Vehicle," was published in the *Journal of American Folklore,* September–October 1979, it rocked the urban legend world. Folklorists had been unaware there was a factual basis for the tales, as Coleman showed. Coleman continued his search for reports of subterranean urban alligators and found them in material from the man who would know the most about the underground waterways of the Big Apple.

Robert Daley's nonfiction book *The World Beneath the City* told of Teddy May, the superintendent of the New York City sewers during the 1930s. In 1935, May began hearing reports of alligators from his inspectors, but did not believe them and refused to approve the reports with the inspectors' notations on alligators. Instead, he hired extra men to watch the inspectors and tell him how they were getting their liquor down in the sewers. The word came back to the "King of the Sewers" that his men were not drinking, yet the reports of narrow escapes from alligators persisted.

Determined to lay the claims to rest, Teddy May decided to go down and have a look for himself. A few hours later the superintendent returned, shaken. His own flashlight, Daley wrote, illuminated the truth behind the rumors. Teddy May had seen alligators two feet and longer in length. Avoiding the dangerously fast currents in the main sewer lines under the major avenues, the alligators had taken to the smaller pipes in the backwash of the city.

The alligators had settled in, and Teddy May was now faced with the task of ridding his sewers of the 'gators.

The methods he used were unorthodox, but then his prey was also rather unusual. Rat poison was employed to get rid of some of the troublesome subterraneans, while others were corralled into the main trunk lines, where they drowned or were swiftly washed out to sea. A few alligators were hunted down by sewer inspectors armed with .22s on their own free time. Teddy May had rid New York City of its alligators in the sewers—or so he thought. Coleman would find that in 1938 five alligators were caught in New Rochelle, and sightings of alligators in the sewers of New York City were recorded in 1948 and 1966.

And then there is this tantalizing tidbit, predating all stories of Florida souvenirs or marijuana harvesters. In 1999, Russell L. Martin III, curator of newspapers at the American Antiquarian Society, passed along some information to University of Utah Professor of Folklore Jan Harold Brunvand. Brunvand, who is a longtime correspondent of Coleman's, passed it on to the cryptozoologist.

"In the course of our work, we recently discovered what may be the earliest example of the classic urban legend, 'alligators in the sewers of New York,'" Martin wrote. "Filed away with our bound volume of the *New York Evening Post* was a single issue of a previously unknown newspaper. The title is *The Planet,* published in Union Village, N.Y., July 18, 1831. It is unclear whether it survived beyond vol. 1, no. 1. At any rate, in the midst of the news and anecdotes is this curious item: 'A live Alligator, it is said, was seen on Friday in the slip between Murray's and Pine street wharves, New York.'"

The final chapter of alligators in the city's sewers mystery has yet to be written. Still, we have to wonder if there just might be a few of these toothy prehistoric reptiles still skulking around down in the dark, steamy effluent of New York's underground corridors, lying in wait for some unsuspecting meal to happen by.

Local Heroes and Villains

"There are new words now that excuse everybody. Give me the good old days of heroes and villains, the people you can bravo or hiss. There was a truth to them that all the slick credulity of today cannot touch." — Bette Davis

Every town has that one person to be proud or ashamed of or, at the very least, amazed by. Colorful characters and local lunatics, their celebrity may extend only to the borders of their own hometown, but within those limits, they shine as bright as any media star.

It would be an understatement to say that New Yorkers are a rare breed of people, and even more of an understatement to say that to stand out among them means you must have done something awfully spectacular, or spectacularly awful, to gain your fame (or in certain cases, your infamy).

Here's to the New Yorkers that New Yorkers have come to love (or loathe). Whether they are performers with strange and unique acts, religious fanatics, obsessive types, or heinous murderers, the following characters have all earned their hallowed place in *Weird New York*.

Speaking to the Dead with the Fox Sisters

The spiritualist movement has a long history in America, dating all the way back to the mid-1800s. This movement holds out the belief that the spirits of those long dead can be summoned back among us and offers "mediums" and clairvoyants to ease the process. It still thrives today, most visibly in the form of the popular John Edwards syndicated television show, on which the charismatic host communicates with the spirits of deceased family members of the people in his studio audience. As Edwards proves, Spiritualism can be a multimillion-dollar business. Who would ever guess that it all started with two teenage girls in a small town in New York?

Kate and Maggie Fox lived with their parents in Hydesville, in a cabin that was regarded by many as haunted. People in the area referred to it as the Spook House and said that years before the Fox family moved in, a man had been murdered in the house and secretly buried in its basement. In fact, the previous tenant had vacated the house abruptly, supposedly because he could not abide the bothersome spirits living there with him.

The Fox family moved into the cabin in 1848 and soon became acquainted with the supposed ghosts. Most notable among the many strange things that occurred were constant rapping noises that kept the unhappy residents up all night. The noises caused great fear in the family, who took to sleeping together in one room. Finally, Kate Fox decided to face the spirits to find out exactly what was going on.

She discovered that when she asked the ghosts specific questions, they would answer with the correct number of raps. Through her questioning, Kate determined that one of the ghosts haunting their house was the spirit of a traveling salesman who had been abducted nine years prior, killed, and buried beneath

their house. It was soon found that Kate's sister Maggie was also skilled at communicating with the deceased presence.

Word of the sisters' unique abilities spread throughout the area, and curious people began coming from far and wide to observe the girls ask questions of the dead and be answered by mysterious knocking

sounds. Soon, their reputation breached the borders of Hydesville. The girls were becoming local celebrities and decided to capitalize on it. Their older sister, Leah, who lived twenty miles away in Rochester, became their manager, leading them on a series of public exhibitions that gained the trio much notoriety and financial success. It wasn't long before the most famous showman of the 1800s, P. T. Barnum, brought the girls to Manhattan, where they put on their show for hordes of curious onlookers. Writers such as Horace Greeley and James Fenimore Cooper marveled at the abilities of young Kate and Maggie. Everyone who witnessed the Fox girls in action thought them to be some sort of hoax, but numerous investigations could reveal nothing of the sort.

By 1852, just four years after the girls discovered their abilities, Spiritualism had more than two million followers. Thousands of people claimed to possess some ability as mediums. And all this sprang forth from two small girls—who were indeed perpetrating a hoax the entire time.

Some years later in life, the Fox sisters told a newspaper reporter the methods by which they had fooled so many thousands of onlookers. Kate Fox discovered at an early age that she had the curious ability to pop her toe joint at will. She mentioned this to Maggie, who discovered that she could do the same thing. Their "talking" to ghosts began as a joke to scare their mother. But the superstitious woman took it all too seriously, and before they knew it, word of their talent had swept the area. Instead of coming forward, they continued their prank and capitalized on it.

In 1857, Leah married a wealthy gentleman and left her two younger sisters on their own. Maggie and Kate suffered from alcoholism for much of their lives. The two are now communing with the dead from their paupers' graves.

Life in a Monkey Cage

New York City is and always has been the gateway to America. For centuries, travelers from far and wide have made their way to the United States through its portals, from the olden days of Ellis Island to the present. Stories of immigrants passing through the city, on their way to better lives than those they left behind, are part of the fabric of our folklore, the very foundation of the American Dream.

One foreign-born participant in New York's story illuminates a more shameful side of the dream. His tale is one of racism, alienation, spectacle, and ignorance. He was an African named Ota Benga, and the account of his time spent in the Bronx is truly strange.

Ota Benga was a pygmy resident of the Belgian Congo. He was enslaved by local villagers until 1904, when American explorer Samuel Verner acquired him along with a few other pygmies. Verner intended to put his trophies on display, most notably at the St. Louis World's Fair. Benga, who was known by those close to him as Bi, meaning friend, was twenty-three years old at the time, weighed 103 pounds, and stood only four feet eleven inches tall. He was marketed as a "boy," but had actually lived a very adult life back in the Congo. He had already been married twice; one wife died after being attacked by a snake, and the other was captured and enslaved by a rival tribe.

Ota's life took a bizarre

turn for the worse when he was bought for the Bronx Zoo by its director, Dr. William T. Hornaday, in 1906. Hornaday had some bizarre views on animals, thinking that they had near human-level thought processes and personalities. On a similar note, he thought that the black pygmy he acquired was little more than an animal. Sadly, this ignorance led to an incredibly weird situation. Ota Benga wound up actually living in the monkey cage of the Bronx Zoo.

Benga was marketed as a "wild man from Africa" and displayed alongside chimpanzees, an orangutan named Dahong, and a gorilla named Dinah. The display became immensely popular almost immediately, and thousands of people made their way to the Bronx to check out the pygmy sensation. Needless to say, this exhibit ignited a firestorm of controversy. It was 1906, and the theory of evolution was still very hotly debated. Church leaders thought the exhibit was an attempt to lend credence to Darwin's theories and condemned the display. African American organizations were rightfully appalled at how the Congan was being forced to live, and they mounted efforts to rectify the situation.

The zoo responded, in a way, to these organizations as well as to Ota's complaints regarding his lifestyle. They gave Benga a white suit and allowed him to walk the grounds of the zoo during the days. However, they made him return to the monkey cage to sleep at night. Even worse, he was still recognized by patrons of the zoo, who would chase him, trip him, and mock him. Not surprisingly, he was terrorized by these jeering locals and responded with threatening behavior. At one point, he began wielding a knife at those who would approach him. At another point, he made a small bow and a set of arrows that he fired upon the more obnoxious and aggressive patrons of the zoo. As he (understandably) grew to be more agitated and violent, zoo officials decided that it was time for Ota Benga to leave their institution. He was released after two hellish weeks as a zoo exhibit.

Although Ota Benga spent some time at a college in Virginia and afterward worked in a tobacco factory, sadly, he was forever scarred by the treatment he endured at the hands of his captors in both Africa and America. In 1916, no longer able to endure this life, he shot himself through the heart, dying at the age of thirty-five.

Tanning the Hide of the Ramapo Cowboy

I thought you'd want to hear a strange story about a murderer named Claudius Smith.

Claudius Smith, known as the Cowboy of the Ramapos, was apprehended in Smithtown, Long Island, in 1779 and brought to Goshen for trial on charges of murder, theft, robbery, and general mayhem. During the Revolutionary War, Smith, his brother Jacobus, and other family members ravaged and pillaged the Rockland and Orange County area, selling stolen supplies to the British and pretty much stealing anything and killing anyone in their path. They were perhaps one of the first dysfunctional families documented in the new United States.

After his trial, Claudius was hung. It is rumored his skull was sealed in the archway of the Orange County Courthouse, some of his bones made into knife handles and his skin was tanned and made into souvenirs. More information can be found with the Orange County Historical Society.

Apparently, in those less politically correct, pre-organ-donor days, this was not an uncommon practice. A few more family members followed him to the gallows over the years, though no others went into the souvenir trade.
—*William Steinmann*

Say You Love Satan with the Acid King

Northport is a quiet town on Long Island, situated on the water. It retains a small-town charm, even today. It's the type of place where you might run into your neighbors at the local hardware store. But twenty years ago, this small town was rocked to its core when it made national headlines as the site of a strange, brutal murder. In 1984, quiet little Northport became associated with killer cults, drug abuse, and the phrase "Say you love Satan." Most famously, it became known as the home of the Acid King.

Ricky Kasso was notorious throughout Northport. A high school dropout, the teenager was a known drug user and dealer. He was also a professed Satan worshipper. Kasso had been arrested a number of times, mostly on petty charges. But in early 1984 he was brought in for grave robbing. He had dug up and desecrated a grave from the 1800s, stealing a skull and hand from the unearthed coffin. He told police that he planned on using the bones in a satanic ritual. Kasso was supposedly linked with a local group known as the Knights of the Black Circle. He was often seen wandering the streets of Northport, monitored by adults and feared by those younger than him, many of whom referred to him as the Acid King.

Kasso's drug dealings brought him into contact with another shady Northport youth

named Gary Lauwers. Early in the year, Lauwers was involved in a drug deal with Kasso, during which he purportedly stole ten bags of angel dust from the Acid King. Kasso began telling his friends that he would get revenge on Lauwers for this wrong. On June 16, he got his chance.

That evening Lauwers, Kasso, Kasso's close friend James Troiano, and an associate named Albert Quinones all found themselves together in a section of Northport known as Aztakea Woods. There, they supposedly spent the night doing a number of drugs, mostly mescaline. Late in the evening Kasso confronted Lauwers about their earlier drug dealing, and things took a macabre turn.

Ricky Kasso produced a pocketknife and lunged toward Gary Lauwers. He began stabbing him repeatedly, each time shouting the phrase "Say you love Satan!" Lauwers responded, "No, I love my mother!" to the wild man as he struggled to defend himself.

By the end of the attack, Lauwers lay dead, stabbed over thirty times, twenty-two of the wounds to the face. Kasso covered his body in a pile of leaves, and the teenagers left the woods, leaving Lauwers behind.

When the body of Gary Lauwers was discovered decomposing on the forest floor some two weeks later, a firestorm of controversy ensued. Rumors swirled of a satanic cult being responsible for the murder. Northport became known as a place where satanists lurked behind the façade of an average suburban neighborhood. Residents began defending their hometown in newspapers and on television broadcasts. Neighborhood kids even came together and began scratching out the graffiti that Kasso had left all over local playground equipment. Most of it was related to heavy metal music. Some of it was satanic in nature, although Kasso apparently was not as into Satan as he claimed. He repeatedly wrote the word Satin instead of Satan, making one wonder if, perhaps, he killed in the name of the silky smooth fabric instead of the lord of darkness.

Ricky Kasso and James Troiano were later arrested for the murder of Gary Lauwers. Kasso confessed and told wild tales of hearing a crow call out while he was stabbing Lauwers to death. Kasso took this as a sign from Satan that murdering Gary was the move to make. Kasso sat in prison until July 7, when he hanged himself in his jail cell. Troiano testified during his own trial that he was simply a witness to the murder and did not take part in the killing. He was found not guilty of second-degree murder and was set free.

Lending a Ride to the Acid King

I had been in school with Jimmy Troiano since kindergarten. He was always a bit hyper, to put it mildly. Ricky Kasso became an acquaintance in junior high school. In my senior year, there was an article in *Newsday* about Ricky being arrested for digging up a grave and stealing a hand. For some reason, I just assumed the story was false.

The high school was pretty big, so it was possible that you could not run into a person for a while, but at the very end of the school year I saw Troiano at a party. I remember thinking that he was being very friendly, or perhaps just socially appropriate. The school was divided into many different social groups, but there was never much friction between them. We were all just a bunch of upper middle class white kids. Some of us liked the Dead, others liked Metal—not too much of a culture gap to bridge. With that said, it was a little odd to see Troiano at this party.

Two weeks later, I was driving down a road that led to Main Street. I saw Ricky and Jimmy walking. I swerved my parents' car over and asked them if they wanted a ride. Jimmy got in the front seat and Ricky got in the back. Again, I found Jimmy amazingly polite. I never had had a conflict with him, but over the years I had seen him behave wildly on many occasions. He was calm and conversational. As we drove down the narrow road that led into town, a moving van blocked the street. It was in a tight spot and it would take about ten minutes before we could pass.

With the delay, the ride was now taking much longer than if the two had walked. They could have gotten out of the car, walked, and been in town in about two minutes. I was not too familiar with Ricky, but I was impressed with Jimmy's good manners. The two politely waited with me. I turned back to Ricky and said, "So, you've become quite a celebrity lately. I read about you in the paper." I was making a joke, but for some reason I had blind confidence that the story could not have been true. Ricky smiled and said something to the effect that he was going to get the guy who set him up.

The van moved and I dropped the two off on Main Street. Jimmy thanked me for the ride and said it was good to see me. Ricky also thanked me for the ride. The following day the two were arrested for murder. The day after that, the Satanic overtones made it a national story and the town was flooded with TV cameras and reporters.

That night, I drove my parents' car with my Mom in the passenger seat. Like the rest of the country, we were talking about the arrests. I said, "Two days ago, Troiano was sitting there and Kasso was sitting there."

"You gave them a ride? How could you give them a ride?" she said. I could see her beginning to worry that I might somehow become entangled in the investigation, which did not happen.

I replied, "When they were getting in, I didn't think to stop and ask them if they had murdered anyone lately. Next time I will."—*Anonymous*

A Cowboy Makes His Mark

"Been walking these streets so long, singing the same old song, I know every crack in these dirty sidewalks of Broadway. . . ."
— "Rhinestone Cowboy," *Glenn Campbell*

Sometimes even the most familiar sights in the city still make us scratch our heads in wonder. Case in point: the locally famous celebrity known as the Naked Cowboy. Each day thousands of tourists and Midtown locals alike bear witness to the weird and wonderful vision of this man standing on a median in the middle of Broadway, right in the midst of the hustle and bustle of Times Square, dressed in nothing but his cowboy hat, boots, white Jockey briefs, and a smile. Day in and day out, year after year, he stands there, happily strumming his guitar and singing his songs.

While the Naked Cowboy might be familiar to most of us New Yorkers at this point, walking past an almost nude character warbling on the crosswalk is still a pretty weird experience, and it still raises the questions: Just who is this musical and muscular fellow with the long blond hair and the briefs? Is he serious about his musical career, and if so, how does he think it's going? And, most curious of all, how does he manage to stand out there singing all day in the dead of winter without freezing his . . . er, boots off?

While finding the answers to all of these questions would probably not be too hard to do, we'd really prefer not to know. We'd rather just continue to wonder, enjoy the show, and appreciate that there are still unique people to be found in Times Square, once a bastion of bizarre behavior, for all of us to marvel at.

Moondog, New York's Viking King

For decades, a blind musical master stood silently on the streets of New York. He is remembered as much today for his eccentricities as he is for his minimalist music. He was called Moondog.

Moondog's real name was Louis T. Hardin. He was born in Kansas in 1916 and lost his sight there in his late teens in an accident with a dynamite blasting cap. He studied music at the Iowa School for the Blind but was mostly self-taught. An aspiring composer as well as a performer, he wrote out his musical numbers in braille.

In 1943, Hardin decided to move to New York City to be closer to the music scene. Having almost no money, he quickly came to live on the streets, sleeping on rooftops and in doorways. He would play his music on the streets, where he initially became legendary—more for his appearance than his music. He wore long robes, Viking hats, and occasionally, masks over his head. He also sported a long beard.

Moondog spent most of his time on a corner on Fifty-fourth Street, playing songs on homemade drums and a few keyboards while reciting his own poetry. He was spotted there by workers at Carnegie Hall, who convinced the musicians in that prestigious theater to let him sit in on rehearsals. Over the years, he met such music notables as Benny Goodman, Charlie Parker, and Alan Freed and began to gain a little fame of his own. Still living on the streets, the New York "Viking" recorded a number of his songs and contributed to many television and movie soundtracks.

In 1974, Moondog left New York after being offered a paying job in Germany. Many who had known him as a permanent fixture on Fifty-fourth Street assumed he was dead, but he was very much alive, just elsewhere. He returned to New York in 1989 as part of Brooklyn's New Music American Festival, where he shared a stage with

such well-known musical figures as Philip Glass. This led to renewed interest in his life and work.

Moondog went from busking in New York to performing throughout Europe, even in front of royalty. His bizarre life, marked by tragedy and determination, had known no limits. Today he is remembered as one of the kings of New York street artists. He died of heart failure in September 1999, leaving a void in the modern music scene—not to mention Manhattan's weird street scene.

He Dances with a Dummy

There are hundreds of street performers, or buskers, vying for the attention, and the money, of passersby in New York's cities. To stand a cut above the rest, performers will go to great lengths. Some have mastered the art of reeling in crowds with creative shouts and catcalls that stop people in their tracks. Others add elements of danger or oddity to their acts.

There is one performer out there who has established himself as one of the true kings of guerrilla performing. And he doesn't have to make a big scene to attract a crowd. All he does is dance. And he has become a legend for it. He is known not so much for his moves, but for his dancing partner.

Julio Diaz has spent many years salsa dancing on the streets and subways of New York with his partner, the lovely Lupita. Lupita, however, is not a real woman, but a mannequin. Outfitted in flashy clothes and full makeup, the dummy stays attached to Mr. Diaz's feet, allowing him to swing her around, dip her, and gyrate her hips wildly. Diaz's moves are so well delivered that upon a casual glance, Lupita appears to be a real woman. Many stop to watch the duo, and when they realize that the female partner is actually a mannequin, their fascination grows even greater.

Mr. Diaz is a Colombian immigrant who sends the money he makes dancing home to Colombia to support his wife and six children. He has not seen them since he left Colombia many years ago. He plans on returning once he has spent enough time in the United States to gain citizenship. The story of how Mr. Diaz came to realize the potential of his dancing doll act is even more bizarre than the sight of him dancing with a doll in the first place.

It all began in the parks of Bogotá, Colombia. A friend of Mr. Diaz's had fallen into a deep depression when a prostitute he had been living with up and left him. One day that man, knowing of Mr. Diaz's talent in doll-making, implored him to make an effigy of the woman for him to burn in an effort to put the memory of her betrayal behind him. Diaz agreed to do so and left to make the doll. By the time he returned, his friend was stone-cold drunk. Before burning the doll, the man proclaimed that he wanted to have one last dance with his lost love. He grabbed the doll and proceeded to dance wildly with her on the streets of Bogotá.

As the two moved, propelled by some music in the mind of the drunken man, a crowd gathered and cheered. Julio Diaz watched their reaction and realized that there might be an opportunity in what was happening. He created his act and made mucho money dancing with dolls throughout Colombia before setting out for New York City.

Mr. Diaz has plied his unusual trade in New York for years now. He became so well known that he was officially sanctioned to perform in the subways by the Metropolitan Transit Authority's Music Under New York program. He performs at different train stations for three-hour blocks at a time—and, rumor has it, he brings in a decent chunk of change doing so.

Father Divine Hated to Do It . . . or Did He?

Today, not many people know the name Father Divine. Those with a mind for history, though, remember him as a strange, cultlike figure who had a massive following during the Great Depression. A charismatic preacher, he worked to find jobs for his followers while promoting a unique form of Christianity. Some people hailed him as the second coming of the Messiah. At the peak of his influence, he had tens of thousands of followers throughout the country.

While Father Divine is usually thought of as a Harlem resident, earlier in his career he worked out of a house in the small town of Sayville. It was here that Divine established himself as a controversial, powerful figure in a showdown he had with the town government that is still talked about today.

Father Divine came to reside in his home through spite. This was 1919, and the house was located in a lily-white neighborhood. A resident of Macon Street in Sayville advertised that he was trying to sell his house to a "colored." (Nothing high-minded here. He was mad at his neighbors and wanted to make them uncomfortable.) After Divine purchased the house, he and many of his black followers moved in. Divine, an early proponent of desegregation, welcomed all people into his movement. Local townsfolk, however, did not share his progressive views. They especially did not like it when large gatherings of Divine's followers would come to his Sayville residence to hear him speak each Sunday and then would chow down at huge outdoor banquets. Fearful neighbors held a town meeting hoping to figure out a way to oust the preacher and his followers.

In November 1931, Sayville police raided one of Divine's banquets, claiming that they were responding to numerous complaints of unruly crowds and traffic backups. Father Divine, along with eighty-eight of his followers, was arrested and charged with disturbing the peace. Most of them pleaded guilty, paid a five-dollar fine, and were allowed to leave. Father Divine paid for their fines with a single five-hundred-dollar bill, which the court was embarrassed to admit it could not make change for. Divine, however, refused to pay his own fine. He opted to go to trial instead, creating quite a spectacle with his commanding presence and fiery oratory. Jurors listened, then came down with the same verdict for Divine as for his followers: guilty.

But Divine's punishment was incredibly more severe:

TUESDAY, NOVEMBER 17, 1931.

RAID ON 'HEAVEN' ENDS MIDNIGHT DIN

The Rev. Divine, Negro and 88 'Disciples' Face Sayville, L. I., Court as Citizens Protest.

55 ARE ASSESSED $5 FINES

Others Will Stand Trial Later— —Leader of Cult Keeps Open House and Feeds All Comers.

Special to The New York Times.
SAYVILLE, L. I., Nov. 16.—There was turmoil in "Heaven" here early this morning. Peace came to weary neighbors only when a group of State troopers, deputy sheriffs, and policemen placed the Rev. Charles Divine, Negro and eighty

"I hated to do it," was all Father Divine had to say on the matter.

Father Divine's comment caused a wave of controversy and press coverage. Rumors of his supernatural powers and godly nature spread far and wide. The incident, despite its eerie overtones, actually helped gain Father Divine thousands of new followers.

Just thirty-three days after he was jailed, Father Divine was released from prison. Calls for a new trial had been taking place for some time, due to the sensational nature of the case and the racist and anticultist prejudices that

He was sentenced to a year in jail and was charged a five-hundred-dollar fine on top of it. His followers were shocked. The judge in the case, Justice Lewis J. Smith, gave a blustery speech proclaiming that those who did not believe Father Divine was some sort of god deserved to have their rights protected just as much as those who did believe in his divinity. The drama was intense. And it would only get worse.

Two days after Father Divine's sentencing, everyone was stunned when Justice Smith, who was by all accounts a healthy man, dropped dead of a heart attack. It was a shocking turn of events in general, let alone when one considered the timing of the unexpected death. People rushed to Father Divine's jail cell, curious to see what their minister would say about the judge's abrupt demise. Father Divine spoke one simple sentence, but the five words he uttered catapulted him from being a little-known religious leader to a great legend.

pervaded the jury box. The new trial never took place, however. Father Divine simply went on his way, and the town officials of Sayville, perhaps tired of the publicity and fearful that they would suffer a fate similar to that of Justice Smith, pursued the matter no further.

Father Divine went on to greater glory, working for his people in Harlem. He was well regarded for his ability to find employment for his faithful followers, even during the harshest periods of the Great Depression. Despite his successes, he was never viewed as completely legitimate and always retained the negative label of "cult leader."

He passed away in 1965, but his wife, known to followers as Mother Divine, continued on with his mission. There are still a number of people who follow the teachings of this legendary individual who went from being an obscure preacher in the suburbs of New York to a national icon. Along the way he helped a lot of people—and scared some others!

Typhoid Mary

Mary Mallon, a cook who worked in New York City in the early part of the twentieth century, will forever be better known by her nickname, Typhoid Mary.

Mallon was one of the first known "healthy carriers" of typhoid, meaning that she spread the deadly disease without ever feeling its effects herself. Her profession as a cook was unfortunate, since handling food was a quick and easy way for typhoid to spread to the unsuspecting. In 1907, after seven places where Mallon had worked experienced a total of over twenty-two typhoid outbreaks, investigators came looking for her. After a number of interviews, marked by anger and cursing, she was quarantined.

Mallon was sent to live out her life in total isolation. She was installed in a tiny cottage on remote North Brother Island, a small piece of land in the East River near the Bronx. (The building, though set off by itself, was part of the Riverside Hospital complex.) There were no neighbors, except for the occasional seagull. Typhoid Mary, as she came to be known, was left to live a life of absolute solitude.

Legal battles ensued. Mallon sued the city, and a number of defenders questioned the legality of isolating anyone in such a manner. Finally in 1910, after three long years, Mallon was allowed to leave North Brother Island. As part of her release, she agreed never to work as a cook again.

Mallon was not heard from for five years. Then, in 1915, the Sloane Maternity Hospital in Manhattan suffered a typhoid outbreak in which twenty-five people became ill and two died. A new cook, Mrs. Brown, was discovered to actually be none other than Typhoid Mary Mallon. The public was outraged. Mallon, who knew her potential for spreading typhoid, had broken her word and become a cook again, an act that was considered by most to be intentional and malicious.

Mary Mallon was quickly recaptured and sent back to her tiny cottage on North Brother Island, where she lived for twenty-three years. She was allowed to work part of the time at Riverside Hospital, but she spent most of over two decades by herself. In November 1938, Typhoid Mary passed away, still suffering the effects of a stroke she'd had half a decade earlier.

Paying Tribute to a Musical Local Hero

It is an almost undebatable fact that there has never been a band even half as cool as the Queens quartet the Ramones. From their general attitude and appearance to the fact that they were once forced to record at gunpoint by notorious producer and eccentric Phil Specter, these heroes of the Lower East Side are unquestionably rock and roll royalty.

Sadly, Joey Ramone, the charismatic front man of the Ramones, passed away at the age of forty-nine in April 2001. But he has not been forgotten in his hometown of New York. Joey Ramone was considered such a local hero that he has been immortalized with his own street name. The next time you're listening to "Beat on the Brat" or "Blitzkrieg Bop" and start to wax nostalgic, or find yourself down in the Bowery near CBGB's, be sure to take a stroll down Joey Ramone Place to pay tribute to this pioneer of punk rock. It's on the corner of Bowery and Second Street.

Entertaining Earthlings with Intergalactic Abilities

Some people will tell you that the Torres brothers came to New York City in the early 1920s from their native Detroit, Michigan. The Torres brothers themselves, however, claimed that they arrived in New York after traveling to Earth from their original homes somewhere in the vast cosmos of outer space.

This was quite a lofty claim. However, the Torres brothers backed it up by participating in a series of feats and experiments that are truly mind-boggling, and still haven't been explained today. Plus, after making many scientists scratch their heads, the two brothers disappeared without a trace. Their whereabouts are still unknown. Perhaps they headed back to their home galaxy?

People first came to know Wilbur and Ralph Torres as two young men in their twenties who had high-pitched voices, wore white suits, and performed a number of inexplicable and seemingly miraculous feats of telepathy. They gained even more notoriety when they came to New York in 1921 and took out full-page ads in *The New York Times* proclaiming, "We are not bound by earthly constraints. We came from another galaxy, and will return there when our work is done. We are free beings."

That did the trick. The brothers got the attention and hype they were after, and stood up to all challenges. Their telepathic claims were put through a battery of tests, and to the amazement of all involved, they passed them with flying colors. Skeptics insisted their so-called gifts were all a hoax, but no one was ever able to prove that.

The Torres brothers became most famous for their supposed ability to mentally communicate with each other over long distances. One of the brothers would lock himself in a room with a witness, and the other would then go to a random floor of a skyscraper with another witness. Every time this happened, the brother left behind was able to guess which floor the other brother was on. This happened without fail, even when the wandering brother switched floors up to twenty times in a single day. The witnesses were completely impartial. Once, the archbishop of a Roman Catholic diocese even lent his word to the authenticity of the brothers' abilities.

The most famous studies of the Torres brothers were conducted by the American Academy of Sciences. Ralph stayed in New York with one team of scientists while Wilbur traveled across the country to Los Angeles with another. An experiment was carried out in silence, to ensure

TELL ME DEAR BROTHER.... WHAT AM I THINKING ABOUT NOW?

I BELIEVE, MY DARLING SIBLING, THAT YOU ARE THINKING WE LOOK ABSOLUTELY DASHING IN OUR WHITE SUITS!

AMAZING, SHARER OF MY MOTHER'S WOMB...AMAZING!

that no one was slipping the brothers any hints or that they were utilizing some kind of verbal trickery to accomplish their task.

A high-ranking member of the Academy of Sciences took a piece of paper and wrote the words "George Washington was the first President of the United States and a major figure in our heritage. He was a man of distinction and his honesty was never in question."

This note was handed in silence to Ralph Torres, who read it in silence. At the exact same moment, in Los Angeles, scientists were astonished to see Wilbur Torres go incredibly pale while gripping his head. He informed the scientists that "my brother is trying to communicate with me." At this point, he grabbed a pad and began writing on it. The words he wrote were telegraphed back to New York and sealed in an envelope. When the scientists there opened it, they were astonished to see that Wilbur had rewritten the message word for word from across the continent. The tests continued, and the brothers baffled everyone by perfectly communicating messages over two hundred words long to each other.

The Torres brothers were modest in the extreme about their achievements. They simply told people that they were from a different planet and that this was the source of their astonishing powers. The mysterious brothers claimed that they came to Earth as babies on a rocket ship and were planning to make a return trip to their home planet very shortly.

Whether or not they went to another planet we don't know. But the Torres brothers did vanish completely in the mid-1920s. Skeptics said that they did nothing more than skip out on financial debts and had hightailed it to a South American country to evade their pursuers. Others, convinced by the amazing feats the brothers had accomplished years earlier, swore that they left our world for their own.

Tracking Down the Rubber Band Man

A friend gave us a tip about something weird going on in a building at the corner of Houston and Broadway in Manhattan. A worker in this particular building was known for his unusual habit of collecting rubber bands. He would get them anywhere he could, then roll them into balls. He became so well known for it that people he didn't know, from all over, began stopping by the building to drop off rubber bands to add to his collection.

This we had to check out. So one day we strolled into the lobby of the building and found a doorman sitting at his post.

"Can I help you?" he asked with a smile.

A little self-consciously, we displayed a number of rubber bands we had collected throughout that day. "This might be weird," we said cautiously, "but we've heard that one of the elevator operators here likes when people stop by with rubber bands."

The man on duty looked suspicious, then broke into a smile. "David!?" he asked. "He makes rubber band balls, sure."

"Guess he's kind of a local legend, huh?" we asked.

The man's tone turned deadly serious in response as he corrected us. "He's *the* legend. He's the Rubber Band Man."

Unfortunately, the Rubber Band Man was gone for the day. His co-worker filled us in, however, on a few choice facts. First, it seems that the Rubber Band Man, also known as Mr. David Martinez, has been manning his post and making rubber band balls for many years. He's also had some interesting experiences with those rubber band balls.

"He broke a Blue Man's face once," Mr. Martinez's co-worker informed us matter-of-factly. We looked back at him, confused. "You know, those Blue Men?" Oh, yes, he was talking about a member of the Blue Man Group, the legendary performance-art trio that for many years has been a mainstay Manhattan show. "One of those guys came in and played with the rubber band ball. It was about as big as a softball at the time. He didn't realize how solid the thing was and bounced it right into the ground and BOOM! It came back up and hit that Blue Man right in the nose. I'm talking blood all over the floor. It was a big fiasco. And it wasn't just any Blue Man," he continued. "It was one of the original guys."

Our intrigue with the Rubber Band Man grew even more, and we resolved to return the next day to interview the man himself. Reentering the building the next morning, we approached the man on duty.

"Are you David Martinez?"

He said he was. "You might be interested in these," we said, dropping a handful of rubber bands in front of him. His eyes sprang to life.

"You came by with a donation! Good looking out!"

From there, he rose to his feet, and we exchanged a series of elaborate fist pounds. He proceeded to fill us in on the story of his famous rubber band ball and its origin.

"I took one rubber band one day and just tied it into a knot," he explained. "Then, I took another and another and tied them around it. I've been doing that off and on for four years." From there, he took us into a back room where there was a rubber band mass approaching the size of a basketball. He allowed us to hold the ball, but only after we promised we would not bounce it. He's gotten cautious since taking out the Blue Man.

To build his balls, the Rubber Band Man places bands one after the other precisely on opposite sides of the ball to ensure it stays perfectly round. He has also found some interesting uses for his giant ball of bands.

"What I do is, I put it in my bag with these ankle weights," he explained. "And I'll do curls with them." He thought a moment about this muscle-building technique. "You know what? I think I'm gonna throw a couple of hammers in there too."

The Rubber Band Man is humble about his status as a growing legend. "Sure, everyone in the building knows me. And people passing by will stop in to see how big the ball has gotten." He grips his rubber band ball with both hands. "They've never seen one so big," he says with the quiet pride of a parent speaking of a child.

To most of us, rubber bands are simply office supplies, used without much thought. But to David Martinez, rubber bands have become not just a hobby, but an obsession—and in the process, an object of unique distinction. From this obsession, Mr. Martinez himself has grown into a burgeoning local hero in his own rubbery right.

Witch of Wall Street

Wall Street is a legendarily fast-paced world of power and greed. Thousands of people have come and gone on the stock exchange floor, forgotten moments after they walk out the door. This being the case, it takes a truly standout individual to be remembered here at all. But one such person long ago rocked Wall Street to the point that she is a legend even today — Hetty Green, the Witch of Wall Street.

Hetty Green earned her reputation by being perhaps the stingiest miser of all time. This title isn't just Wall Street gossip. Hetty is listed in *Guinness World Records* as the greatest miser the world has ever known.

Hetty was born in 1835 in New Bedford, Massachusetts. Her family owned a large whaling fleet but were practicing Quakers, so Hetty lived a comfortable but simple life. Then in 1865 her father and her aunt died within months of each other, and both left their inheritances to her. This gave Hetty Green close to $10 million, equal to roughly $185 million by today's standards.

One would think that coming into possession of such a vast sum of money would lead Hetty to a life of luxury and relaxation, a life without a care in the world. In fact, the exact opposite became true. Instead of being content with a mere $10 million, Hetty became obsessed with expanding her fortune. She immediately began playing the markets, an unheard of thing for a woman in her day. And she was a skillful player. Her first major windfall came by buying depreciated U.S. bonds at the end of the Civil War.

For all her wealth, Hetty was incredibly stingy with her money. She appeared every day in the same black dress. She wore her underwear until it was in tatters. She never turned on the heat in her homes, and she ate cold oatmeal, unwilling to spend the pennies it would take to warm it up. One story says that she once stayed up an

entire night searching for a lost stamp that she had spent two cents on.

But Hetty was not only cheap, she was downright mean-spirited. She would lash out at people, insulting them in foul-mouthed language and accusing them of trying to cheat her. Her behavior made her nearly universally hated by all who encountered her. And it led to her infamous nickname, the Witch of Wall Street.

Hetty actually managed to marry. The lucky bridegroom was wealthy, of course—a businessman named Edward Green. Even in her marriage, though, Hetty seemed to rule the roost. One of the most famously shocking incidents occurred with her son, Ned. The boy had injured his knee, and when Hetty learned of it, she refused to take him to a doctor. Instead, she tried to treat the injury herself. Hetty was fond of her son, but not to the point where she'd actually spend money on him.

She proved to be a poor physician though, and Ned's knee remained painful and swollen. Still not relenting, Hetty dressed her son in the clothes of a pauper and took him to a free clinic as a charity case. When the staff there realized that she was the famously rich Hetty Green, they refused to treat the boy without payment. Again she refused to spend her money and left the office in an absolute rage. At the time, she was worth approximately $50 million. The boy's leg was eventually amputated.

You can be as much of a miserable miser as you like in life, but as the saying goes, "You can't take it with you when you go." Hetty Green died in 1916, not surprisingly due to an attack suffered while engaged in a screaming match. (Legends say that the argument erupted with a maid over the virtues of skimmed milk.) She left behind over $100 million, or what would be close to $1.5 billion today. Ned spent his share of his inheritance lavishly.

Hetty Green was an infamously wealthy, infamously greedy, and infamously strange woman. She was also America's first true female tycoon, though we'd imagine that few would hold her up as a shining role model.

Matchmaker, Matchmaker, Take Me Uptown

New York is a city of singles. But in such a big, impersonal place, finding the right person to date is not as easy as you'd think. One man has taken it upon himself to help the lonely singles he comes across—from the front seat of the taxicab that he drives.

Ahmed Ibrahim began matchmaking for his passengers a few years back, when a female passenger was bemoaning her inability to find a man worth dating. Ibrahim realized that he had heard similar tales of woe from hundreds of previous passengers and, on a whim, created a matchmaking service right there on the spot. He asked the girl for her cell phone number and a bit of personal information about herself. He began doing the same to other customers, matching up those he thought might hit it off. By now, he has matched hundreds of people on dates. He hasn't kept track of them all, but he knows that one couple has been dating for well over six months.

Ibrahim doesn't offer his services to all his customers. He has a strict screening process, mostly to eliminate those he thinks aren't serious or trust-worthy. If he decides a rider is match material, he produces an audio recorder and asks a few simple questions. He then plays the answers for subsequent riders to start attempting a match. On average, he arranges roughly four matches a week.

Ibrahim doesn't collect any money for his service, preferring to do it for the pure satisfaction of making his customers happy. Ibrahim himself is unmarried, although he is dating a woman he met in his cab.

The Real Birthplace of Free Love

Today people know the town of Oneida only as a sedate, secluded town east of Syracuse. But anyone who knows anything about Oneida knows that its history is rooted in secrecy, sexual deviancy, and an outright rejection of societal standards: all of this in the service of a utopian ideal called Perfectionism.

Oneida was the chosen home of an enigmatic young preacher named John Humphrey Noyes and his followers. Noyes's mother raised him to be a preacher, but from an early age he rejected the usual notions of shepherding a Christian flock. Noyes had another idea, a philosophy he called Perfectionism, in which men and women would live together communally, sharing everything equally, including themselves.

Noyes began his efforts to gather a flock in 1834. He made his way throughout the Northeast, preaching fervently yet failing to gather a significant number of followers. Eventually, he had a nervous breakdown, brought on perhaps because his most faithful

John Humphrey Noyes

follower and lady love, Abigail Merwin, left him and married another man. Ironically, this nervous breakdown led to Noyes's publishing a series of articles that managed to attract the flock he so desperately desired.

Noyes's famous articles appeared in a fledgling publication known as the *Battle-Axe*. In them, he outlined a number of unusual ideas. Among the most noteworthy was his criticism of the institution of marriage. Noyes promoted a lifestyle in which people were sexually free; no one was bound to any other individual. (He also hinted that he was an agent of God himself sent to earth.)

His articles began generating interest, most notably in Harriet Holton, the granddaughter of a wealthy New York politician. She and Noyes eventually married, though the preacher carefully let his bride know that their marriage was only spiritual and that they would be living under his progressive sexual policies. Holton used portions of her family fortune to fund her husband's efforts, and Noyes began promulgating his views on a wider basis. He also began arranging marriages between his followers, some of whom were his own brothers. The foundations of what would become one of the nation's most influential cults were being laid.

In 1848, the group was large enough and wealthy enough to purchase its own compound in Oneida. For his followers, Noyes bought twenty-three acres of farm and forest land, including a handsome house. The relative

Harriet Holton

seclusion of the new property was not accidental, since the group knew well that its practices would make them pariahs among outside society.

The Oneidans lived by a number of unusual doctrines that set them apart. Among the mildest was something called Mutual Criticism. This practice dictated that any member of the community could be called before a governing council, who would then take it upon itself to harshly and publicly criticize the individual in question. The only person at Oneida exempt from Mutual Criticism was John Humphrey Noyes himself, as he decreed that it was unhealthy for a community to publicly doubt its leader.

Mutual Criticism, while no fun for the unfortunate person being targeted, was not a completely unknown practice. Other religions, including the usually benevolent Quakers, had similar practices. But other Oneidan practices were of a more sexual nature, and these were what threatened to create outrage in the surrounding communities.

The most famous of the Oneidan principles was known as Complex Marriage, which advanced the idea that every man and woman of the Oneida colony would in effect be married to each other. Every adult could have sexual activity with any other, and exclusivity between couples was highly discouraged.

With all this activity going on, Noyes and his followers had to come up with something to hold down a potential population explosion, so they developed the practice of

Male Continence. This was a form of birth control that required a knack for, shall we say, very good timing on the part of the men. Older women in the group, presumably immune to any problems created by a slipup, helped the young men develop their skills.

With good times being had by all, it's no surprise that the Oneida community grew steadily until the late 1870s. What started out as an experiment involving only eighty-seven people would become a group of over three hundred. From all reports, the community lived in relative harmony. They had land to farm, a sawmill on their property, and a growing trade in producing silver flatware for the dining tables of the wealthy.

The peace and harmony—and good times—came to a screeching halt in 1876 when John Humphrey Noyes handed over leadership of the community to his son, Theodore.

Theodore Noyes was an authoritarian who attempted to control the Oneidans with a tight fist when it came to sharing the wealth and an iron fist when it came to enforcing the rules. This was not responded to with many warm feelings by those who had been a part of the community for a substantial amount of time. Factions formed, and the structure of the community suffered. John Humphrey Noyes returned, but it was too late. The combination of internal dissension and disapproval from residents of surrounding areas caused the community to collapse.

By 1880, many of the Oneidans had settled into traditional marriages and were actively avoiding the doctrines that had made their community unique. In January 1881, the effort at Perfectionism came to an end. The Oneida Community was broken up, and a joint stock venture known as Oneida Community, Limited, was created in its place. This company still exists today, manufacturing furniture and silverware in many of the buildings that once housed one of America's most famous utopian communes.

The most famous of the Oneidan principles was known as Complex Marriage, which advanced the idea that every man and woman of the Oneida colony would in effect be married to each other.

The Oneida community c. 1865–1875

The Twisted Tale of Albert Fish

One of the most deranged criminals ever to walk the face of the earth was a man named Albert Fish, and his story is as disturbing as they get. When he was finally captured, he appeared to be nothing more than a broken-down elderly man. Nothing could be further from the truth.

Albert Fish was born in the 1870s near Washington, D.C., and raised in an orphanage. There he was exposed to strict discipline and sadistic acts that would affect him for his entire life. Nevertheless, Fish managed to make something of a life for himself. He held a job, married, and had six children. Early on, though, it became clear that he was a severely disturbed man. For one thing, he had a taste for being flogged with a board with a nail sticking out of its end.

In 1917, things began to get very bad. Fish's wife left him for a younger man and his children would later testify that after his wife's desertion Fish started displaying some terrifying behavior. He would eat large amounts of raw meat, especially during full moons, and rave on about being a Christ figure. And it was during this period that Albert Fish launched his career as a child molester and killer. It's known that he killed at least six, and possibly up to twelve people. And it's estimated that he molested over two hundred children between 1917 and his death.

Fish gained the most infamy, however, after murdering a young New York City girl named Grace Budd. In 1928, the Budd family was living a life of poverty in lower Manhattan. In an attempt to find work, the patriarch of the clan, Albert, took out an ad in a local paper offering the services of himself and his eighteen-year-old son, Eddie, in hard labor.

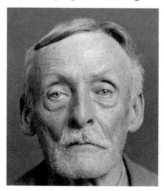

Albert Fish, a.k.a. Frank Howard

The afternoon the ad was published, a well-dressed older man arrived at the Budd's home. He introduced himself as a Long Island farmer named Frank Howard who needed help tending his farm. He offered both Albert and Eddie jobs on the spot. The family was overjoyed at this turn of luck. Mr. Howard vowed to return later with more details.

When the man returned days later, he said he would come back that night to bring Al and Eddie out to his farm for their first day of work. He had to spend the day, he said, at his niece's birthday party uptown. He asked Grace if she would like to accompany him, as there would be other children her age at the party. The girl was thrilled at the idea, and her parents, overwhelmed by Mr. Howard's kindness, gladly agreed to let her attend the party.

They never saw Grace, or Frank Howard, again. This was because there was no Frank Howard. It was the diabolical Albert Fish. He had walked into the Budds' home and abducted their daughter right under their noses.

When Grace didn't return at the appointed time, the Budd family went to the police. A manhunt ensued, but to no avail. After months of media exposure and constant searching for the young girl, nothing turned up. It would be six years before the family heard anything of Grace again.

On November 11, 1934, a disturbing letter arrived at the Budd home. The writer claimed to be the man who had abducted Grace six years earlier. He claimed that he had encountered a sea captain who taught him the finer points of eating human flesh. After this, he became interested in the idea, so he had kidnapped, killed, and eaten Grace Budd. For the Budd family, the letter was devastating. For investigators, it was a

The scene of the crime, located in Greenburgh, New York. Fish occupied the house on the far left. The murder took place in the cottage

occupant of the chauffeur's room had used some of this stationery to write the letter sent to the Budd family.

The hunch turned into pay dirt. King found that a man who had used the room in question fitted the description of the man the detective was looking for. But the owners of the boardinghouse said the man's name was Albert Fish. He no longer lived there but did return periodically to collect his mail.

The next time Fish stopped by for his mail, the boardinghouse workers delayed him and called the police. Detective King arrived in time to arrest the man, who quickly confessed to killing Grace Budd. He also confessed to a half-dozen other murders and made vague references to many more.

Little Grace Budd's remains were later recovered from the foundation of an abandoned house in Westchester County, just where her killer said they would be.

Albert Fish was found guilty of his crimes and sent to Sing Sing Prison in 1935, sentenced to die in the electric chair. Fish, who was addicted to pain, told the press he was happy about this, referring to the experience as an untried adventure. On January 16, 1936, he was executed, one of the oldest inmates ever put to death in the history of American justice.

new impetus to track down this crazed killer.

The lead investigator on the case was Detective Will King, who used the letter to follow a long shot that eventually cracked the case. In tiny script on the note's envelope were the letters NYPCBA, which King found out stood for New York Private Chauffeur's Benevolent Association. First, King assumed the killer was himself a chauffeur, and he interviewed every member of the NYPCBA who might fit the bill. He seemed to be striking out. Then one member confessed a small crime that gave King the lead he needed. He said that he had routinely stolen supplies from the NYPCBA, including a large number of envelopes. He had left some of the stationery behind at a boardinghouse on Lexington Avenue. It was possible, Detective King decided, that the next

Grace Budd

Personalized Properties and Visionary Environments

"private property began the instant somebody had a mind of his own."—e.e. cummings

The American dream lays out a very specific vision of the perfect home. A white picket fence, a well-manicured front lawn, two cars parked in the driveway, and two and a half kids playing somewhere nearby. It's an idyllic vision that has come to be part of the nation's mythology.

But there are those out there who rail against this vision of the perfect life. These people see their surroundings as canvases upon which to express their individuality. Why have just a front lawn when you could dot that lawn with strange, expressionistic statues? Why settle for just a white picket fence when you could instead build a giant tower peppered with freaky-looking children's toys?

The bottom line is that there are many people who want to present their true selves to the world, not someone else's idealized version. And for some reason or another, they have decided that the best way to accomplish this is by altering the very

physical environment in which they exist. Normal buildings and landscapes are so routine.

To stumble upon these environments is always interesting. Sometimes, it's fun to see something so playfully set apart from the norm. Other times, these works are truly unsettling, clearly the result of some sort of residential dementia. Whichever they are, personalized properties such as the ones described in this chapter may soon be a thing of the past. The recent Supreme Court decision supporting the government's right to seize private property makes it more possible every day that odd places like these could be destroyed.

Some of them are already gone, remaining only in people's memories and photographs. But many still remain, publicly and steadfastly defying the norm. Please visit, honor, and appreciate any that you can while the opportunity is still available, but always bear in mind the rights of the owners to their privacy.

Opus 40

Opus 40 is a stunningly beautiful collection of sculptures set in a pastoral area in Saugerties. The site is serene and would be completely weird-free if not for the fact that it was built entirely by hand and, on top of that, entirely by one man.

Harvey Fite worked on Opus 40 for decades, turning an old abandoned bluestone quarry into a six-acre surreal environment, the centerpiece of which is a nine-ton monolith. He expected to put forty years (hence the name Opus 40) into building his massive sculpture. Fite used nothing but hand tools and blasting powder to build the beautiful structures. The creation includes finely fitted stone ramps and swirling terraces around pools and fountains carved out of the rock bed.

Fite took a while to come to his destiny in life. He was born in 1903, attended law school, and went on to study for the ministry. Then he decided that acting was more his thing, but he soon grew bored with that. Eventually, he turned to sculpture and found his true calling. Despite working full-time at Bard from 1933 to his retirement in 1969, he would find time to build Opus 40.

In 1938, Fite found the perfect place to work as well as a perfect source of sculpting material: an abandoned bluestone quarry. He bought the twelve-acre property and built a house and studio there. During this same period, he was invited to do restoration work on an ancient Mayan sculpture in Honduras. The Mayan influence is evident in his work. When he returned to New York, he began clearing away the rubble and brush in the old quarry and started building.

The idea was to carve pedestals for his sculpture out of the bluestone, but soon the terraces took on a life of their own. The statues displayed include a two-ton *Tomorrow,* a four-ton *Quarry Family,* and a half-ton *Flame.* No mortar or cement was used anywhere in their construction. The focal point is a nine-ton monolith, which was raised into position in the 1950s using methods employed by the ancient Egyptians. Fite had planned to carve the piece, but once it was in place he decided to leave it as it was. He then moved the other sculptures to the nearby woods and let the ramps be the main work. In the early 1970s, Fite built a museum for his collection of quarryman's tools and artifacts.

Obviously, Opus 40 was a true labor of love for Mr. Fite, and something of an obsession. Perhaps it is only fitting, then, that its creator actually died on the site. In 1976, while riding a lawn mower, Fite, then seventy-three, was catapulted over the side of the quarry when the machine got stuck in gear. Now his sculptures stand as a reminder of the passion of one man, played out in decades worth of work.

Opus 40 is located in Saugerties on County Road 32. To stand in the open air, soaking in the beautiful scenery, realizing that one obsessed man built it all himself before being thrown over a cliff nearby is a truly overwhelming, weird experience. Opus 40 is open from noon to five p.m. daily.

Easter Island in Rockland County

The stone faces stare out at unsuspecting visitors. All who pass by are surprised upon their first encounter. Some of the faces are ominous. Some appear to be in pain. All stand out from their otherwise sedate, almost sterile environment.

You don't have to travel all the way to the South Pacific to experience this sensation. Instead, head out to Haverstraw to Ted Ludwiczak's house. He's the artist who has created what many refer to as "Easter Island on the Hudson."

Ludwiczak's home and yard are covered in stone faces he himself has carved. He positions them so that they are visible from the road as well as from the banks of the Hudson River. He has been carving these stone countenances since 1988. It's a hobby that began randomly. While building a retaining wall, Ludwiczak noticed a large piece of rock sitting on the ground, and for some reason he was drawn to it. He began carving away at it with a bent lawn mower blade that was lying around. When he was done, a face had emerged. He has continued this activity for close to two decades now, and he still uses the bent lawn mower blade for the majority of his projects.

Ludwiczak has made money selling his faces through a gallery in New York City. He doesn't enjoy this fully, however. He sees it as "breaking up a family" of stone faces. Every time he sells one, he immediately carves a replacement face to stand in its stead.

Haverstraw is a quiet, suburban town to which Ted Ludwiczak's creations add a unique flavor. They'd really fit in more on some tropical island or at a Native American tribal ceremony than they do in Rockland County. But everybody's got to be somewhere, right?

The Garden at Sixth and B

The East Village, in Manhattan, is not known for its lush gardens, and it's certainly not known as an outdoor art lover's paradise. But a small plot of land at the corner of Sixth Street and Avenue B brings both of these things to one of New York City's most urban neighborhoods.

The garden was created after the city acquired the land from previous owners due to unpaid taxes. Residents of the community, seizing an opportunity, cleaned out the piles of garbage lying around and set out to create a garden. Eventually, the spot became a place for locals to meet, walk, and commune with nature, not an easy thing to do in downtown New York. Inevitably, the city tried to sell the land to real estate developers, but locals set up a determined effort to save their garden, which had become an integral part of their community. The city came around and allowed the little patch of green to stay as it was. Now the Sixth and B site is an official city park. And this is in many respects due to the efforts of one man with a vision: local character and sculptor Eddie Boros, who has built many strange, controversial sculptures in the famous garden.

He's also the man responsible for the turn it's taken toward the weird. Most famously, he created a titanic wooden tower and has hung hundreds of weather-worn children's toys from it.

Eddie is a local who has called this neighborhood home all his life. He is a longtime collector of found objects, scouring the city for discarded items he deems of value. These items have come into play in the sculptures he has erected in the park. One can't miss Eddie's work—it's impossible. Turning onto Avenue B off of Sixth Street, the entire block seems crammed in tightly together; everything is brick and asphalt. Then, soaring dozens of feet into the sky, is a huge latticework of wood, rising up to form a gigantic tower. Sun-bleached stuffed animals stare out from the dark recesses created by the intersections of wood that make up the tower. Carousel horses hang, slowly spinning in the wind, their once bright faces dulled by sun, rain, and wind, giving them a somewhat creepy appearance. Beloved characters such as the Muppets peek out from different corners of the edifice. To many visitors, this imagery is not only unusual but somewhat disturbing.

Boros's tower is one of the most bizarre sights in a neighborhood already known for being very eccentric. To stand out as weird in the East Village, a place well accustomed to the more outlandish sights the city has to offer, is a true accomplishment.

Ave. B Tower Looks Even Weirder When You're Drunk!

There are a lot of things in the East Village that make me uncomfortable. It feels like one of the final areas to resist Giuliani's efforts to make everything about Manhattan sterilized and squeaky-clean. It's the only part of the city that I ever really feel intimidated in, the only place where I feel like I really have to watch my back.

There is one spot on the East Side that makes me more uncomfortable than any other. At a community garden on Avenue B, there is this tower that has freaked me out a number of times. It has all these toys and other objects hanging off of it. It looks completely out of place. It looks evil—like something you'd expect the bad guy from *The Never Ending Story* to live inside of. Or the type of place you'd tell a little kid a witch lives inside, and she'll eat you if she catches you—warped childhood levels of evil. Walking home drunk past this thing is really disconcerting.*—DSS*

The Collyer Brothers

Homer and Langley Collyer started out their lives on top of the world and ended them buried deep within their own world—both literally and metaphorically.

The two brothers were born into one of New York City's most prominent families. Homer, born in 1881, and Langley, born in 1885, were the sons of a noted gynecologist and a well-educated mother who was an expert on the classics. Both sons lived opulent lives at the family's mansion on Fifth Avenue at 128th Street in Harlem. Homer had a degree in engineering, and Langley became a lawyer. The Collyer brothers seemed bound always to live on easy street.

After 1909, the boys' idyllic world started to fall apart. Their parents divorced, a rarity at that time. The brothers continued to live in Harlem with their mother, who eventually passed away, leaving the boys on their own. The neighborhood and economic climate began to change. Harlem became poorer and more crime-ridden. Most dramatic of all, Homer went blind in 1933.

For unknown reasons, the two brothers retreated into their home and spent almost all their time there. Perhaps because they were running short of money, or perhaps because they were losing some hold on their sanity, they had the water and power shut off. Every few days Langley would emerge and walk four blocks to a park, where he would fill containers with water from a fountain. Other than this, the brothers were rarely seen. They boarded up all their windows and set up a vast series of booby traps throughout their home to fend off any who might try to enter. Langley devised a diet of oranges, bread, and peanut butter that he insisted would give Homer his sight back.

Langley Collyer

The world heard little of the Collyer brothers. In 1942, they defaulted on their mortgage and bank representatives traveled to their home in an effort to evict them. They were met at the door by a screaming Langley Collyer. Police were called and smashed the door in, only to find that it was blocked by a titanic pile of junk and newspapers. The dispute was settled when Langley handed over a check that paid off the mortgage in full. The Collyers again retreated into their own strange world.

Then, on March 21, 1947, police received a call from a man calling himself Charles Smith. He informed them that there was a dead body inside the Collyer brothers' residence. Police arrived at the scene, but the doors were locked, windows were boarded shut or covered in iron, and there was no doorbell or phone. Police broke the door down, only to face a solid wall of newspapers, beds, old sewing machines, and various other forms of junk. An attempt to climb a ladder and enter through a second-floor window met with similar results. The only option was to reach into the window and repeatedly throw out handfuls of newspapers mixed with other garbage.

Finally a large enough space was cleared to allow one policeman to climb inside. He began toppling over more

mystery increased: Where was Langley Collyer?

Every day police would delve farther into the house, tossing more junk and newspapers out the windows, and would report that Langley Collyer had not been found. Sightings began to pour in across the nation as the story's prominence grew, but the accounts were all false.

Finally, on April 8, after over two weeks of searching through the home, workers pushed aside a pile of junk and found the body of Langley Collyer being gnawed on by a rat. He was only about ten feet from where his brother, Homer, had been found, but due to the density of junk throughout the house, it had been impossible to locate him. It was quickly determined that Langley had most likely fallen into one of his own booby traps and was pinned

piles of newspapers as he searched through the area with a flashlight. Eventually, he stumbled upon the body of old, blind Homer Collyer. He was dressed in only a bathrobe. His head was pressed to his knees, and his unkempt hair fell below his shoulders. He was immediately pronounced dead.

The brothers' status as local legends had long been established. On this first day of the search of the Collyers' home, over six hundred spectators gathered. The crowds grew bigger as the house was further emptied out, and the

underneath it, where he died. Homer, blind and unable to navigate his way around the house on his own, slowly starved to death ten feet away.

All in all, over 136 tons of junk were removed from the Collyer brothers' home. Most of it was in the form of newspapers. Langley had been saving them for Homer so that when his sight was restored he could catch up on current events.

The home of the Collyer brothers was torn down after the discovery of their bodies. Today the site is a parking lot.

The Land of Broken Dreams

Liverpool lies along the New York Thruway off Exit 38. It is a small, quiet town and, to many, is not much more than a point on the map just outside Syracuse. But to those who know a little more about it, this strange place has come to be known as the Land of Broken Dreams.

The Land of Broken Dreams is the brainchild of one Bob Smith, known more popularly to locals as the Whirligig Man of Exit 38. For the past forty years, Bob has been constructing a vast art yard consisting of root sculptures, large decorated fences, and found objects. Among these found objects is a neon cowboy that once stood as a roadside icon outside the DeWitt Ranch Motel in Syracuse. Smith rescued him from destruction and has put the cowpoke on display. However, he has not fixed him so that he functions properly. The homeless cowboy doesn't light up; he just sort of stands there, propped up against a tree, aimlessly lassoing overgrown vines with his lariat. Smith says that this fits the theme of the Land of Broken Dreams quite literally.

Other "broken dreams" found scattered throughout the property include discarded rocking horses and other broken children's toys, bathroom paper towel dispensers, street signs, vintage hubcaps, garage sale oil paintings, dolls, a tree trunk festooned with broken clocks, discarded home decorations, electronics and sports equipment, puppet heads suspended on sticks, and naked mannequin legs wearing high spike heels. Anything you can think of is probably somewhere to be found squirreled away in the Land of Broken Dreams.

Smith has created pathways throughout the cluttered yard using old carpeting and has constructed small buildings in which to house rabbits and live birds. The art yard has actually become something of a bird sanctuary as well, attracting many fowl, which make their nests among the dozens of strange sculptures dotting the landscape. But there are several other buildings throughout the property that we wouldn't recommend that anyone or anything inhabit: Scattered around in a seemingly haphazard layout are numerous sheds or shacks that seem to be standing by sheer force of their own goodwill. Most of the wood and glass structures seem to serve no real purpose other than to house a few more busted-up artifacts. But standing there, leaning precariously to one side or another, windows and doors open to the curious wanderer, they seem almost like shrines dedicated to all things that have been used up and thrown away, as almost everything in our daily lives eventually is.

There's an old saying that one man's trash is another man's treasure, and that might be put to the test here in Liverpool. Is Bob Smith's Land of Broken Dreams just a junkyard, or is it, like the Island of Misfit Toys, a metaphorical statement about all that we as a society value and then discard? Might it, in fact, be a scrap heap that stands as an homage to our disposable culture and material excess, or is it just a collection of worthless stuff? The next time you're traveling along the New York Thruway, get off at Exit 38 and pay a visit to the Land of Broken Dreams. Have a look at Bob Smith's place, and decide for yourself.

Socrates Sculpture Park

Another, more formal, but no less strange sculpture park sits in a very unusual location, on the bank of the East River in Long Island City in the borough of Queens. Located at the intersection of Broadway and Vernon Boulevard, Socrates Sculpture Park is one of New York City's only notable venues for the display of outdoor art.

Up until 1986, the land at the corner of Broadway and Vernon was completely abandoned. Desolate and foreboding, it was being used as a landfill. Then, under the leadership of artist Mark di Suvero, a group of artists and community activists banded together to clear the lot and establish an area for an outdoor display that would become Socrates Sculpture Park.

Weird New York, along with some friends, visited Socrates Sculpture Park in the summer of 2005. The theme for the entire park during our visit was sports. The displays were large and numerous. One was a boxing ring, made out of concrete and metal pipes, with metal gloves left inside the ring. Another was a tower, some thirty feet tall, atop which a football player stood. Embedded within the tower were various pieces of sporting equipment, as if they had been excavated from the earth. One sculpture was simply a metal pole with a number of thirty-five-pound weights stacked on it. A nearby placard explained that the artist purchases each weight in Manhattan, then walks across the Queensboro Bridge carrying it. He makes his way through Long Island City with the weight, then places it on the pole. He has vowed to continue doing this, one weight at a time, until the entire pole is covered with the heavy metal objects.

The park is a strange, hidden oasis in a rather desolate part of Long Island City. Because it is shrouded from view by a large row of bushes and bracketed by a large parking lot, you'd probably drive right past it if you didn't know it was there. We felt hidden from the outside world when we

were there. Other guests were few and far between. Many of those we encountered had brought picnic lunches and sat eating along the East River. One man felt comfortable enough to find himself a corner of the park to sunbathe nude. The entire place feels like one great big secret, inside and out.

And yet the park is world renowned, with the work of dozens of artists on display. Some of the pieces are traditional, while some are truly weird. Tens of thousands of people visit the installations each year. The park is open until dusk, three hundred and sixty-five days each year. It also offers an outdoor cinema program, sculpting programs for kids, and special exhibits throughout the year.

Long Island City isn't usually associated with cutting-edge, outdoor art. Most people probably still think of this area as a landfill perched on the river. Socrates Sculpture Park breaks the stereotype by replacing an urban wasteland with a surrealistic wonderland.

Terrillion Ranch

Veronica Terrillion, a resident of the tiny town of Indian River, is a small, bespectacled woman who looks more like a grandmother than a visionary folk artist. But Ms. Terrillion has come to be known as just that—her property is adorned with hundreds of handmade sculptures, making it a famous roadside stop for thousands of travelers each year. Terrillion made her first sculpture in 1954 and hasn't stopped since. She began with a concrete figure of the Virgin Mary. In the five decades since that first effort, her mere three acres have become home to over four hundred sculptures. She has even built her own pond, containing two islands, which are home to even more sculptures. Many are of a religious theme. Others are of animals, relatives, and friends. Terrillion is also an oil painter.

The Terrillion Ranch is like an oasis in the rural environs of Lewis County. It sits on Route 812 and is visible from the road.

From Automobiles to Furniture

Steve Heller is the owner and driving force behind Steve Heller's Fabulous Furniture, a store standing in Boiceville, near Woodstock. The name of Heller's store doesn't even begin to hint at the strange items to be found on sale there and on the surrounding property.

Steve Heller's Fabulous Furniture opened in 1973, but Mr. Heller's fascination with crafting sculptures began many years before. At the age of twelve, Heller started searching for downed trees every day after his paper route. He would take the trees and shape them into odd sculptures and functional objects. Some of these original sculptures still stand at Fabulous Furniture, which has come to be a showroom for Heller's works. These days, Heller is still crafting objects out of wood. He also works with metal, using scrap he rescues from the local dump.

Most intriguingly, he has made dozens of art cars, rescuing junked Cadillacs from the 1950s and crafting them into weird-looking pieces. His sculptures are on sale at his store and also dot the landscape surrounding it. It is not hard to spot a Heller piece or Steve Heller's Fabulous Furniture. The bizarre works that surround his store are impossible to miss.

Heller's art-from-automobiles are his most famous pieces. On his website, www.fabulousfurnitureon28.com, Heller speaks of his downright obsession with rescuing cars and turning them into other objects:

"I love wood and metal, but in my heart I'm a car freak. The Cadillacs of the 1950s are the cars I love the most. I've collected dozens of them over the years,

and have incorporated them into furniture and sculpture, hoping to keep them from going to the crusher (perhaps the most evil piece of machinery ever invented). I have made cedar chests, entertainment units, beds, lights, and other pieces of usable furniture out of these once rusting piles of metal. I am, after all, my father's son."

Heller's taste for old cars is probably genetic. His father was known as an antiques dealer, but on his own website Heller lovingly refers to him as more of a junk collector. Heller's dad collected tons of materials over the years. When he died in the late 1980s, Steve's mother asked him to remove his dad's stuff. But on the way to the junkyard, Heller realized that it was all material he could use in his sculptures. From that point forward, he worked in the mediums of both wood and metal.

In addition to his off-the-rack pieces, Heller also builds commissioned works. So if you're looking for something specific or just want to see some of the most bizarre objects made of wood, metal, or former cars, head up Route 28 in Boiceville. Steve Heller is the man you want to meet.

Schroon River Figures

On Schroon River Road, just six miles north off I-87 at Exit 23 (Warrensburg), there are a series of bizarre papier-mâché characters. From the looks of it, they might have once resided in an amusement park, but the truth remains unknown. I tried to contact the owner of the house where the figures are located, but was yelled at to "Keep out!" from within the darkened house. Needless to say, I didn't pry any further.

As far back as I can remember, those odd figures have always stood along the field and nearby the house, without caving in or falling over. The most memorable to me as a kid were always the Bigfoot and the trees with faces. I think this was because they seemed like a sort of homage to the dark side of upstate NY.

With all of the weird things to find in upstate New York, these "lawn ornaments" are a testament to the weirdness that abounds.–*Clayton J. Gibbs*

The Pratt Rocks of Prattsville

Just when you think you've seen it all, another tidbit of weirdness springs forth and grabs you. While hiking in the nearby Catskill Mountains of New York State recently, I came across a mini Mt. Rushmore—well, kind of. Located about a half mile up a steep hillside beside the exceedingly rural Route 23A, relief carvings in the cliffs snared my "weird" eye and prompted my closer inspection.

Here's what I found out: Pratt Rocks was a lifelong work in progress for one Zadock Pratt, founder of the largest tannery in the world back in the 1830s. It was so large, in fact, that it spawned the town of Prattsville to house its workers. Nearly every achievement and major landmark in Pratt's life was recorded in stone here, carved into the rock by a local sculptor under his employ.

What's there, you ask? Well, there is a family coat of arms, Pratt's own bust, various pivotal dates and events, sculpted horses, an arm and hammer, a shrine to his son (killed by Confederate fire in the Civil War), and inscriptions of all sorts. But the coolest thing is a carved-out "tomb" that was intended to house Pratt's carcass for eternity. Word has it that it was found to leak, so Pratt ultimately abandoned the idea. Of course, this raises the obvious question, Why should a few drips matter to a rotting carcass? But remember, this was a very wealthy man who, by virtue of constructing this stone monument to vanity, had already proved to some (not I!) that his thought processes were—shall we say—just a tad offbeat?

Presumably, locals have since painted the rock sculptures white; that, or they used very good paint back in the 1800s! It's a short hike up to the cliffs, and the trail is easy to find from the road. When last there, my biker pal Dave claimed to hear ominous sounds coming from the tomb area; but then, Dave is at least as weird as the place itself, so I took his comment with a grain of salt.

But haunted or not, this spot deserves a visit and certainly ranks high on the weirdness scale. Enjoy, foot soldiers. —*Jeff Bahr*

Wing's Castle: For Sale for a King's Ransom

One of the most famous personalized properties in the entire state is up for sale. And it ain't cheap!

Wing's Castle is an eclectic, handcrafted castle built in Millbrook by Peter and Toni Wing. Construction began in 1969 and was finished nearly three decades later. Since its completion, the castle has become a curiosity visited by thousands of people each year. It's perched on a hill with a spectacular view of the beautiful Hudson Valley below.

The giant castle, both interior and exterior, is adorned with found objects, strange faces, and architectural oddities that leave most visitors scratching their heads in wonder. Inside, there are three bedrooms and two bathrooms. One of those bathrooms is in the shape of a three-leaf clover. The home also features a fireplace shaped like Buddha, as well as a moat that serves as a swimming pool.

As of this writing, Wing's Castle is for sale, and the asking price is $7,900,000. This may seem like a ridiculously steep price, but the castle is located on prime real estate and is a truly beautiful building. It is not just the home of the Wings but of an annual Shakespeare festival that uses the castle's fantastical appearance as a backdrop for the old bard's plays.

The creative force behind the structure, Peter Wing, was born in the Hudson Valley but left it to join the United States Navy after being ejected from high school at the age of seventeen. He toured the world, and many of the things he saw in the Mediterranean and Asia have been incorporated into his designs for the castle. In a recent

edition of the *Poughkeepsie Journal*, Wing wrote a column explaining the impetus that led him to build the castle, his connection to it, and what it has come to mean to the community of Millbrook and beyond:

"Why did we create it? I have tried to answer this question to no avail. However, it may well be the Hudson's vista—the mind and spirit soar, imagination takes flight up here. Look over history: the Dutch, French, English colonists, fighting to hold it; Native Americans probably did the same among themselves. The sunsets of color can stir you on."

Wing obsessively adds on to the castle that bears his name. Even with the main building completed, he continues to devise new additions. He recently told the *Poughkeepsie Journal* of plans for an outdoor section:

I'm finishing a garden complex and small court that bed-and-breakfast guests can enjoy. There are stone angels, faces, Greek gods and strong Asian and Spanish influences. The castle proper was finished eight years ago. The garden complex has taken that long so far, with another two years to complete. As I walk the paths of the first construction, vines and flowers and birds have overtaken it. It seems it has always been there.

Visit www.wingcastle.us for more information if you are interested in Wing's Castle and have $8 million to spare. Be sure that you're the right type of person before you commit to buying the place, though. Wing's Castle is fit only for a king.

The Tragic Tale of Boldt Castle

Located on Heart Island in the St. Lawrence River, Boldt Castle is a partially finished architectural masterpiece with a very sad story to tell. All who visit are struck by the beauty of the building, the peacefulness of the surrounding island, and the deep tragedy that led to the building's being left in its uncompleted state.

George Boldt was a manager at Manhattan's famous Waldorf-Astoria Hotel. In 1900, he decided to take a huge part of his fortune and dedicate it to building the most magnificent house he could imagine in honor of his wife, Louise. He selected the location on Heart Island and had workers begin building the structure immediately.

After four years, Boldt had spent over $2.5 million on his wife's castle. There was a children's playhouse, a yacht house to shelter the family's numerous boats, and a network of tunnels connecting the main building to the servants' quarters. Everything seemed perfect. The wealthy family was constructing a fairy-tale life for themselves on Heart Island. Then, without warning, it all came crashing down.

Louise, George's beloved wife and the muse behind the castle, died suddenly in 1904 from heart failure. Upon hearing this sad news, George acted without any hesitation. He immediately sent a telegram from New York City to the island, ordering that all work cease. The project was on the verge of completion, but upon receiving the telegram, workers were ordered to stop immediately. They laid down their tools on the spot and walked away.

For seven decades, the castle remained exactly as it had been left. Entirely abandoned, it stood unfinished, a testament to the love George Boldt had for his wife, Louise, and to the suddenness with which death took her away from him. George himself never again returned to Heart Island and never saw the castle he had commissioned.

Eventually, Boldt's Castle was opened for tours. Admission is $4.25 for adults and $2.50 for children. It is accessible only by boat, available at Alexandria Bay, New York. The building and surrounding grounds are open for self-guided tours between May and October. For no charge beyond admission, weddings can be held outdoors on the island. It seems only fitting that Heart Island, a labor of love, would be so accommodating to young brides and grooms.

Mushroom House

Powder Mill Park in Perinton, just southeast of the city of Rochester, is notable for its secret history. It was originally a hidden location where gunpowder, dynamite, and artillery shells were manufactured by the Acadia Power Company.

While that interesting tidbit speaks to the fact that this area has always had a weird element, there is something in the park today that is a much more visceral representation of how strange the place can get.

There is an odd private residence at 142 Park Road that rises above a stream at the entrance to Powder Mill Park. The house has come to be a head-scratcher of a sight for the generations of people who grew up in the surrounding area. Visible from the road, the building appears to be a number of mushrooms growing out of the wooded hillside.

Though it is commonly referred to as the Mushroom House, architect James H. Johnson actually fashioned this unique dwelling after a stem of the Queen Anne's lace plant. Built in 1970 for Robert and Marguerite Antell, the home's distinctive retro-modern "pod" design earned it a designation as a Perinton landmark in 1989.

Johnson had studied with Bruce Goff, a professor of architecture at the University of Oklahoma, who combined unusual materials in unexpected ways to create buildings that are both futuristic and plantlike at the same time. Johnson has been the architect of dozens of custom-designed homes and numerous religious buildings throughout New York and around the world. The Mushroom House consists of a series of pod units, which look similar to lily pads from beneath, suspended on stemlike stilts. There are even underground pods, a car-pod garage, and a mosaic-lined interpod tunnel. According to a home owner who lives in another house designed by the architect, "Jim Johnson's houses are like sculptures. We're living in a sculpture."

To us, it seems more like life in the ape city from *Planet of the Apes*. Or perhaps like inhabiting one of the fantasy toadstool-like landscapes depicted on an old album cover by the band YES.

The Doll Death House

I grew up in Astoria, Queens, and had always heard that there was a house close to Astoria Park (right near the East River) that had dolls hanging by their necks on the bough of a tree. Of course, I found this to be intriguing. So back in my late high school/early college days, my friend and I drove past this house on many an occasion to get a closer look at its oddities and perhaps its owner.

What we saw was a feast for the eyes! There were those baby dolls hung precariously by their necks in a gruesome lineup. There were also cutouts in the tree trunks that served as shelves for various tchotchkes and knickknacks. Not to mention lawn ornaments, weather vanes, and a small tomb in front of the house that had our imaginations spinning out of control!

The owner's wife, according to rumor, was buried right on the property. One day, we stopped the car in front of the house and were marveling at all of its attributes when we suddenly realized we were being watched . . . by the owner! Needless to say, we peeled out of there and never returned.

Last year, another high school friend and I visited the house. It's still standing and still pretty odd. It looks somewhat different now, but I think it still qualifies as weird! I live for this stuff!—*Janice Wolk*

Gone the Way of the Giant Chicken

Just an update about the Astoria Doll House. I live two blocks from where the house used to be. It has been torn down, and they are planning to build a new set of row homes where it stood.

I remember when the house was there, and I can attest to the fact that it sure was creepy. Some dolls were actually nailed into the trees, along with stuffed animals of every kind! This area is an old section of Astoria, and there are a lot of old houses and mansions dating back to the nineteenth century, including one that was recently refurbished and turned into apartments, where my wife swears, when she was a kid, she found giant chicken tracks all over the yard.—*Dave L.*

Poor Man's Penthouse

Located in Syracuse, it can be spotted clearly on the east side of Route 81 just north of the city. From what I've heard (the most sensible explanation as far as I am concerned), the owner had a clause in his will that forbade the destruction or removal of the house from the property. So when the property was acquired for construction of the pictured warehouse, there was only one possible solution. The big sign was added years later, I'm assuming to hide the house.
—*Bruce Bertrand*

Anyone who runs a restaurant knows that décor is as important to business as the cuisine that is served. High-end eateries spend many thousands of dollars making sure that their layout is arranged in a way that both is comfortable for their clientele and will increase sales.

But there are restaurants that go in the opposite direction, trading the traditional or even the advisable for the memorable. Some of the most impressive personalized properties in the entire state of New York happen to be restaurants. Who knows what compels these business owners to take their establishments from routine to bizarre? Whether it's to offer consumers a little bit more bang for their buck or just to catch their eye in an effort to get them to come inside, the following two eateries have gone from delicious to delirious when it comes to décor.

Rosemary's Texas Taco

Located on Route 22 in the tiny Putnam County town of Patterson, Rosemary's Texas Taco is as bizarre a restaurant as any. Inside, spicy Mexican food is offered up, as one would expect from the name of the establishment. But there are also hundreds of found objects hanging from the walls and scattered about the restaurant, some left as they were discovered and others altered to make them appear more artistic or warped. A number of robots and mannequins stand throughout the dining room. The interior of the restaurant is weird enough, but the land surrounding Rosemary's Texas Taco is even weirder.

Dozens of pink flamingos, pushcarts, old bicycles, and other random junk stand in front of the small building. A truck usually sits outside, covered in similar materials. In back, things get even stranger. A massive sculpture garden, filled with more junk and tons of peculiar statuary, is crammed

onto the land directly behind Rosemary's. Music blasts from speakers affixed to trees on the property. Parrots, a lemur, and a caged monkey live in this outdoor fantasyland, making it even more bizarre.

Rosemary herself is an integral part of the establishment. Her outlandish makeup, outfits, and hairdos add to the legend of her Texas Taco stand. If you're ever in Putnam County, just a stone's throw from Danbury, Connecticut, make sure to stop in, say hello to Rosemary, soak in the décor, and eat a Texas Taco or two.

Pizza and More at Pollywogg Hollër

Believe it or not, the best place we've found to eat in New York State is called Pollywogg Hollër. It's also the hardest to get to. Pollywogg Hollër isn't so much weird, but rather surreal. It's a pizza restaurant in the middle of the woods, off the electrical grid, surrounded by sculptures that have been left by students at the local art college.

The place is located in the town of Belmont. To get there you have to take Route 244 west and make a right onto North Road (dirt) and drive about a mile. Park and follow a hiking trail for five minutes, past a thirty-foot geodesic dome, and you will come upon a woodstove pizza restaurant in the middle of the woods. Bill Castle, the proprietor, built this place by hand and with lots of sweat. The Pollywogg Hollër official website tells the story of how Castle ended up out here in the middle of nowhere:

"Pollywogg Hollër is the birth of a dream that started back in 1976 when Barb and Bill Castle entered this enchanted forest with their three young children, a bunch of hand tools, and a vision to establish a home site and life style that would be in harmony with nature—a reprieve from our hectic modern life."

After building their

own little hideaway in the wilds of upstate New York, the Castles decided to open their woodland oasis to the public as what they call an "eco-resort." According to Bill and Barb, "After opening our doors as an Eco-Resort in '86, we owe our continual growth and thanks to the constant flow of adventurous guests that discover our path each day. We continue to grow in love as a family business and invite all that are interested to come and share this love at Pollywogg Hollër."

When I went, I ordered a Bill's Golden Garlic Pie, which was topped with garlic, black olives, feta cheese, mushrooms, and red peppers. After the first bite, I can only describe it as a big piece of garlic with some pizza on top of it. Also offered is some of Bill's homemade wine, a hearty red you can get by the glass or the bottle. The pizza was $7, and the wine was free, with donations accepted. To pay for it all, there's a cigar box on the bar counter, and you make your own change.

I was sitting on the back of an old tractor eating the last bite when Bill, who was having a lively discussion with a familiar patron, came around the bar and lifted his shirt to expose his large, extended belly. The guest responded by lifting her shirt and exposing her finer points to him and the rest of the crowd. (Sorry, no pictures!) All the while, bluegrass music was blasting from speakers hanging from the trees. Sunday afternoons and Wednesday nights are the hours of operation, if you're interested.

The rest of the thirty-plus acres is a sculpture garden (for lack of a better term), which seems to be a depository of all the big, bad, discarded ceramics projects from the

art school, just sprinkled around the grounds. The PH web page paints a more highbrow picture of the art collection:

"The work of over one hundred artists—many from the world-renowned New York State College of Ceramics at Alfred—is displayed along the wooded trails that encompass the camp. Here, you may stroll undisturbed through towering figures that pop with color and contrast. Fern covered knolls cushion glass ornaments. Pottery encrusted with moss sprouts from the earthy surroundings."

After your pizza and stroll through the sculpture garden, if you'd like to spend more time at Pollywogg Hollër there are a number of small cabins scattered throughout the woods that are available to rent. The Castles describe an overnight stay at their eco-resort this way:

"The morning sky will greet you through skylights overhead, and ample room for two is provided in the luxury of a heated spring water shower. A hearty breakfast prepares you for another day of weird wonders."

Weird wonders indeed!

—Thanks to WNY *correspondent Brett Stern*

Praise the Lord and Pass the Pie at John's Pizzeria

Usually, a so-called "personalized property" qualifies as weird because of alterations made to a building or landscape. Sometimes, though, it's the alterations you don't make to a piece of property that qualifies it as weird.

John's Pizzeria, located on West Forty-fourth Street, in the heart of Manhattan's Theater District, is unlike the hundreds of other pizza shops in the area. While most are small, cramped, and have limited seating, John's is an expansive space. It stands within a decades-old church that the owners altered little in the making of their restaurant.

Paintings portraying New York City scenes still dot the walls. A large dome, once the centerpiece beneath which an entire congregation gathered, is now a beacon to New Yorkers looking for delicious thin-crust pizza. Ornate, highly detailed sculptures still protrude from the walls and ceiling. It feels almost sacrilegious to eat here, as if you had waltzed into a church and started chowing down. Ultimately, though, even God wouldn't argue with eating high-quality pizza, would He? I mean, why else would He have invented it in the first place?

John's has floor seating, a bar, and a second level that affords one a close-up look of the artwork adorning the walls. The cavernous space is a surreal place to eat a very common type of food. Besides its unique setting, John's serves up what is inarguably one of the best slices of pizza in all of New York City. Stop by to satiate your hunger and kneel before God all in one trip.

Roadside Oddities

American culture has traditionally been a car culture. Who among us has never climbed into a car for a classic road trip? Our nation is crisscrossed with highways, byways, and back roads, all of which reflect this attachment to automobiles.

It's no wonder at all, then, that so many odd things can be found literally right along the roadside. From huge and strange signs that can be read at 60 miles per hour to campy attractions meant to suck in summer travelers, the American roadside has come to be a collection of attention-grabbers that turn heads and make drivers hit the brakes.

Some of the sites sitting along New York's roadsides are goofy, quirky, or simply claim to be the largest of whatever they are. Others seem to have a more sinister side, a darker edge. Still others have stories associated with them that you would never dream of unless you heard them straight from the mouths of the locals. Regardless of the particular classification of the following sites, it's inarguable that New York's roadsides are chock-full of strange, intriguing attractions that are well worth a detour.

Dolly Dimples

The giant girl statue in Silver Creek is named Dolly Dimples. I grew up there and saw that statue my whole life. Just thought you would like to know her name. She has been there for the thirty years I've been in the area. I think she came from a drive-in restaurant down the road. It used to be called Pat's Drive Inn, but that was before my time. The business that has her now is Valvo's Candy. They make candy and concrete and composite statues. They have the best sponge candy in the world! *–Letter via e-mail*

Thinking BIG

New York has always been known for having the biggest, best, and the most of just about everything. Heck, New York City is even called the Big Apple! Sure we've got some of the tallest buildings in the world and lots of other grand-scale landmarks to crow about. For now, though, let's take a look at some lesser known icons of New York culture — grand not only in size, but also in terms of their weirdness.

The Mighty Big Duck

The Big Duck is a Long Island landmark known well beyond the borders of Nassau and Suffolk counties. This pumped-up bird is one of the finest remaining examples of mimetic roadside architecture. In fact, similar types of buildings, shaped like animals, food, and so forth, are called "duck architecture" in reference to this structure.

The Duck started out as a store where farmer Martin Maurer and his wife sold their Peking ducks. From the 1920s to the 1950s, three quarters of American ducks were produced in Long Island. In the 1950s, there were more than seventy other duck farms nearby. But today there are only four such farms left on Long Island.

The Maurers got their idea while on a trip to California, where they were inspired by a teapot-shaped luncheonette. During the Depression, they hired a couple of unemployed theatrical designers to make their featherbrained idea a reality. The plans were drawn from an actual duck tied to a porch with a piece of string. Construction was completed in 1931. The duck is twenty feet tall, thirty feet long, fifteen feet wide, and weighs ten tons. Ford Model T taillights were used for the eyes (they still work and glow red at night). Today the interior is used for the Big Duck souvenir gift shop.

The Duck has been moved a few times. In 1936, it was moved from Riverhead to Flanders, where it continued to sell eggs and processed duck. In 1988, it faced demolition and was moved to Hampton Bays. It's possible that it may return to its Flanders site in order to give the property a national historic site designation (the Duck is on the National Register of Historic Places) and thus preserve a dozen old farm buildings. There is a nice miniature replica (still rather large) at Island Green Golf Center in Selden. These days, the Duck is the home of the Long Island Tourist Information Center as well as a welcome sight for all who drive past its roost.

Nipper Watches over Albany

A giant watchdog guards the state capital of Albany. This pooch looks friendly enough, but you would be smart to watch out—he sure is big.

The dog is a representation of Nipper, once the RCA Victor mascot, made famous in the "His Master's Voice" ad campaigns of yesteryear. He sits atop the former RCA building just north of downtown, where he has been perched for five decades. At one time there was another RCA spokesdog, in Baltimore, but that massive mutt was removed years ago, putting Albany's four-ton canine in a breed all his own.

Nipper, a fox terrier–bull terrier mixed-breed dog, is modeled after a painting where the dog is posed with an ear cocked toward an old-fashioned Victrola. This twenty-five-foot-tall likeness, the largest man-made dog in the world, was built in 1954. It has a steel frame and composite body and weighs four tons. His name is inscribed on his collar. Originally, there was also a Victrola box with a horn.

Arnoff Moving and Storage bought and renovated the Albany building and Nipper in 1997. Because of his height, he has an aircraft beacon on his right ear. A steep set of stairs inside Nipper allows for changing the bulbs.

Bottlegate Farm in Kent has two eight-foot-tall and two four-foot-tall bottles at its entrance. We assume this place was once a dairy farm.

The Milan Fork is thirty-one feet tall and made of steel. It was built in 2000 as a pun on its location at a fork in the road.

That Needle and Button Are Sew Big!

Located in New York City's Garment District on the northeast corner of Thirty-Ninth Street and Seventh Avenue, this giant needle and button were built in 1995 as part of the Fashion Center Information Kiosk. The Claes Oldenburg–inspired sculpture has a thirty-one-foot-long needle and the world's largest button. The octagonal kiosk was designed by Pentagram Architectural Services and was awarded the 1995 Art Commission Award for Public Architecture.

Big Leather-Wearing Guy

This statue on Route 30 in Mayfield originally stood in front of Alvord's House of Leather, which closed its doors in 1998. Decked out in his hippest 1970s suede fringe jacket and knee-high boots, he now welcomes customers to a new store, the Adirondack Leather Shop. He still seems right at home, though, judging from the serene (and somewhat lecherous) smile on his big face. Sporting an oddly groomed beard, combed-over mop of brown hair, bushy sideburns, and black horn-rimmed glasses, he looks something like Austin Powers disguised as a radical university English professor circa 1972. Groovy baby, groovy!

The Big Hippie Dude

I have just come back from a vacation in the Adirondacks. This is the Big Man located on Route 30 in Mayfield. Besides the novelty of being a Big Man, I always had the impression that he was made to look specifically like someone, perhaps the original owner—I think it's the glasses. My husband has been taking this trip since the '60s, and the Big Guy was always there. They used to call him the Hippie Dude.

The other roadside attraction is the Tree House, also on Route 30 as you approach Northville. I don't know the origin of this one, but it's weird to see a house built around a tree!—*Geralyn Colvil*

Land of the Giants and Diving Horses

The Magic Forest is an amusement park located in Lake George that promotes itself as a park for young children. Featuring over twenty-five rides and a number of shows throughout the day, the park does provide everything it promises as far as children's entertainment is concerned. There are other aspects to the Magic Forest, though, that are not as well advertised—some really odd things.

For starters, the Magic Forest is the home of one of the world's greatest collections of Muffler Men, which any roadside aficionado should appreciate. The term Muffler Man refers to a type of fiberglass statue that is found along roadsides throughout the United States. These bizarre statues, which generally have outstretched arms, often holding items advertising the stores they stand outside of, are undeniably eye-catching. They're often painted to depict famous figures from American folklore. The figures first began appearing in the early 1960s and have been part of the fiber of American roadside culture ever since.

The Magic Forest features several of these great giants, standing along trails that make their way through the woods. In addition to the often seen Paul Bunyan–type characters, there is an Amish Muffler Man, also holding an axe, who resembles *MAD* magazine mascot Alfred E. Neuman but with an Amish-style beard. Probably most disturbing of all, though, is the giant Technicolor Muffler Man painted as a clown.

Besides Muffler Men, the Magic Forest is also the home of the world's largest Uncle Sam statue. This thirty-eight-foot-tall tribute to patriotism stands in the parking lot.

Statues are not the park's only claim to

The world's tallest *Uncle Sam* was purchased from the Danbury Fair in 1981 and placed in the Magic Forest parking lot back in 1982. He is thirty-eight feet tall, weighs 4,500 pounds, and is made of fiberglass. He was repainted (red, white, and blue, of course) in 1992.—Debra Jane

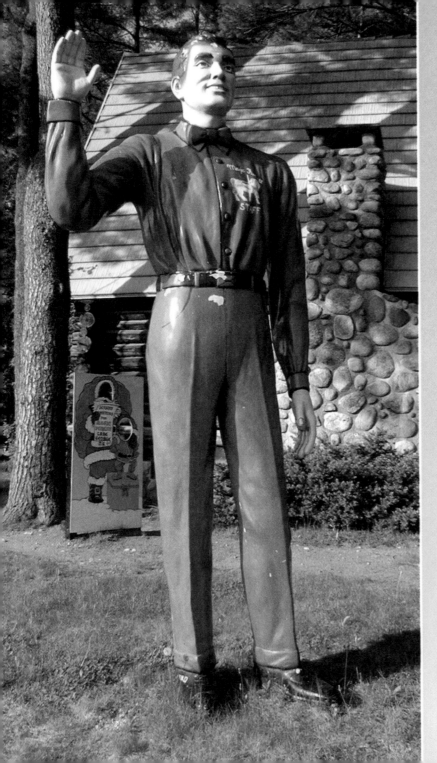

oddity fame. The Magic Forest is also the home of a genuine live diving horse. The original diving horse, Rex, began his act at the theme park in the late 1970s. Now his son, named Lightning, has been trained to carry on his father's legacy. Without the use of prods, trapdoors, or trickery, Lightning climbs to the top of a wooden platform and dives nine feet down, headfirst into a fourteen-foot-deep pool of water. Lightning then swims across the pool and climbs out, to the delight of watching children. Horse dives take place at the park twice daily.

A visit to www.thedivinghorse.com, run by the proprietors of the Magic Forest, serves as an informational guide on Lightning's diving, as well as a defense against the many animal rights activists who have spoken out against the diving horse show. The Magic Forest fervently denies that the act is in any way inhumane. They also invite people who have condemned the act without having ever seen it to come and watch the show for themselves before they continue to criticize it. Not a bad idea.

Attack of the Fifty-Foot Men!

The Magic Forest has four giants created by the International Fiberglass Company, the Michelangelos of giant fiberglass statuary: three Bunyan types (a traditional Bunyan, a dark-skinned "Pecos Bill" cowboy, and a very unusual and somewhat disturbing clown) and one Half-Wit (modified to look like an Amish man). Paired with the Amish Man is a crude (non-International Fiberglass) lumberjack.

Burger Family

They may not be the biggest roadside giants out there, but they are arguably the cutest. Mama Burger (below) worked the Coney Island boardwalk while Papa Burger (above right) resides at Mr. Bill's in Glens Falls, a drive-in restaurant offering carhop service. Baby Burger (top left) and Teen Burger (bottom right) are both from the Magic Forest in Lake George.

If He Only Had a Heart . . . Oh, Wait, He Does

This Tin Man stands out in front of Just Like Grandma's in Vernon, which specializes in selling and restoring antique cast-iron stoves. It appears that this statue is made entirely from stove parts.

Injuns of Long Island

Long Island is home to not one but two very notable Native American–themed roadside attractions. This first is a Muffler Man–style statue that guards the gates of the Riverhead Raceway. Perched at the raceway's entrance, this statue strangely seems to be giving a solemn and serious Nazi salute.

Riverhead Raceway

The island's other Native American has stood for many years on Sunrise Highway. Flanked by a bear and a horse, the statue is known as Big Chief Lewis and, according to a nearby handmade sign, was built by a Pennsylvania resident named Rodman Shutt. The statue stands for peace, and visitors are encouraged to touch the nearby totem pole while making wishes.

Chief Towaco

The Middletown Indian, a.k.a. Chief Towaco (according to the base), has seen better days. Apparently, he's been duct-

Chief Towaco

taped together and repainted many times. He stands in the Indian Village area of the Orange County Fairground in Middletown. We suspect his rather out-of-the-way location makes him vulnerable to vandalism.

The Indian of the Taconic Parkway

Travelers on the Taconic Parkway have long been terrorized by a large Native American who lies in wait along the busy road. Have no fear, though. This is no Wild West tale, and the Indian in question serves as more of a head-scratcher than a head-scalper. While riding on the parkway near the town of Claverack, keep your eyes peeled for this guy. He's an oversized stone bust, representing a member of the Mohawk tribe, who sits on the property of a local artist along the highway.

The TePee of Cherry Valley

The TePee Souvenir and Gift Shop was built in 1950 by Ken and Iris Gurney. It was actually on old Route 20 (the entire highway was relocated) and moved when the road did. At that point, the TePee was rebuilt on a larger scale. It is now fifty feet tall and forty-two feet wide. There used to be a stuffed horse bucking nearby, but that has been replaced with Buffy, the fiberglass buffalo, who has been standing out front for the past twenty-five years. According to Dee and Margate Latella, the current owners and operators of the TePee, the horse was actually a real stuffed animal that visiting children loved to climb on and then have their pictures taken. After the horse "died," it was buried out back, behind the TePee.

The TePee used to have a galvanized steel finish, but it was painted light yellow in 1996. Somewhere between 2002 and 2004 the lacing was painted on the front of the building. Today, as in days of yore, the TePee is home to a gift shop specializing in Native American souvenirs. The Latellas are dedicated to keeping the TePee going as one of New York State's premiere roadside landmarks.

The TePee of Cherry Valley

Wigwams of Jasper

The Wigwams Free Museum and Restaurant used to have Gulf pumps out front. It currently serves as the Jasper Historical Museum.

Wigwams of Jasper

Left, smoke shop Indian located in the Cattaraugus Indian Reservation territory in Irvington

Some people might think that peculiarities are somehow shameful, things to be kept hidden away, out of sight. Not so here in New York, where we proudly put our home state's oddities on display in museums, at fairgrounds, and in public parks, inviting all to see just how strange we really are.

The House of Frankenstein

The village of Lake George is one of the most popular vacation destinations in the entire Northeast. Every summer thousands of tourists find their way to this serene small town nestled away in the Adirondack Mountains. The main drag of the village, Route 9, reflects the town's status as a vacation spot. The street is packed with restaurants, gift shops, and video arcades. Basically, Lake George is full of the usual summer resort town fare.

But there is one building right in the middle of all this tourism that stands out as truly unique, not in a subtle way, either! Screams and moans emanate from the building, and occasionally a large man dressed as Frankenstein terrorizes passing children by lifting them into the air by holding on to their ears. This venerable institution is the House of Frankenstein.

The House of Frankenstein is a wax museum that has been in operation for over thirty years. It is truly a bizarre place, a favorite of kids who visit the Lake George area. Inside are over fifty exhibits depicting numerous forms of torture. The exhibits feature not-so-realistic-looking mannequins in various uncomfortable situations, such as being eaten alive by ants or split into pieces by ancient weapons.

The House of Frankenstein is a true must-see for anyone interested in strange roadside attractions. For an insider's look at this odd place, we asked *Weird New York* reporter Clayton Gibbs—who worked there for a number of years—to give us his take on it. From his experiences, it's clear that there's more going on at this museum than meets the eye.

Real Horror in House's History

The House of Frankenstein Wax Museum is the creepiest wax museum I have ever been in. I began working there in 1991, when I was fifteen. After being there for seven years, I soon found out why it always felt so creepy.

The museum is very large—and very dark. It's not meant to be the typical intentionally scary horror house, but is more of a true-to-life depiction of medieval torture and famous murders/monsters. Located in the heart of Lake George Village, it was the first business property to replace a local house. The house that it replaced had a horrific history of its own. Two brothers had once resided there, and both committed suicide in the early 1970s, just three years before the HOF was erected. The house was torn down, and the lot was purchased by Canadian owners.

Centuries before the House of Frankenstein was constructed in 1973, the area where it now stands had been used by English Colonists as the town gallows. Opposing French forces along with traitors, Huron Indians, and an array of religious heretics were slaughtered and tortured within this square of land. Over one thousand people were executed on the soil that later became the location of the House of Frankenstein.

The two-story wax museum opened in 1974. It seems odd that a majority of the exhibits revolve around methods of execution and torture. Given the history of the land long before the museum's construction, I find it more than coincidental that the theme therein is so gruesome. Although the history is not widely known, I wonder if in fact the owners of the museum had

access to the information. Stranger still is the fact that the owners are descendants of French Colonists. Since many of the people who suffered on these grounds were French, it seems another odd coincidence that they should choose such a location. Too odd to believe, really. It is my belief that they were drawn to it, somehow needing to re-create the horrors suffered by their ancestors by gruesomely displaying the methods used against them.

In the first three years of the museum's operation, five employees committed suicide, although not at the museum itself. One woman parked a car that she had stolen by the lake at Shepards Park, dug a hole during a full-blown rainstorm, covered the hole with a tarp, ran a hose from the tailpipe of her car into the hole, and then lay in the hole to choke. The girl's ghost is said to still roam the halls. I never saw her, but I did notice a few terribly cold spots throughout the museum, notably one directly adjacent to an exhibit called the Druids, which portrays human sacrifice.

Every morning when the place was opened, before the squeaking of moving motors and the screams of the soundscapes, I could hear footsteps on the floor above. The same happened at night when everything was shut down. Too often, I would notice that the angle of a wax figurine's head had changed from one day to the next. And stranger still was that whenever I was alone and walking about, I always thought I saw a shadow disappear around the corner ahead of me no matter how fast I tried to catch up.

The areas that stick out most in my mind as the creepiest are the first-floor Torture Chamber, near the guillotine; the Witch Burning exhibit, on the second floor; the Crypt exhibit, also on the second floor; and an area once known as the Strange Planet (now the Lost Jungle), also on the second floor. Within these areas, I felt not only colder, but a deep sense of dread.

Within the Grim Reaper exhibit, a small journal was found recounting another employee's bad feelings when he neared the Strange Planet attraction. Admitting that he had never felt so bad in his life, he vowed to hang himself there on August 10, 1987. There were no further entries, and a cross-reference check with the local newspaper revealed that an employee had died unexpectedly on that day.—*Clayton Gibbs*

Secret Caverns

Despite its name, the roadside attraction known as Secret Caverns is no secret at all. Due to its infamously obnoxious signage and its reputation as bizarre, this place does attract a certain number of visitors each year.

This weird place is just a stone's throw (no pun intended) from the more established Howe Caverns. For decades, Howe Caverns has been beckoning visitors from far and wide to experience the wonders of its underground caves. Secret Caverns is a less spectacular, less well-run version of the same concept: dark caves snaking through the underground. And its workers are famously honest and bitter about their more well-to-do neighbors.

One of the most notable things about Secret Caverns is the abundance of signs they have placed along local highways to lure in passing travelers. The signs are all hand-painted and feature strange patterns and figures. Like everything else about the place, even the signs leading up to Secret Caverns qualify as odd. Many a traveler has stumbled accidentally into Secret, not realizing that they had missed Howe by a few miles. These unsuspecting few are treated to the wonders of Secret Caverns instead.

Secret Caverns versus Howe

Life is a study in contrasts. Black and white, good and bad, right and wrong—we're never far away from things, or events, that beg for our comparison. That's just the way of the world. Within this study, there are those entities that compare favorably (let's call them the winners) and the ones that don't quite make the cut, the nonwinners. (To say losers just seems too cruel!)

About thirty-five miles due west of Albany, a version of this comparo-fest plays out each and every day, for this is the land of subterranean wonders, home of the dueling caves. Secret Caverns, situated at the hindquarters and slightly downwind from neighboring Howe Caverns, plays David to giant Howe Caverns' Goliath. A ride past each on a summer weekend illustrates the comparison perfectly. Where typically you'll find hundreds of vehicles in Howe's enormous lot, Secret Caverns is lucky to have fifteen or twenty.

In fairness, Howe does enjoy the advantage of having been discovered many decades earlier. Still, that can't fully account for this disparity in popularity. Perhaps being located first on the only road leading to both caverns has helped Howe gain an advantage. Be that as it may, it would be foolish to base your opinion of this cave solely on its number of visitors. In fact, to do that would be to miss the point entirely. You see, Secret Caverns' most endearing quality is its lack of sophistication.

Where Howe is glossy, slick, almost sterile in nature, Secret is blue-collar, decidedly low-tech, and hokey. It's just the kind of offbeat place for those of us who don't pass the Grey Poupon. And it only gets better as the tour commences. Our guide, fresh out of high school and acting every bit of his eighteen years, was refreshingly comical, both intentionally and not. As he led us through the winding labyrinths, he made it known that he had an ongoing gripe with another tour guide. He displayed this by calling him names (no expletives, just silly taunts), with malice in his voice, and let the echo carry his message. It was hilarious when we heard similar heated words floating back, as if on time delay.

Comparing the two caves from an aesthetic sense helps bring Secret Caverns still closer to our hearts. Howe may have a short underground boat ride, but, by golly, like the giant killer it is, Secret Caverns has a one-hundred-foot-tall, in-your-face underground waterfall! As far as natural formations go, Secret's are a bit sparse, but the lively commentary of the guides more than makes up for any missing stalactites and stalagmites.

VISIT NATIONALLY FAMOUS SECRET CAVERNS

100 FOOT UNDERGROUND WATERFALL

When the tour is over and you make the obligatory visit to the gift shop, you really can't help feeling compassion for this operation and its staff. For no matter how much humor is injected into their tour, resentment toward that other hole in the ground is ever present. In the gift shop, we noticed a large photo of a building ablaze. Our guide said it was Secret Caverns' former gift shop, and an arsonist was to blame for the fire. We didn't even get the chance to ask who might have done it, before he pointed his finger (the middle one), in the general direction of Howe Caverns and launched into a diatribe of name-calling and allegations!

Whew! Now we ask you, where the heck do you find that kind of entertainment value nowadays? Yes, my friends, Secret Caverns is truly a diamond in the rough, begging for your visit. Here's hoping they never smooth out! There really is an intimacy to the smaller operation that can't be matched by its larger neighbor.

If you plan to visit, schedule your trip for the warmest months of summer (remember—no crowds here), and enjoy the exhilaration of standing at the base of the infamous one-hundred-foot waterfall, in the spray, as it cools you off. I can think of a lot worse ways to spend a day.—*Jeff Bahr*

The Unisphere Welcomes All to Queens

The largest globe in the entire world stands in Flushing Meadows Park in Queens. Visible from the Van Wyck Expressway, the Grand Central Expressway, the Long Island Expressway, and from planes coming into both LaGuardia and Kennedy airports, this massive silver representation of the earth is a true icon of New York's roadside culture.

A remnant of the 1964 World's Fair, the globe is known more commonly by its nickname, the Unisphere. It is 140 feet tall and 120 feet wide, and weighs in at an impressive 900,000 pounds. The Unisphere was built as a symbol of world peace and is officially dedicated to the idea of "peace through understanding."

Promise of a Brighter Tomorrow

The New York State Pavilion is also located on the site of the 1964 World's Fair. The original guidebook description of the site said:

> Above a huge "Tent of Tomorrow," housing state exhibits and shows, rise three towers, one of them an observation tower 226 feet high. Various displays are sheltered under the world's largest suspension roof, made of translucent plastic and hung from sixteen 100-foot columns. . . . On the main floor the Texaco Oil Company has inlaid a mammoth map of New York in terrazzo, and here visitors gather to watch school and community groups perform.

Today the overgrown and undermaintained fairgrounds languish by the roadside, still promising a future that has long since been and gone.

Fondly Remembers Days of Future Past

I remember vividly the 1964 World's Fair. I still drive by on occasion, and at one point I did stop and walk into the N.Y. Pavilion. It took me back to the time as a boy I was able to locate my hometown of Kingston on the floor map, during that magic summer of 1964. The image was still there!–*Letter via e-mail*

Flushing Meadows: The Final Frontier

Over the last twenty years, I've been photographing the ruins of the 1964–65 New York World's Fair: the U.S. Pavilion, the N.Y. State Pavilion, the Fountain Lake Amphitheater (also known as the Aquacade), and the U.S. Space Park.

Back in 1964, when I was eight years old, I was amazed by all the technology—the race to the moon, nuclear power, even Formica. My dad worked for General Motors where the Futurama exhibit showed this huge machine rolling through the jungle, lasers cutting down trees, leaving a completed road already with traffic.

Space Park still stands, and you can still see the first stage of the huge Saturn 5 rocket. I wish they had the entire rocket there; you'd be able to see it from miles away.–*Phil Buehler*

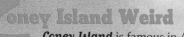oney Island Weird

Coney Island is famous in American lore as the epitome of fun and merriment. From the shore crowded with bathers to Nathan's hot dogs to the Cyclone roller coaster, Coney Island has come to represent the ideals of leisure and amusement in the minds of many Americans.

But don't be fooled. There is a dark underside to Coney Island. Some of the strangest things in the entire state of New York call this place home.

For one thing, Coney Island houses the Coney Island Circus Sideshow, one of the nation's finest and last remaining freak shows. Besides being the home of performers such as Eak the Geek and Insectivora, among many others, it also features a museum detailing the history of freak shows and displaying many wondrous items, including one of P. T. Barnum's famous Fiji Mermaids. Those interested in actually partaking of the freak lifestyle can enroll in the sideshow's school, where they will be taught fire breathing, snake handling, human blockhead techniques, and myriad other skills that any freak worth the price of admission must know to succeed in this bizarre business.

The Coney Island Museum is also the home of a

memorial to Topsy the Elephant, a pachyderm who made history by merely defending herself and meeting a tragic fate in return.

At the turn of the twentieth century, Topsy was among the most popular of the elephants who roamed the grounds of Coney Island's Luna Park. People came from miles away to the amusement park to marvel at the elephant's size and exotic nature. Unfortunately, Topsy was considered a problem child by those in charge at the theme park. She was known for lashing out at her handlers and had managed to kill three of them in just a three-year period. It was decided that, despite her popularity, keeping Topsy around was not worth the risk she presented. The elephant was to be executed in a public ceremony right out in view for all to see. This was decided despite the fact that, when lashing out at the people around her, Topsy was simply responding to the treatment she received. The handlers she killed were no saints. Topsy attacked one of them after he fed her a lit cigarette. Still, in those less correct times, the abuse Topsy was enduring was never taken into account when her fate was decided. The execution was planned and put into action—a few times, in fact.

Those charged with killing Topsy found that it was easier said than done. They tried to poison her, but the elephant was too tough to be susceptible to something like cyanide. Then it was announced that she would be publicly hanged at Coney Island. After it was pointed out that New York had recently done away with hangings in favor of the new electric chair, it was decided that more attention could be garnered if Topsy was electrocuted instead of hanged. Luna Park wanted to be sure that this time the job would be done correctly. They went straight to the electricity big guns. None other than Thomas Alva Edison was called in for assistance.

Edison had been embroiled in a war with his main

competitor in the field of electricity, Samuel Westinghouse, over the use of AC versus DC currents. Edison maintained that Westinghouse's AC methods were deadly, even if they were less expensive and more viable for public use. He even referred to being electrocuted as being Westinghoused.

Edison used Westinghouse's AC methods to create the electric chair as a way of showing the deadliness of his competitor's product. Instead, the chair was embraced by the government as a more humane way to enact capital punishment upon convicted killers. Since the inception of AC, Edison had been maniacally trying to prove his point by publicly killing off dogs, cats, and horses near his West Orange, New Jersey, laboratory. When those at Coney Island contacted him about killing Topsy, he figured the challenge of killing a beast as big as an elephant would do even more to hurt the public standing of Westinghouse. He agreed to help kill the hapless elephant.

The death of Topsy the Elephant was also to be filmed so that even those who could not witness the act firsthand

could share in the moment through the magic of one of Edison's other inventions, the motion picture.

At the appointed time, Edison's technicians sent high voltage coursing through poor Topsy, who jolted upright when she felt the current surging through her body. Smoke emerged from the bottoms of her feet, and after only ten seconds of exposure to the lethal voltage, Topsy the Elephant toppled over dead. It was one of the most brutal and most public cases of cruelty to animals ever to take place on American soil.

These days, Luna Park is gone (it burned down years after Topsy's death). All that is left to remind us of the elephant's fate is the memorial at the Coney Island Museum and ten truly disturbing seconds of film footage. So the next time you're enjoying a hot dog and a ride on the Wonder Wheel over at Coney Island, have an extra bag of salted peanuts in memory of poor Topsy.

Shooting the Freak at Coney Island

In the early part of the last century, Coney Island was bigger than Disneyland is today. A million visitors came every day during the summer of 1920. Between 1897 and 1904, three amusement parks opened: Steeplechase Park, Luna Park, and Dreamland. Today, many of the rides stand abandoned and slowly fading away, like the summertime memories of carefree youth. But there is still some weird fun to be had out at Coney, on the world's first boardwalk. Next time you visit to ride the world's only Wonder Wheel and the rickety eighty-year-old wooden roller coaster, the Cyclone, don't forget to take some time to have a Nathan's Famous Frank and then Shoot the Freak!

Shoot the Freak is a live-action interactive game that is fun for the whole family, if you happen to be from the Manson family, that is. The object, as the helpful boardwalk barker instructs you through a squawky amplified headset, is simply to "Shoot the freak. Shoot 'em in the head; that's what he likes." After you pay your ten dollars, you are then handed what looks like a high-powered assault rifle, and the freak is set loose for the hunt.

Hey, let's face it, times are tough at Coney Island, and folks do whatever they can to eke out a living in the face of increased competition from newer, more high-tech, and just plain better amusement parks elsewhere.

But the carnies of Coney are a steadfast breed and will do whatever it takes to turn a buck and pinch a mark. And that's how Shoot the Freak, perhaps America's only target shooting game employing live human targets, was born.

Set in the rubble of a demolished boardwalk building, the Shoot the Freak "arena" looks like a postapocalyptic set from one of the Terminator movies. Crumpling concrete and brick walls surround the Freak's graffiti-scrawled enclosure, allowing the wretched creature nowhere to run and nowhere to hide. When the buzzer sounds, the Freak is set loose and the hunter is given the opportunity to live out his or her homicidal fantasies armed with a paintball rifle. The Freak, a young man dressed in helmet, pads,

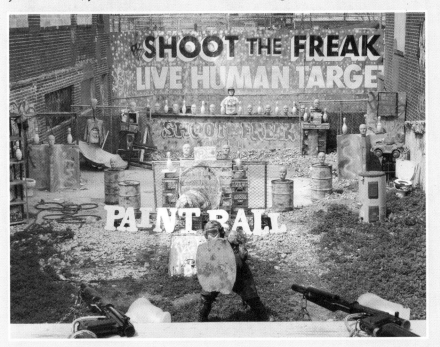

and goggles and looking something like Robocop, brandishes a wooden shield to ward off the splattering onslaught of paintball fire. He darts and dashes around the ruined building foundation, constantly dodging fire from behind the rusted steel barrels and discarded toilets. He bobs and weaves as the paint projectiles pop on and around him.

"Shoot him in the HEAD!" the carny barks repeatedly. "That's what he likes—that's what he wants!"

There doesn't seem to be any real goal to the game, other than shooting a living person in the head, and after it's over you'll more than likely find yourself wondering who's the winner and who's the loser—regardless of which end of the gun you happened to be standing at.—*Mark Moran*

Rocks in Their Heads

New York is the home of a number of interesting painted rocks sitting along the roadside. Something must be in the air above the Empire State, because there's no real explanation as to what has compelled playful graffiti artists to repeatedly paint and repaint these roadside stones over a number of years.

One New York painted rock is the Elephant Rock of Hague. This large boulder has not only been painted but also carved into a shape resembling an elephant. Locals have painted it time and time again over the years, making it a well-known local landmark and source of pride.

Another famous rock sits on I-84 in Fishkill. It's been painted to look like a race car with a white number on the side and white stripes on the hood. Locals refer to the famous painted stone as Volkswagen Rock.

The World's Largest Quartz

Rock City, in Olean, bills itself as the "world's largest exposure of quartz conglomerate." This place is the home of huge rock formations that were created millions of years ago that look like pebbles in concrete.

You can find boulders with interesting names like "teepee and pulpit rock" and "fat man's squeeze." It has been a tourist attraction since 1890 and was always an adventure, since there are no guardrails or barriers. There's only a worn white line with a spray-paint warning not to walk within six feet of the precarious ledge.–*Brett Stern*

Staten Island's Stonehenged Shores

Walking along the windswept southern shoreline of Staten Island, between Page and Sharrot avenues, one is suddenly transported to an alien landscape as hundreds of stone towers, roads, rooms, and driftwood monoliths rise from the beach. The curious sculptures, which are composed of materials found along the high-tide line, rise seemingly out of nowhere. Upon seeing the thousands upon thousands of stones painstakingly piled meticulously atop each other, one can only wonder, Why?

What is this rocky place doing way out here on this barren, desolate shore, far from the nearest house? Is this the work of some mad hermit who has made his home on the remote sands of the Raritan Bay as if a castaway?

The stony shoreline is the creation of artist Douglas Schwartz, who says the half-mile stretch of coast is an experiment in ecological art. Whether or not Mr. Schwartz is in fact mad is up to viewers to decide for themselves. If you'd like to meet the artist, Mr. Schwartz can be found working on the project every Sunday and Monday morning. The stones can be found there 24 hours a day, 7 days a week, 365 days a year.

Lots of folks dream of traveling the world, gazing upon the many wonders in far-off lands, sampling strange cuisines, and mingling with the natives. But if real globe-trotting is just too much of an effort, New Yorkers can experience quite a few exotic sights without ever leaving the confines of their state. That's right, friends, in a single day you can see the Great Sphinx and then travel to the Far East, if only to grab a quick hot dog!

Something Sphinx on Long Island

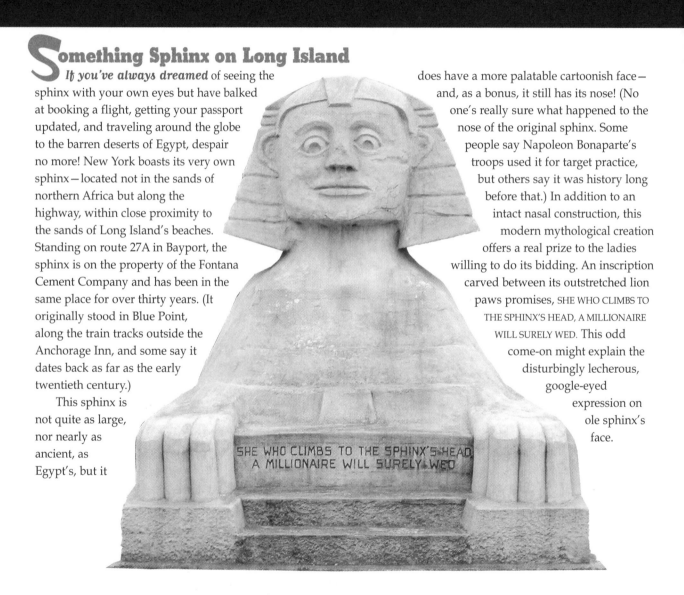

If you've always dreamed of seeing the sphinx with your own eyes but have balked at booking a flight, getting your passport updated, and traveling around the globe to the barren deserts of Egypt, despair no more! New York boasts its very own sphinx—located not in the sands of northern Africa but along the highway, within close proximity to the sands of Long Island's beaches. Standing on route 27A in Bayport, the sphinx is on the property of the Fontana Cement Company and has been in the same place for over thirty years. (It originally stood in Blue Point, along the train tracks outside the Anchorage Inn, and some say it dates back as far as the early twentieth century.)

This sphinx is not quite as large, nor nearly as ancient, as Egypt's, but it does have a more palatable cartoonish face—and, as a bonus, it still has its nose! (No one's really sure what happened to the nose of the original sphinx. Some people say Napoleon Bonaparte's troops used it for target practice, but others say it was history long before that.) In addition to an intact nasal construction, this modern mythological creation offers a real prize to the ladies willing to do its bidding. An inscription carved between its outstretched lion paws promises, SHE WHO CLIMBS TO THE SPHINX'S HEAD, A MILLIONAIRE WILL SURELY WED. This odd come-on might explain the disturbingly lecherous, google-eyed expression on ole sphinx's face.

SHE WHO CLIMBS TO THE SPHINX'S HEAD, A MILLIONAIRE WILL SURELY WED

Cleopatra's Needle

Want to see some more genuine ancient Egyptian artifacts? Still no need to travel halfway around the world! The oldest man-made thing in Manhattan doesn't come from the days of Native Americans or the earliest European settlers. No, the oldest object in Manhattan dates back much further than that. Known as Cleopatra's Needle, it's an ancient obelisk that found its way from Alexandria, Egypt, to Central Park, New York.

The red granite stone stands over seventy feet high and weighs in at between twenty and thirty tons. It, along with nine other obelisks, was constructed during the reign of the pharaoh Tuthmosis III sometime between 1504 and 1450 B.C. It survived Roman occupation and removal from its original site and, along with one of its doppelgängers, stood in front of the Caesarium Temple in Alexandria for centuries. Then a massive earthquake struck the area in A.D. 1301, toppling one of the monuments. During the nineteenth century, the remains of the fallen obelisk were sent to London, while the other one was shipped to New York City's Central Park. It was sent to the United States by the government of Egypt as a sign of appreciation for U.S. assistance in the construction of the Suez Canal.

East Meets West in Mamaroneck

Though it might look to all who see it like a pagoda from the Far East, Walter's is actually a good ole American hot dog joint. The weird local landmark originally opened in 1919, selling hot dogs and apple cider. It moved to its present location at 937 Palmer Avenue in Mamaroneck in 1928. The sign spells out WALTER'S in hot dogs arranged in pseudo-Oriental letter characters. Today the eatery continues to sell its specially formulated "splits" (hot dogs made of beef, pork, and veal, split down the middle) and grainy mustard with pickle bits. There was talk of franchising in the 1990s, but the business is still a family-run operation.

Walter's was declared a historic landmark in 1991 and listed on the County Inventory of Historic Places as typifying a 1920s roadside stand. It even has its own web-site (www.waltershotdogs.com), where you can view postcards sent by loyal patrons over the past eighty years. Included in the collection are cards from President Calvin Coolidge and one from a member of Admiral Byrd's 1929 Antarctic Expedition, supposedly sent from the South Pole.

Grafton's Peace Pagoda

In the tiny town of Grafton is an ornate outcropping of buildings known as the Peace Pagoda. Dedicated to Buddhist philosophies, they sit on a desolate hillside, appropriately removed from the hurly-burly below. Visitors looking for it will notice signs placed along Route 2. After following a trail and passing through a thick forest, there is a clearing where obelisks and a number of small temples are located. These temples are used for meditation purposes and to teach those unfamiliar with Buddhism about the religion's practices and beliefs.

The Peace Pagoda in Grafton has a sister pagoda in Leverett, Massachusetts, and a third one is being built in Tennessee. The pagodas were constructed by an inspirational Japanese Buddhist nun named Jun Yasuda, of the Nipponzan Myohoji order. An organizer of peace walks throughout the world, she has become a cult figure, revered by many. In 1978, she joined a group of Native Americans who marched from San Francisco to Washington, D.C., as part of what they called the Longest Walk. This walk, like all of Yasuda's strolls, was dedicated to spreading peace around the world and as a protest against violence.

After the 1978 walk, a New York landowner approached Yasuda with a proposition. He was willing to donate a chunk of land he owned in Grafton, on which she was invited to build a monument dedicated to peace. Construction began in the autumn of 1985, and shortly thereafter the Grafton Peace Pagoda was born.

The Peace Pagoda of Grafton is open to one and all. Whether you want to practice yoga, have a quiet place to meditate, or simply explore a religious oasis in the serene hills of New York State, the Peace Pagoda can accommodate your desire.

There are a lot of people in the state of New York who are trying to get a message out to anyone who will listen. Sometimes, though, it's anyone's guess what their strange sign language is trying to say.

The World's Largest Living Sign

Whether you're driving your pickup through or flying your plane over Canisteo (Steuben County), you can't help but notice the world's largest living sign, certified in the *Guinness Book of Records*. Created in 1933 by planting 260 Scotch pine trees, the icon measures 300 feet by 90 feet, with each letter 30 feet wide and 70 feet tall. The trees form letters that spell out the town name. The two locals who designed and planted the sign thought it would aid pilots. A service crew of the New York State Department of Correctional Services now maintains it. You can't miss it. It's right behind the elementary school. Just look up (or down, depending on your vantage point).

Moan and Groan Road

This road sign is in Hope (Adirondacks) right off Route 30.

Kould This Be a Koinkidenke?

This strange and possibly scary sign is located on Route 5 in Herkimer. Is that wordplay simply a way to attract the attention of passing motorists . . . or could it be a symbol of something far more sinister going on?

This Bus Stops for Alligators

This shot was taken up in the Adirondacks in New York State. I'm reluctant to give the exact location—last time I submitted something, the MOAN AND GROAN ROAD sign disappeared mysteriously right after I sent the picture!
—*Steve Gorny*

Where Superheroes Go for Their Shopping Needs

As any fan of comic books knows, many superheroes call Manhattan their home. Spiderman scales the city's famous skyscrapers. The Fantastic Four live in one. And the Avengers have hung out in Manhattan since their first appearance. Many others also make the famous borough safer for all of mankind—in comic books. Who knew that to get their crime-fighting supplies, these superheroes had to hop on a subway and get off in the borough of Brooklyn?

The Brooklyn Superhero Supply Co., in Park Slope, makes many passersby scratch their heads at its outlandish storefront window advertisements. Inside, the adornments promise, one can find capes, nets, alter egos, shrinking gas, and dozens of other necessities no

working superhero can afford to be without.

The strange store features a secret door that opens to a much unexpected locale—a tutoring center for kids. The Superhero Supply Shop is actually the brainchild of author Dave Eggers (known for his book *A Heartbreaking Work of Staggering Genius* and for being at the helm of the popular magazine *McSweeneys*). In San Francisco, Mr. Eggers runs a similar store based around a pirate theme. The idea behind the odd themes of these tutoring centers is that kids will come more willingly to a superhero supply shop than they would to an average, bland tutoring environment. Still, the real purpose of this very strange storefront does not take away from its status as a true roadside head scratcher.

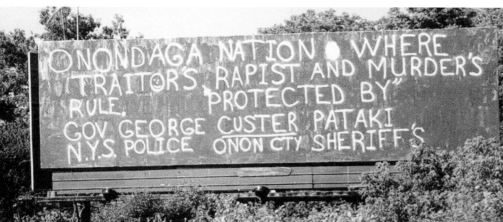

Onondaga Roadside Rage

If you are ever in the area near Syracuse, you need to head south a few minutes down the highway to check out the Onondaga nation's signs. I don't know what happened to get these people so mad, although I bet it has to do with hundreds of years of oppression and the decimation of their culture and whatnot. No matter what the specifics are, something really pissed someone off. The nation has put up a huge wooden sign with hand-painted accusations toward the federal and state government all over it. The best part is when they refer to Governor Pataki as Governor George "Custer" Pataki. It's not road rage—it's roadside rage.—*TL*

Anatomically Incorrect

The Giant Vagina of Rockland is a big sculpture that stands in front of the County Courthouse. This sculpture was erected sometime in the 1970s and was regarded at first as modern, abstract art. It used to stand in front of the County Courthouse and faced the main street. In the 1980s, people started complaining that it looked more anatomical than abstract. Suddenly nobody could look at it and NOT see a vagina, so the legislators swiveled the offending side of the sculpture away from the street and toward the courthouse. And there it stands today!—*Robert Martens*

Very Well-Endowed Fountain

Get a load of this picture. This is a statue that is on our "campus" at One Blue Hill Plaza in lovely Pearl River. The lake you see in the foreground also has a fountain in it. You can only imagine what it looks like when the fountain is turned on! *–Michael Mahle*

A Roadside Tribute Gets Put in the Doghouse

A barn on I-88 East in Emmons stands strong as a roadside memorial to the roadside attraction it used to be. Years ago the barn was emblazoned with an image of the beloved Peanuts character Snoopy. It was written up in a local newspaper, which was then brought to the attention of Snoopy's creator, Charles Schulz. He sued the creator of the image, who was forced to remove it. He then replaced it with the image of a shooting star and the words Dog Gone, followed by what appear to be birth and death dates; they are the years that Snoopy once stood here.

The Fountain of the Planet of the Apes

This is an actual name of a fountain in Flushing Meadows. Why?–*Joey Vento*

Hands off My Fountain, You Apes!

It turns out that this strangely named Fountain of the Planet of the Apes is merely a tribute from one freethinking man to one of his favorite movies.

The fountain was built next to the Queens Wildlife Center for the 1964–65 World's Fair and named the Fountain of the Planets. When Parks Commissioner Henry J. Stern came along a few years later, he ordered that the plaque adorning the fountain be altered to contain the words "of the Apes." After a year of its going unnoticed, someone finally complained to the city about the strange alteration, but Stern refused to change his decision. "It's a great movie," he offered up as justification for his action, "which is also a treatise on the dangers of war."

An adjacent fountain in the same park is named the Fountain of the Planet of the Grapes of Wrath. Stern figured that if there was a fountain named after an animal-related pop culture reference, it was only fair to have another containing a plant-related one as well.–*Chris Maget and Robyn Miller*

Headless Horseman Bridge?

No one can really be certain what bridge Ichabod Crane might have ridden his horse across in Washington Irving's classic work of fiction *The Legend of Sleepy Hollow*. But that didn't stop the citizens of Sleepy Hollow (formerly North Tarrytown, formerly Beekmantown) from taking it upon themselves to designate one bridge as the legendary crossing. Located on Route 9 adjacent to the Sleepy Hollow Cemetery and Old Dutch Church, the bridge was originally wooden but has since been rebuilt using stone and has a plaque dedicating it to the memory of Irving. Nearby a sign, which looks very much like a historic marker, proclaims THE HEADLESS HORSEMAN BRIDGE DESCRIBED BY IRVING IN THE LEGEND OF SLEEPY HOLLOW FORMERLY SPANNED THIS STREAM AT THIS SPOT.

The Jell-O Museum

Most people don't need to know much about that wonderful substance called Jell-O, except that it's delicious and jiggly. But there are people in this world who want to know all the subtle nuances and entire history of their favorite gelatinous dessert. They want to know the incredible rate at which Jell-O is sold on an average day in the United States (that's thirteen boxes per second) and what exactly Jell-O is composed of (mostly boiled cow bones and hides). And there are those who aren't content with simply eating Jell-O—they need to celebrate it!

These people head to Le Roy, New York, to visit the official Jell-O Museum.

Jell-O was produced in Le Roy up until 1964, when the company moved to a more modern facility a few states away in Delaware. When the Jell-O people left, they took with them over three hundred jobs and effectively crippled the town's economy. But a few years back, Kraft Foods, the corporation that makes billions from its Jell-O sales each year, donated $50,000 to the town of Le Roy for the development of this memorial to the shaky stuff.

The museum opened its doors in 1997. Among its many attractions are century-old oil-painted advertisements for Jell-O, exhibits on the making of Jell-O, and perhaps best of all, an exhibit known as the Jell-O Brick Road. The museum is located at 23 Main Street in Le Roy. Admission is $3 for adults and $1 for children.

The Mystery Spot of Lake George

A number of years ago, while at a roundtable discussion of Acoustical Anomalies and Decibel Equations in Munich, I had the good fortune to meet Professor Gregory Mauch, who is well known for his radical theories on Atomic Distillation and the accompanying Gravitational Tempest. But during dinner, he told me of a spot in New York State where the known laws of spatial time and acoustics did not apply.

"Balderdash!" I exclaimed.

Mauch smiled and poured another tequila.

He insisted that not only had he heard of such a place but could give me the exact location. I was all inebriated ears.

After he told me the coordinates, I realized that this place was not only in New York but actually in downtown Lake George. I was stunned.

This past year, following the tipsy bar napkin scribblings of Professor Mauch, I went in search of this amazing spot. And, believe it or not, I found it.

Walking up to the spot, I saw a compass cut into the ground. A huge circle, it was obvious where one was to stand. Being the brave guy that I am, I told my companion to walk into the center first.

"Do you feel anything strange?" I asked. "If you do, get the hell out of there."

"I don't feel anything— wait, holy s%$t!" she blurted.

"Come in here. You gotta hear this!"

I walked into the center, and then I heard it as well. A glorious echo filled my ears. I yelled at the top of my lungs. A huge echo returned. But the people standing outside the circle heard just my voice. The mysterious echo could be heard only from the center of the ring. Professor Mauch was right. Son of a gun!

So if you're ever in the Lake George area, take a walk to the Mystery Spot. To find it, you just have to head to where Canada Street and Million Dollar Beach come together. Walk east, along the lakeside of Million Dollar, for about a hundred feet or so and turn to the left, where the small stone wall offers a view of the lake. Look on the ground and you'll see a giant ring that has a compass etched into it. Then walk to the center and start yelling your head off.

— *Dr. Seymour O'Life*

Roadside Religion

The Shrine of the North American Martyrs

Isaac Jogues, Rene Goupil, and John LaLande did not experience happy deaths near Auriesville in the 1640s. Far from it. Christian missionaries, these three men became official martyrs of the Roman Catholic Church after their efforts to convert Native Americans to Christianity went badly awry. The three were tortured mercilessly (including having their fingernails chewed out of their hands), suffering pain and humiliation over a long number of hours before finally being killed. While their deaths were gruesome, the shrine that has been built near the sites of their demise has grown into a massive roadside attraction that draws thousands of religious faithful, Native Americans, and curious travelers each year. A museum details the horrific circumstances of the men's deaths, along with graphic descriptions of the final hours of many other missionary martyrs. Besides the museum, the grounds of the shrine are filled with ornate religious statuary and an abundance of crosses. Christians come to the spot to remember the martyrs. Native Americans come to visit what was once their land. Other visitors come for the strange ambiance that this clash of cultures created close to four centuries ago.

Long Island Gets Religious Too!

The Shrine of the North American Martyrs isn't the only place roadside fans can go for their spiritual fix. Another well-known roadside religious shrine stands in Eastport, Long Island. This park is free for all to experience. It features a giant statue of the Madonna perched on a boulder, a walk-through portrayal of the stations of the cross, and perhaps most innovative of all, a rosary walk with bushes strategically placed to represent each bead on a rosary. If you're looking for redemption or simply want to spend a day in a religious theme park of sorts, Eastport is the town to head to.

A Little Religion on the Lake

What may be the world's smallest church can be found resting upon a small wooden platform in the middle of a small lake off Sconondoa Road in the small town of Oneida, near Syracuse. It's known as the Cross Island Chapel, but don't let the name fool you. There's no island. The tiny church just sits on a sort of makeshift dock in the middle of the lake. A few feet away, a wooden cross is wedged into a pile of rocks that do breach the water's surface and may qualify as an island.

According to a sign posted on dry land nearby, the nondenominational Cross Island Chapel was built in 1989 and dedicated as a witness to God. The sign also states that it is open to the public upon request and available for special occasions and meditation. Although regular services are not held in this odd little chapel, which measures about three feet by six feet, ceremonies can be scheduled by appointment. You'd better have a pretty small family, though, if you're thinking of booking it for a wedding. It has only two seats and can barely hold a bride, groom, and minister, let alone a wedding party.

Roads Less Traveled

"Improvement makes straight roads; but the crooked roads without improvement are roads of genius."
—William Blake, English poet, painter, and mystic

Some roads are great because they get us quickly from one place to another. Other roads are great because they are beautifully scenic. But some roads have a special quality, not designated on any road map, for less tangible reasons. They carry legends that travel with us on our journeys and stay with us long after we've reached our destinations.

New York, perhaps more than any other state, has an abundance of these storied byways, each with its own unique and often terrifying tale to tell. These are roads shrouded in mystery and local lore, where strange creatures lurk, violent deaths occur, and only the bravest explorers dare venture after darkness falls. The next time you find yourself traveling through this great state of ours, try getting off the highways and onto the back roads. You might have a journey you'll remember the rest of your life— if you live to tell the tale, that is.

Misery Stalks Sweet Hollow Road

In Huntington, Long Island, there is a small area south of Jericho Turnpike that seems to hold more than its share of ghostly tales. *Weird New York* correspondents John and Laura told us about two roads in particular that seem to host an unusual number of ghostly wayfarers.

Mount Misery Road and Sweet Hollow Road, John and Laura report, are less than a mile apart at their farthest points. Both are narrow, winding ways pinned in and overshadowed by thick woods. In the old days, you could turn off your headlights and drive down these roads in complete darkness, but now civilization has intruded; lights have been installed, and the woodland has diminished somewhat. But the roads still give off the eerie feeling that anything can happen there.

Odd stories have been circulating about this particular area since before the American Revolution. At least two Native American tribes may have considered it taboo. But this is not how Mount Misery Road got its name. In olden times, the road was rutted and bumpy and passed through infertile land unable to support a farm or flock. Many a traveler snapped a wagon wheel in its treacherous pits. To them, the trip was a misery, hence the name for the road and the area.

In the mid-1700s, a small mental asylum was built near the road. Our forefathers believed the best way to deal with mental illness was to shut up the afflicted so as not to upset other members of society. Suffice it to say the treatment was not exactly therapeutic, and there are many accounts of screams and moans ringing out from the asylum. Then there was the fire that shut it down, and the beginning to the strange legends.

Supposedly, John and Laura tell us, one of the female patients was going through a bout of depression and managed to set her room and herself on fire, burning down the entire hospital. This unfortunate woman can be seen at times, wandering the roads, still wearing her white hospital gown, with her hair wild and askew.

Actually, this Lady in White is many legends in one, merged by centuries of oral tradition passed from generation to generation. Some say she was a patient of the hospital. Others claim she was a woman walking home from work who was killed by a car in the dark of night. Whichever, she seems to be a spry little ghost who likes to jump in front of cars at night.

The Lady in White is not the only specter around this haunted area. The overpass of the Northern State Parkway above Sweet Hollow Road is the site of many strange reports. According to one story, some teens hanged themselves from the overpass bridge, and if you park near there and flash your lights, they will appear. Another woman, who is never seen, haunts the bridge. It is said that she was killed in a head-on collision in the '70s and now protects other drivers from the same fate. Sweet Hollow is narrow and winding at that point, so it is easy to believe a collision could occur. This particular ghost is benign. If you park under the bridge and put your car in neutral, she will push you to safety, supposedly uphill.

But that's not the strangest thing that might happen to you along this road! If a policeman should pull you over one dark night, check the back of his head. If he has no skull there, you have just met another of Mount Misery's ghosts.

Spectral humans are not the only spooks to look out for around Mount Misery. According to some tales, there also is a creature called a Hell Hound. It lurks in the trees by the road and stares out with fiery red eyes. Its fur is black as night, and some say that seeing the hound is an omen of imminent death.

Tales about the Mount Misery area have been passed on from person to person for over two hundred years, so it stands to reason that the stories will change and grow. Do demonic dogs wander the same roads as the eerie Lady in White? Only the roads themselves know for sure. But whether you are a believer in the legends or not, it is indisputable that there are more oddities reported in this small neighborhood than in any other on Long Island.

The Burning Asylum of Mount Misery

Mount Misery Road has no street sign. The name is painted in white on a tree at the start of the road. Ten years after a fire destroyed a mental asylum there, the hospital was rebuilt, but only a few months later another fire broke out. Fearing another event, the town decided not to rebuild again and just used the land for housing. There are still some houses there, hidden deep in the woods, but only a very few.

The legend is that if you find the right trail that will take you to the spot where the main hospital once was, you will see burning ghosts running and screaming. One of them slowly dances along the side of the road. I've been there several times and have seen nothing. The one strange thing that I noticed is that at the end of the road, there is a big tree stump lying across the road. It's meant to block off anyone from going into the woods beyond that point. I wonder what could be in those woods beyond.–*Anonymous*

Sally Sits Up on Mt. Misery Road

There is a legend I heard of when I was growing up which was the story of Mt. Misery Road, located in Huntington. The road starts in an affluent residential section and then continues into a large county park and ends. The road is said to be haunted and hostile to unwelcome visitors.

Another oddity on the road is the ghost of Sally, who was an unfortunate individual who was killed when her car hit a tree. The story is that when the headlights of your car flash past this tree you see a shadow sit up. Some say that it is a trick of a car's lights; some say that it is Sally. Mt. Misery Road was a favorite road to travel as a high school student and each time there was always a new story to tell. Perhaps if you ever find yourself in the Huntington area at night, you too might travel along it and have a new story to add to the tale.–*Arthur Criscione*

Terror Along Federal Hill Road

Mysterious murders. Satanic rituals. Ghosts floating to the surface of a cursed pond. And an infamous tree that sprouted not only branches and leaves, but the very image of Jesus himself. All this can be found along a dark, imposing road in Brewster that for some reason has become an epicenter of strange tales and tragic happenings.

The Jesus Tree

Legends of Federal Hill Road have persisted for decades now. There's something about it that seems to attract the dark, the strange, and the netherworldly.

The most famous legend of the road (which becomes Joe's Hill Road when it crosses the border into Danbury, Connecticut) is that of the Jesus Tree, which was said to feature a naturally formed image of Christ hanging on a crucifix. Surrounding the large, bulbous tree were twelve other, smaller trees, spaced evenly apart. These were said to represent Jesus' twelve apostles.

Stories of the Jesus Tree quickly spread throughout the area. It was near a body of water appropriately dubbed Blood Lake, where on some prom night of yesteryear a girl was said to have drowned. Her ghost still haunts the wooded road, trying to hitch a ride from unsuspecting passersby. Another story says a high school boy was shot and killed nearby when he stopped to help some people in what he thought was a broken-down car, but turned out to be a lure for the unsuspecting. To add to the legend, there have been an unusual number of accidents in the area near where the tree once stood. It was cut down in the early 1990s, in the hope that removing it would remove the evil presence.

There are other stories of strange activity on Federal Hill Road entirely unrelated to the tree. A secret satanic church supposedly operates out of the buildings on the grounds of the Morefar Golf Club, which, the story goes, is

nothing more than a front for their evil operations. These satanists are rumored to be responsible for terrorizing those who travel on Federal Hill Road and are even said to be associated with a handful of murders that have occurred along the street.

Murder on Farrington Pond

One of the road's murders occurred in the late '80s, when a man was found shot to death in his car, which was parked along the banks of Farrington Pond—the site of a number of gruesome incidents, this murder being just one of them. The pond's mysterious evil has been spoken of for years and seems to begin with tales of the death of a young girl. Supposedly, a high school girl was on her way to her prom and was driving down Federal Hill Road. While passing Farrington Pond, her car went out of control, veering straight off the road and into the body of water itself. The girl struggled violently but could not free herself from the sinking vehicle. She drowned inside her car, dying in the prom dress she'd hoped to dance in.

Since that incident, dozens of accidents have occurred at Farrington Pond. Many have said they felt strangely drawn to its dark waters just before crashing near it. More eerily, others have claimed to have been distracted from their driving by the image of a spirit clad in a white dress emerging from the surface of the lake. Some of these distracted drivers have crashed into the pond itself, just like the prom-going girl of many years ago.

High at the Sweet Jesus Tree?

There used to be a tree on the border of Brewster, NY, and Danbury, CT, that looked like Jesus and was surrounded by twelve smaller trees. But they cut it down. And apparently, mostly it was visited by people who went there to get high, so that might be why they saw Jesus.–*Kevin H.*

Beware the Disciples of the Tree

Federal Hill Road is definitely an eerie place. Some really aggressive types used to hang out there looking for trouble all the time. They considered the road, specifically the area around the Jesus Tree, their territory, and they wouldn't hesitate to come after you if you didn't respect that. I think they were skinheads or something. That never stopped me and my friends from driving by on weekend nights to see if we could catch a glimpse of Jesus' face on the side of that tree. I have to say, it was pretty odd; it really did look like Jesus on the side of that tree!
–*Deena Felding*

Jesus Tree Cut for a Killing

I'm from Redding, CT. And yes, there DEFINITELY was a Jesus Tree, and yes, they cut it down. BECAUSE (plot thickens) a young man from Redding named Mike killed someone there.–*Curtis Gwinn*

Zapped Where the Tree Once Stood

I had heard the Jesus Tree was cut down and needed to see it for myself, so I made a detour down Federal Hill one night while I was out in that area anyway. When I got to the spot where the tree used to be, all the electrical systems in my car turned off for no reason. All the lights, the radio, you name it, dead. RIGHT NEXT TO WHERE THAT TREE ONCE STOOD.–*S. Stovitz*

Whiskey Hollow: Where the KKK Hangs Out?

Baldwinsville is a small village roughly twelve miles northwest of Syracuse. In this quiet, remote town is a particularly quiet, remote road. The five-mile-long thoroughfare is known simply as Whiskey Hollow. There are no businesses or homes along the road. It simply cuts through the woods, connecting two, more well-traveled, streets. However, all is not as quiet as it seems, for legends say that at night, Whiskey Hollow is used by evil groups of people for nefarious purposes.

The most persistent legends of Whiskey Hollow are that it has for many years served as a meeting place for both the KKK and an aggressive band of Satan worshippers. They have claimed the road as their domain, particularly the mile-long, unpaved stretch in the middle. Many murders and satanic sacrifices are rumored to have taken place here in the remote recesses of the woods. Others have seen not the KKK or Satan worshippers but, perhaps more terrifyingly, the ghosts of the victims these clandestine cults have killed along Whiskey Hollow.

According to legend, a large number of those who lost their lives along Whiskey Hollow were children. The spirits of these unfortunate kids still make their presence known. Many have encountered the ghosts of small children wandering along the road. Sometimes they seem confused. On other occasions, they have asked passersby for help, then have disappeared.

Whiskey Hollow Road is closed to traffic at night. Is this because too many travelers have made their way down the road after dark, searching for children's ghosts? Whatever the reason, it's safe to say that Whiskey Hollow Road is a strange and mysterious place.

> **The most persistent legends of Whiskey Hollow are that it has for many years served as a meeting place for both the KKK and an aggressive band of Satan worshippers.**

Saw Sacrificial Evidence on Whiskey Hollow Road

Supposedly, a series of murders occurred in the woods near Whiskey Hollow Road, and it was severely haunted because of this. Guys in my school used to drive us down the road to try to scare us. They would tell us about kids who were hung in the trees and how you could see rope burns in the limbs from the hangings. After a couple trips, I started to get numb to it. I began to suspect that maybe the stories were just made up by guys who wanted a good make out spot to take gullible girls like me to. That all changed one day during my junior year.

I was dating a guy who took me down to Whiskey Hollow. Bored by the whole thing by this point, I decided to call his bluff. "Why don't you get out of the car?" I asked, in that flirty way only a bored, evil high school girl can manage.

He stopped dead in his tracks. "What?"

"I dare you to get out of the car, walk down the road for thirty seconds, then back." I smiled at him.

"Why?" he asked.

"Why not, are you scared?" That did the trick. If word got back to our friends that he was scared to take a dare from a girl, he would never live it down.

"Okay," he said as he zipped up his sweatshirt and opened the door. As soon as he stepped out, I hit the automatic lock button, locking him out. When those locks dropped, he spun around, giving me the evilest eye I have ever received. I laughed.

He made his way up the road, walking at a brisk pace. I was timing him on my watch. About thirty feet away from the car, I saw him jump straight back and throw his hands over his head. He stumbled backward and landed right on his butt. I was freaked out but laughing at him. He got up and ran back to the car. After a few seconds of playing like I wasn't going to unlock the door, and him yelling at me, I popped the locks. He climbed in, breathing hard.

"What is it?" I asked.

He looked back at me wild-eyed, fumbling for the keys. "You don't want to know!"

"Yes, I do. What happened?" I asked.

"Fine, look," he said. He drove forward to the spot where he had fallen and pulled off the road enough that the headlights illuminated a truly grisly sight. Sitting on the roadside, just at the edge of the woods, was a four-foot-wide circle of animal bones.

This wasn't roadkill. There was no blood, and the bones had been stripped of all fur, all skin, all muscle. Most eerily of all, there were a few different animals all piled on top of each other. It looked like a deer was included, because there were some big bones, but there were smaller skulls in there too. I'm no zoologist, but I'd say there was a raccoon and perhaps a possum. I screamed, and he drove away.

Now, I know enough about nature to know that there's no way a number of different species are going to get together to die within a four-foot circle. And there's no way those animals are all going to stay undisturbed by scavengers long enough to have all the material decompose completely off their bones. As we sped down Whiskey Hollow that night, every story I had heard about the Satan worshippers doing rituals there came back to me. And I certainly never made anyone ever get out of the car again.—*L. Krash*

Followed on Fuller Road

This quaint and sometimes dark road gives you a forbidding feeling the moment you set foot on the ground. There have been several stories about Fuller Road in Carlton from many people. One person states that in mid-October he was walking down the street to go to his friend's house. The ground was covered with leaves, which made it hard to walk without making a lot of noise. He was almost halfway down the road when he felt that he was being followed. Since the road is virtually covered by a canopy of overhanging trees, there is a lot of shade and strange shadows are cast on the pavement before you. Thinking he was just being paranoid, he continued to the end of the road.

As he reached the end of the street, he turned back to see if there was anything following him. Halfway up the road he saw a dark, silhouetted figure standing in the middle of the street at the spot where he had started feeling strange.

Another account was from a young woman riding her bike down the road. Out of nowhere, an old beat-up truck started following her. She went faster to try and get away from the truck, but it still gained on her. Suddenly the truck slammed on its brakes. She turned around to see what was happening to the vehicle, and it was nowhere to be found.

Many other people say that on bright moonlit nights you can see silhouetted figures just standing in the front yards of people's houses, in the road, and in the trees.—*Tim Davis*

House Road

House Road stretches several miles from Riches Corners Road in Albion to West Lee Road in East Shelby. Many people who venture out on the road at night say that they hear screaming and gunshots and see shadows that move with no apparent source. To add to the oddities, a Victorian-style house, known as White Pillars or the Old County House, for which the road is named, sits in a remote area, west of Gaines Basin Road. Sanitariums, or county houses, were mental institutions where the insane, unstable, and freaks of society were held. This monument stands today as an apartment which has recently become abandoned. It is sometimes hard to imagine the things that may have gone on in the house.–*Tim Davis*

Happy Valley, Not So Happy at All

Perhaps the most ironically named area in New York is the section known as Happy Valley, a piece of Oswego County bordering Williamstown and Albion. A little research into the dark history of this area reveals that there is actually nothing happy about it. Instead there are deaths, diseases, and mysteries that linger to this day.

At one time, many years ago, within the area that is now the Happy Valley Wildlife Management Area, there was the small town of Fraicheur. The tiny community, which lay along Happy Valley Road, seemed to exist much in the same manner as all of the surrounding towns of the area. Then at some point around the turn of the twentieth century, something happened that led to the abandonment of the entire village.

Many say that the town was struck by a mysterious disease referred to as black water fever. Most residents died during this epidemic, and those scant few who didn't succumb quickly fled the area. One legend states that the town's water supply was poisoned by a local resident, who nursed some grudge and was hell-bent on destroying the town. Fraicheur was reclaimed by the forest, and the area was later designated as a wildlife management area. All that remains of the former towns of Happy Valley are the remains of a schoolhouse and a cemetery.

These days, rumors persist that Happy Valley is haunted. Its twisting roads are said to house the ghosts of those who died suddenly in this lonely place. Locals avoid the area by night, and you might be well advised to do the same.

Gravity's Pull

There is a road in Rockland County that is called Spook Rock Road. It is a long, twisting road that starts in Suffern and eventually ends at Route 202. When you get near the end of the road, it looks like it is descending downhill. If you park your car about the middle (or toward the end) of the road and turn it off and leave it in neutral, you will roll uphill.

It is pretty neat. No one knows why a car would roll uphill, but it does! A while back a few people studied it, and their conclusion was that the last stretch of the road was an optical illusion. It only LOOKS like a hill that is going down—it is really a hill that is going upward. You could have fooled me. How could something that looks like a hill really be a hill in the opposite direction?–*Bonnie*

Haunted Places, Ghostly Tales

*"So many ghosts, and forms of fright, Have started from
their graves to-night, They have driven sleep from mine
eyes away; I will go down to the chapel and pray."*
—Henry Wadsworth Longfellow

hosts aren't real. Or so we were told from a very young age,
on those dark sleepless nights when something
nameless was keeping us awake. If ghosts aren't real,
then why are stories of them so pervasive?

New York State is the uneasy home of many allegedly haunted
locations. Restless souls, perhaps tormented by the manners of their
deaths or their circumstances in life, refuse to move on. Instead they
linger here, drawing us into the shadowy folds of their half-life.

There are people who have seen ghosts for themselves. Others
dismiss the very idea as hogwash, saying there is a scientific explanation for everything. Some publicly profess a disbelief in the supernatural. How many of those same folks, we wonder, in their heart of
hearts, would secretly like to be proved wrong? For to believe in
ghosts is to accept the idea that there is more to this world than we
mortals comprehend.

The following stories are actual accounts told by ordinary people
who have had experiences they cannot explain. Certainly we will not
venture to try. It is up to you, dear reader, to decide if the phantasms
described in the following pages are simply the product of people's
overactive imaginations or if there is much more to them than that.

On the Trail of Abigail West

Ever since I can remember, I have heard the legend of Abigail West. The tale has always interested me, so I did my own research in 1996 at the Crandall Public Library of Glens Falls.

Apparently, Abigail had lived in an isolated area of West Mountain in Queensbury around the 1900s on what was once a potato farm (now the man-made Butler Pond). One night she was struck by lightning and killed on what is now known as Butler Pond Road. Weeks passed before she was discovered, and when she was found, her body was not at the location where the lightning had struck. It was assumed she had survived and managed to crawl away from the location, even though it was a good half-mile away.

People have said for ages that on a stormy night, Abigail can be seen on Butler Pond Road, right off Goggins Road adjacent to exit 20 of I-87. Residents living at the base of Butler Pond Road have reported having things in their houses moved, and one resident even told me that at one point, his wife's sewing machine would operate all on its own. Of course, with all of these strange stories circulating, I had to take my own little exploration trip and see what I might arouse.

One night in August, beneath a full moon, three friends and I decided to hang out by the pond, just to get away from things. To the west of the pond, about three quarters of a mile along the trail, there is a circular clearing in the trees, which is oddly full of dead and twisted branches. The four of us decided to use only the light of the full moon to guide our way through the forest. When we arrived at the clearing, we all fell suddenly silent as a wind pushed its way through the barren woods, making an awful creaking wail through the tall, dying trees.

THORNY ACRES

Though bloom the rose
To beautiful red
So brilliant a color
To plant for the dead
Beware the allure
For at the base of its hood
Is the prickly thorn
Which draws out the blood

The noise was startling at first, but soon we got used to it, knowing that it was only the trees. Before long, however, there was a massive pounding sound beneath the ground, getting closer to where we stood. The noise was like giant footsteps approaching us. It veered from where we stood, only to stop suddenly behind a huge oak tree. The wind had died completely by this point, and without a word, the four of us bolted out of there. On our way back to the car, we saw several flashes of lightning, and soon some of the trees near the pond began falling. When we reached my car, we were all spine-chilled and speechless. I remember thinking that if I had spoken, whatever was pursuing us would know my exact location and be able to grab me quicker. After that night, the four of us barely spoke about the event.

But then in 1998, my good friend Jason and I decided to investigate the house where Abigail West had lived on a nearby street known as Clendon Brook Road. Surprisingly enough, we found a tall chimney at the side of the road. Beneath it was a deep black hole filled with twisted black branches similar to those found in the clearing in the woods. There were no trees nearby that matched the dead branches. Also, many red and white candles had been melted over an indentation in the chimney that was in the vague shape of a triangle. Someone had taken a piece of coal and written strange symbols on the rock beneath the candles.

Jason wrote down the symbols and later transcribed the chalky message. It was in an alphabet known as Transitus Fluvii, and it read only one word: Samhain. When we went back about a month later, the chalk had washed away, but there in the opening of the fireplace was a burnt piece of thick paper with a strange poem on it. It read as pictured at left.

Though it wasn't signed, we were both

sure that it had something to do with Abigail West. My friend submitted it to the historical society, and I've often wondered if anyone would come forward to claim it.

One day a jogger directed me to a clearing on Butler Pond Road where the supposed grave of Abigail West was located. Surprisingly enough, I found the clearing, but beyond it, hidden from the road, was a path lined with stacked rocks. I couldn't help but be drawn into the path and keep walking, even though the grave might have been right in front of me. The woods seemed to come alive the farther in I got. Black birds gathered in masses, and strange artifacts like women's dress shoes littered the overgrown path.

When I reached higher ground, I heard something rumbling, much lighter than what I had heard on that horrible night years ago. As I stopped, I smelled sweet perfume suddenly, and it seemed more potent the farther in I went. I sensed something moving in the woods, and I decided to head back in fear of a hunter mistaking me for a deer.

On my way back, I saw off to one side something made of bright white fur hanging from a tree. I got closer, looking the fur over, and noticed that it was fresh and there was blood on the opposite side. To me, it looked like a dog's scalp, since I couldn't think of any other animal with such clean white fur, other than perhaps a skunk.

I took two pictures with my digital camera. I looked beyond the fur and saw that there were many other furs hanging from branches deep into the woods. Some were black, some brown, and one even looked blond. It was a disturbing sight. I tried to take another picture, but the camera died. After I changed the batteries, the camera was still not working.

Needless to say, I was not so much worried about hunters anymore, but something worse.

Of course, when I got back to my car, the damned camera worked just fine. The next day I decided to go back and snap a few pictures of the strange area. The scalps were gone, except the bright white one. I inquired about Satanism, even with local police, but they said they hadn't seen anything like what I described since the early 1980s, and they laughed when I told them where I had found it. They thought I was nuts to go up there alone. *–Clayton Gibbs*

Symphony for a Specter

I grew up in an old farmhouse in upstate New York. The house was over a hundred years old and had been built by my great-grandfather. I took piano lessons growing up, and our piano was in the front room of the house, the living room. One day, I was about ten or eleven at the time, I was sitting there practicing. I had two piles of books on the bench with me, one of books I'd practiced from and one I had yet to play from. Now, neither pile was very large, only a couple of books in each, and both piles were squared off on the bench.

As I played, the pile on one side just fell off the bench . . . not like the top book had slid off, but the whole pile fell off. I stopped playing for a moment and looked down at them, but then resumed practicing. A moment later it happened again with the other pile, and again I stopped playing and looked at them. For no real reason I could figure out, I stopped playing and turned around—and there she was. . . .

The only way I've been able to describe her is as a shadow, but with features. I remember her as probably around five feet tall, in a long, flowing dress. She was facing the front of the house, at a right angle to me. I blinked my eyes, shook my head, and she was still there. She didn't look at me, just stared straight ahead. She then moved toward the front of the house, and poof, she disappeared.

Needless to say, I didn't set foot in that room for a few days. I asked my parents about ghosts in the house, but neither of them had ever heard tell of any. I know there was at least one. *–J. B., Boston*

Eerie Amherst Synagogue in Erie County

The quiet town of Amherst in Erie County is home to what is easily the scariest place I have ever visited. It's called the Amherst Synagogue.

The stories of the abandoned synagogue start before it was even built. Many years ago this area was plagued by a sadistic serial killer who targeted children. He would abduct innocent kids, take them to a densely wooded area, and murder them. On that land now stands the Amherst Synagogue.

For many years, rumors spread that the area was haunted by the ghosts of the kids who died there, and the area was largely avoided. Then it was decided that the synagogue should be built there. During its construction, three men were killed when a wall toppled over on top of them. People said the ghost kids were angry and knocked the wall over.

I have been to the synagogue at night, twice. I will never go back again. This place is not to be trifled with. The building itself is pretty nondescript. But behind it

are trails, woods, and the supposed hidden graves of the children who were left dead there.

The first time I visited, I heard shrieks come from the woods. I felt ice-cold winds rush past me even though it was a warm summer night. And I saw streaks of light in the distance that I absolutely could not find a rational explanation for.

I decided to return, more curious than I had ever been about any supposed haunted site. On the second trip, I was easily the most scared I've ever been in my life.

When my friends and I arrived on our second night, we split up into smaller groups. One set of friends claimed that they saw the apparition of a young boy slowly emerging from the ground. They took off to wait at the cars. The rest of us thought they were just trying to scare us. I wish I had left at that time too.

As we made our way around a bend, I heard a terrifying yell and saw a man with a hatchet quickly walking toward us. He seemed totally off—looking almost through us instead of at us. We took off running. He continued his fast-paced walk. We got to the cars and took off, completely and totally freaked out. We called the cops, who made us meet them in front of the synagogue. They searched the grounds and found no evidence of the axe-wielding maniac.

As they left, one of them offhandedly told me, "It's always great when you kids go looking for ghosts and actually find one." I asked if that meant other people had seen the hatchet man before us. He smiled and nodded and left.

I don't believe in most hauntings, and I have been to the majority of supposed haunted places in western New York. The Amherst Synagogue is the only one that I fully endorse as real.—*PirateVsNinjaVsRobot*

The Ghost of Murdered Grace

Big Moose Lake is nestled in the Adirondack Mountains, and even today it remains quiet, hidden, and tranquil. But the peace and tranquillity of the lake were shattered almost a century ago when a gruesome murder rocked the area. A sensational trial followed, filled with scandal and violence. And many say that the sad spirit of one of the story's principal players still appears above the waters of Big Moose Lake, mourning her fate and that of her unborn child.

This is the story of Grace Brown and Chester Gillette. It is a tale of love gone awry, of multiple mysteries, and ultimately, of lonely deaths.

During the summer of 1906, Chester Gillette was spending a lot of time working at his uncle's skirt factory in Cortland. During his time there, he began a whirlwind romance with another worker at the factory—a nineteen-year-old girl named Grace Brown, who came from a local farming family. Their affair was extremely intense but also quite brief. As summer wound down, it became clear that Chester was uninterested in continuing his courtship of Grace. He was avoiding her around the plant and was

seen pursuing other girls. Grace knew how to take a hint and tried to move on with her life.

This proved to be impossible. Grace soon realized that she was pregnant. It could only be Chester's child.

This was a scandal of the highest caliber. Remember, it was 1906, in the small world of rural New York. To be pregnant out of wedlock was deeply shameful in those parts at that time.

Grace informed Chester of the circumstances that had developed. After hearing the news, he told her to pack for a trip. He was going to take her on a sojourn to the Adirondacks. Naturally, the girl assumed that Chester was taking her to a romantic location to propose marriage to her. She couldn't have been any more wrong.

Grace and Chester traveled to the Hotel Glennmore at Big Moose Lake. Chester registered as Carl Grahm, while Grace used her real name. Soon after arriving, Chester rented a small boat and told his pregnant companion he was going to treat her to a secluded picnic. But they never made it to any picnic. Chester piloted the boat into the South Bay area of the lake, the most isolated and one of the

Hotel Glennmore at *Big Moose Lake, where Chester Gillette murdered Grace Brown (inset). The book* An American Tragedy *by Theodore Dreiser and the film* A Place in the Sun *are based on the story of the murder*

deepest portions of the body of water. What happened next has long been disputed. The results, however, are irrefutable. By the end of that boat trip, Grace Brown was dead. And Chester Gillette was on the lam.

Chester was found three days after Grace's body was discovered. He'd gone to Eagle Bay to pick up an advance on his pay and was now having a little vacation in the town of Inlet. He was quickly charged with the girl's murder. A trial was held at the Herkimer County Courthouse, which became a mob scene, packed with spectators and Grace's grieving family. Letters Grace had written were held up as evidence against Chester. Unfortunately, little physical evidence could be produced, as the county medical examiner mistakenly allowed the body to be embalmed before an autopsy could be properly performed. Still, the prosecutors pressed on in their case against Chester Gillette.

They claimed that upon arriving in South Bay, Chester struck Grace on the head, opening up a gash on her forehead. Rocked by the blow, Grace was easy prey as Chester pushed her out of the boat and into the waters of Big Moose Lake. Disoriented from her injuries, and thus unable to swim, poor Grace sank beneath the surface and drowned.

Chester Gillette's defense claimed that Grace had

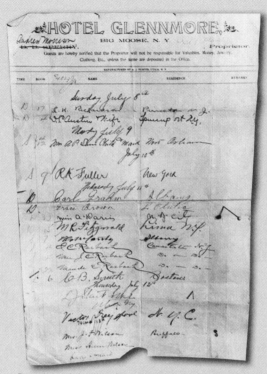

Page from the registry book for the Hotel Glennmore that shows Chester Gillette registered as Carl Grahm

actually committed suicide. According to Chester, Grace leaped from the boat on her own. He had never struck her.

Not surprisingly, the jury didn't buy his story and sentenced Gillette to die on March 30, 1908. His mother attempted to gain a reprieve from the governor, but to no avail. Chester Gillette was executed in the electric chair as scheduled.

The story of Grace Brown and Chester Gillette has never been forgotten in these parts, for a number of reasons. Obviously, the immense amount of tragedy and drama involved in the affair is intriguing. But perhaps the biggest thing forcing people to remember what happened to those young lovers so many years ago is the frequent reported appearances of Grace Brown's ghost around Big Moose Lake.

Many who have visited the lake, especially the area around the Covewood Lodge in Eagle Bay, have witnessed a glowing white female entity floating just above the surface of the water. Others don't see the ghost herself, but do report experiencing intense feelings of sadness while they are in the area. Workers at the lodge have reported hearing stories from guests who encountered the spirit without even knowing her tale. It's thought that Grace's death came at such a young age, and the heartbreak of her unborn child dying with her was so intense, that her soul has been unable to pass on to the afterlife. Instead, it lingers here, where her faithless lover retreated after murdering her.

Haunted in Haverstraw

When the hurricane hit New York a couple years ago, my best friend's house on the Hudson River got devastated. She and her family had to find a new place to live while they rebuilt their old home. They found a nice old two-story brick house in Haverstraw, off Route 9W. They didn't know it wasn't quite as empty as it looked.

After moving in, they had a family get-together. Everything was going well until a glass figurine from shelves on a wall decided to take flight and crash into the wall on the opposite side of the dining room! Now that the mood was set, a plate of yams cooking in the kitchen suddenly burst into a yam inferno! That, thankfully, wrapped up that evening's entertainment . . . but there was more to come.

The longer my friend and her family stayed, the stranger things got. They would put boxes of stuff in the attic, later that night hear stuff thumping on the floor, and the next morning find the things that were in the boxes thrown around the room like a child had been playing with them. Both my friend's mother and little sister were "shoved" down the stairs by something. Luckily both of them were relatively unharmed.

One day my friend found that one of her perfume bottles was missing. She naturally thought one of her sisters had taken it, but they never produced the bottle. For the next three weeks, my friend would suddenly get a whiff of her perfume while she walked through the house, even if she was the only one there. Then one day the bottle showed up in the pocket of the robe she wore every day. If she had absent-mindedly put it there, there's no way she would not have noticed it before.

I was lucky enough to explore the house on Devil's Night. Nothing happened, but there were many strange things about the house itself. In the basement, there was a room used for coal storage back in the 1800s. It had a dirt floor, and all the windows were bricked over. Torn clothes were found half buried in this room. Who knows what else might have been buried there? The room looked like it came straight from a movie—the perfect place for torturing and killing someone without anyone finding out. I didn't like being in that room at all, and I'd never had that kind of reaction to a place before.—*Patrick Birmingham*

Haunted Highway

We live in Manhattan, and we have seen the oddest thing on some nights coming off the 125th Street ramp from the Henry Hudson Parkway. It's this ghost who stands on the side of the road.

He usually appears on the left side of the road as if he is standing on the guardrail. He wears a puffy parka and disappears just as you get close to seeing his face. He also has a distinctive hairstyle. We have seen him on more than one occasion. I think it's a reminder not to drive too quickly down the road.—*Kim and Victor C.*

Still Making the Rounds at St. Marks

During Manhattan's earliest days, when it was still New Amsterdam and dominated by the Dutch, the undisputed father of the colony was Peter Stuyvesant. Stuyvesant spent the last twenty-five years of his life living in what is now the Bowery area of the Lower East Side of Manhattan, presiding over the colony as the commander of the Dutch West India Colony.

Stuyvesant had had a long career that had taken him around the world for many adventures. By the time he came to preside over New Amsterdam, he was famous for both his no-nonsense demeanor and his wooden leg, which he kept wrapped in silver bands. Stuyvesant's impact on what is now the East Village area can still be felt, as buildings, a square, and other sites there are named after him.

Stuyvesant helped establish the original church that once stood where St. Mark's Church now stands, at Tenth Street and Second Avenue. Many church attendees, visitors, and staff have reported encountering a strange presence over the years. Most often, distinctive footsteps are heard — including the unmistakable sound of a peg leg echoing throughout the halls and pews of the historic holy building. People have seen strange

movements and shadows within the church's windows while passing by on the street. The bells at St. Marks have rung at strange times, often accompanying a sighting of the ghost.

People have been reporting seeing Peter Stuyvesant's ghost ever since his death in 1672, easily making his specter one of the most enduring phantoms of New York.

Verizon Ghost

I work for Verizon, and one of our buildings sits in the heart of Richmond Hill, Queens. Once, while working a 12–8 tour there, I heard someone talking, so I turned around but didn't see anyone. An hour later I heard the same voice again. As I turned around to look in a different part of the building, I saw a guy walking down one of the aisles. I quickly called out to him. He turned and looked at me for a couple of seconds and continued to walk away. This was very funny to me because after twenty-five years of service I know almost everyone in Queens, but I had never seen him before. He was dressed very old-fashioned: white shirt and tie, pocket protector, etc. I went looking for him, but could not find him on any of the five floors in the building.

The next day I called the control center to see if anyone was assigned to Richmond Hill that night, but no one was. A few days later I told one of the other guys at work what I saw. He started to laugh and said that was one of the old switchmen who used to work there. I asked him if he lived around there, and he told me he died forty years ago. Many people have seen him, and now when they ask me if I have, I can tell them yes.

The ghost of the switchman was just finishing one more job. *–Joey V.*

Ghostly Footprints in the Snow

Balthasar Kreischer was a wealthy businessman back in the mid-1800s here on Staten Island. Perched on a hill overlooking Arthur Kill Road sits the spooky, majestic Kreischer Mansion. It is reported that there were two mansions originally built on the property, one for Kreischer and his wife, the other for Kreischer's son and his wife. Tragically, Kreischer's son and daughter-in-law died in their sleep as their mansion succumbed to a fire.

My friends and I would sometimes drive past the Kreischer Mansion, but although we fancied ourselves a somewhat crazy bunch, none of us was ever brave enough to get out of the car and climb the hill to the mansion.

In the early 1990s, a couple of daring folk decided to open the mansion as a restaurant. The venture didn't last long. There were reports of cold spots in areas of the dining room, doors slamming, and a fireplace tool flying across the room.

About a month ago I was out for the day with my six-year-old son. I stopped on Arthur Kill Road and asked if he wanted to take a walk with me to the mansion. He said that he was eager to see it, so we walked past the iron gate and trudged along the snow-covered driveway. I was amazed at how huge the place was up close.

When we arrived at the house, I became very spooked but remained semi-calm for the sake of my son. I was tempted to try the door, but decided to depart instead. As my son and I walked back down the winding driveway, he asked what that sound was. There was a sound of crunching snow, which was counter to the sound we were making with our footsteps. It was so clear that it was unmistakable. The hair on the back of my neck was standing up, and I was glad to get back to the car. We departed promptly.

I am convinced there is haunted activity at the Kreischer Mansion. Initially, I thought I would be more calm about actively pursuing strange and possibly haunted places, but I must say that it takes a bit more than interest to see these matters through.–*Chris Roschbach*

Ghost of the Well

Have you heard of the ghost of Spring Street? It concerns the murder of a young woman who haunts Spring Street in Manhattan to this day. Seems that a young woman named Gulielma Elma Sands was murdered on the night of December 22, 1799, and her body was found in a well a few days after Christmas. Levi Weeks, her fiancé, was a blacksmith who had been the last person seen with her. He was accused and was probably guilty of the crime. The couple had gone by

sleigh supposedly to be married (she had told her cousins, but it was a secret). The next morning she was found murdered.

Her ghost rose from the well soon after the crime and to this day continues to be sighted near where the well was. The Manhattan Bistro on Spring Street is in front of where the well is today; the spring still runs under Spring Street into the Hudson River.

Construction workers have seen the girl's ghost, and she is usually trying to say something. Sightings have occurred in the restaurant, along with reports of glasses breaking and beer taps that just start flowing. I've tried to see the ghost myself, but now the well is blocked off by a bunch of fencing and construction signs. Supposedly, the best time of day is really early or around nine or ten p.m. It is a very creepy spot.–*Kim Catano*

Ghostly Paces Just Beyond the Door

Dominican College in Orangeburg is a small private college that caters mostly to commuter students but also has living quarters for those who want to live away.

My friend Gary, who was a dorm student, would usually ask me to stay overnight when we were engaged in some activity at school. This time was for a drama rehearsal. He had a single room, and I was on the floor in a sleeping bag, eye level with the floor and the outside hallway.

At around three a.m., I opened my eyes and noticed something walking back and forth in the hallway, right outside Gary's door. Again, to make this clear, I saw the feet, I didn't hear them. I just thought that it was someone going to the bathroom. But these mysterious feet kept going back and forth for about an hour and a half, and it seemed too weird that it was constant and never stopped. I tapped Gary on his leg and told him what I saw. He just dismissed it as if I were nuts. Then after about ten more minutes of this "thing" walking back and forth, it finally stopped in front of Gary's door. I jumped up and now vigorously shook Gary to wake up. He finally did and told me to relax and that it was nothing, but he'd go see. I then fell to the floor and covered myself with the sleeping bag, only exposing my eyes to see what was going on.

I still had my eyes on the feet on the bottom of the door as Gary went for the doorknob. I begged him not to open the door, and as soon as it swung opened, the feet disappeared. I jumped out from the sleeping bag, ran to the hallway, and looked in both directions and saw nothing. Gary thought I was nuts, but I know what I saw. –*Robert Zampella*

Dylan Thomas Haunts His Favorite Bar

In 1953, renowned writer Dylan Thomas entered the White Horse Tavern on the corner of Hudson and Eleventh streets in Manhattan. He proceeded to drink eighteen straight shots of whiskey.

"I've had eighteen straight whiskies," he uttered. "I think that's the record. Then, he famously dropped dead right there in the bar.

Since that day over five decades ago, staff and patrons of the White Horse have reported running into a ghost they believe to be the spirit of the famous poet. He is known to linger around the fireplace and to spin a table in a certain corner, said to be his favorite haunt in life.

Ghost Horse of the Adirondacks

I experienced the most intense ghost visitation during the summer of 1992 in the Adirondack Mountains, where I worked. It was at a resort on Indian Lake, in Sabael, along NY Route 30. The resort was the only thing for many miles along this stretch of two-lane road. I was employed as a wrangler, so I spent my days taking guests on trail rides around the area.

Every evening after staff dinner, my co-worker Kath and I would go for a run along Route 30. The track ran one mile down the road, and 1.2 miles back through a trail about a hundred feet into the woods. We would run down on the road and then sprint back along the trail, racing the setting sun.

One night it was already quite dark when Kath and I got to the entrance of the trail in the woods. We decided to go for it anyway and began sprinting back to the resort. I would run behind Kath, staring at her feet to make sure I didn't step on her. Well, as we entered the trail, Kath's feet slid to a stop, like in a cartoon. I looked up, and galloping toward us was a very large white horse. It was at least seven feet tall and all white.

We could feel the thunderous pounding of his hooves on the ground, and he was headed right for us. Kath and I turned on a dime and ran screaming into the road. There we stood, winded, laughing hysterically, waiting for the horse to emerge. It should have been right behind us, but several minutes later, the horse still had not shown up.

Kath had turned around so quickly that her hat blew off and stayed in the woods. We decided, giggling, to go fetch the hat. Into the woods we crept, listening for the horse. But there were no sounds. We kept going, deeper and deeper in, shocked by the absolute silence as well as the absence of any kind of tracks in the dirt trail. THERE WAS NO HORSE!

Being the resort wrangler, I knew for sure it wasn't one of ours. Throughout the remainder of the summer, Kath and I tried to figure out where the horse had come from, to no avail. This is remote Adirondack wilderness we're talking about. Gigantic white horses are not normally sighted running freely, without tack. Kath and I are convinced we saw a ghost.

–Jen Wroblewski

Boogeymen in the Bronx

In the Bronx, there is a huge park called Van Cortlandt Park. It stretches all the way into Yonkers as well. The park is full of trails and woods and at night is completely pitch-black. The park plays host to many activities during the day, but as soon as the sun goes down, almost everyone leaves.

I went to a part of the park outside the woods one night. I was looking for my friend's sister because she had his house keys, which we desperately needed. Bored out of our minds waiting for her, we stumbled across a hose that stretched out from an underground pump. We turned it on, and since it was the middle of summer, started to hose each other, playing around. I looked toward the fence where the baseball fields ended and the woods began.

I was shocked to see a white, ghostly figure floating around the fence, almost as if it was pacing back and forth. I kept looking and noticed that I could see only the limbs of the person. It was as if he were wearing black shorts and a black T-shirt. After alerting my friend, we watched the figure for about three minutes until he stopped dead in his tracks. With no hesitation, we both ran out of the park.

After that ghostly experience, I was told that the park had been a huge battlefield during the Revolutionary War, and you can sometimes find musket balls under the rocks. There is even an old mansion that is open to the public, named Van Cortlandt Mansion, which was owned by a victorious general during the war. It closes at night, but many workers say that strange sounds and footsteps have been heard. A lot of workers are afraid to go to the upper levels, and some even hear discussions about war strategies. Van Cortlandt is home to many, many legends and scary stories. Dead bodies always turn up, and creepy people always walk around at night. As if the Bronx wasn't scary enough! *–Mike O'Keefevan*

Spirits in the Mausoleum

The city of Troy might just be the weirdest in the whole state of New York.

No one ever wants to discuss Troy's Pinewoods Cemetery (a.k.a. Forest Park), because this one is so haunted that some say you can never leave once you enter. It's true, actually, because the memory stays with you.

About thirty-three years ago, I walked through this abandoned cemetery with my cousin. We went through some tall grass surrounding a deeply rutted and, for the most part, unpaved road to an interior mausoleum vault, which was open. We decided to go into the mausoleum, which had broken windows all around, to get out of the sun.

When we got inside, there were empty marble vaults where coffins had once been. The temperature was so cold we could see our breath, and there was frost coming down the sides of the interior of the vault. Just a little light came in, even though there were plenty of broken windows all around. We stayed there for about a half hour, because we couldn't leave—we felt as if something was holding us back, spinning us around in the mausoleum. I took pictures on my Instamatic, and, par for the course, they did not come out! When we left, we felt fear and then calm. I knew that was probably my first true visit from spirits, yet I was not afraid at all. After that experience, I started walking through other cemeteries at night, just to see if I could get the same feeling at another cemetery, but I could not.–*Adriana Delia Collins*

This one is so haunted that some say you can never leave once you enter.

Ghostly Green Glow of the Troy Mausoleum

Back in the '80s a group of us (about five people) went at night to a cemetery in Troy that we heard was haunted. We went in there armed only with flashlights. The gates of the cemetery were wrought iron and grown over with plant life. The place had not been taken care of in years. We made our way farther into the cemetery and found an old mausoleum that had no roof. All of the bodies had been removed, but you could see the spots where they had been. We were just hanging out when someone said, "Hey, look over there." So we all looked at the empty concrete holders for the coffins, and exactly in the middle was a small glowing green light about the size of a half dollar.

I went over to have a closer look to see if it was a reflection or something. It wasn't. There was no shadow, no moon, no flashlights on—nothing—just a green, glowing light with no apparent source. We got kinda freaked, so we decided to leave. Well, on the way out, my friend felt something pulling on the back of his shirt, and he turned around and there was nothing there. This cemetery is a VERY creepy place; you feel goose bumps just being there. It is definitely a place to check out.—*Amy*

It's Not Just the Mausoleum That's Haunted!

The Pinewoods Cemetery has long been closed to the public (since the '30s I believe) and overgrown by woods. Supposedly, as legend has it, this followed a few unexplained incidents, including one where the bodies that were being held in the mausoleum disappeared without a trace sometime in the '20s or '30s. One of the creepiest statues in the place is the one that stands around ten feet tall; it's an angel standing in front of a cross, but its head is missing.

Venturing into the wooded area, which most of it is, is like walking through a scary movie. You'll take a few steps through some trees and stumble upon a child's headstone. There are a lot of cold spots, and I've even had friends who were chased out of there right up to the edge of the woods by something—a shape or entity that they couldn't describe as anything other than a dark figure.

My friends Steve and Don (two very tough ex-marines) decided to venture in one night and ran out, after going only a few feet past the entrance, when the bushes started rustling and they heard the laughter of several small children. The spirits there seem to be in some state of purgatory. It was listed in *LIFE* magazine as one of the top ten most haunted cemeteries in America. If anyone plans to visit, you have to be very careful; there are a lot of NO TRESPASSING signs, and the entrance is heavily patrolled by police (and as legend has it, by the spirits themselves!). You can, however, gain access to it with permission from the town of Brunswick.—*Jack Marshall*

Cemetery Safari

So we go inside, and we gravely read the stones; all those people, all those lives, where are they now? With loves, and hates, and passions just like mine— they were born, and then they lived, and then they died. —"Cemetery Gates," *The Smiths*

D*eath*, to paraphrase the popular cliché, is one of the few certain things in life. Each of us who knows life will someday know death. This is indisputable. Perhaps that's why so many of us are fascinated by the graves of those who have lived and died before us. New York is riddled with interesting tombstones and fascinating cemeteries. Whether it's a haunted graveyard that fills you with fear or a strange tombstone that makes you scratch your head in wonder, New York has a plethora of final resting places that have become truly legendary.

There's no getting around it. Whenever people discuss cemeteries, the conversation always seems to turn to ghosts. And why not? Graveyards are, after all, not only where the mortal remains of the deceased are interred for all eternity, they are the places we go to when we want to honor and remember the dead. Throughout New York, there are tales of spirited cemeteries filled with spooks and the specters of former residents who cry out to be remembered, sometimes in the most hair-raising ways.

Goodleburg

Few cemeteries in the world have as many legends associated with them as the Goodleburg Cemetery in Wales, New York. This small patch of land off Goodleburg Road is the home of centuries-old tombstones, as well as a number of well-documented ghosts.

Essential to the spooky atmosphere is the ominous abandoned house that stands across from the entrance to the cemetery. Most of the legends about the place relate to activities that supposedly took place there many years ago. At one time, stories say, a doctor lived in the now-deserted house. He performed illegal abortions there, and the unborn babies he removed are buried throughout the grounds of the graveyard. On a number of occasions, the surreptitious surgeries were botched and the pregnant women died along with their babies. The doctor would remove the bodies of these young women from his house under the cover of night, take them to the pond at the back of Goodleburg Cemetery, and dump them in. These events are all said to have taken place in the early to mid-1800s. Now, some two hundred years later, rumor has it that Goodleburg is still cursed by the aftermath of these grisly events.

Goodleburg Cemetery these days is often referred to as one of the most haunted spots in America. Hundreds of curious people visit the graveyard each year, hoping to encounter the legendary ghosts that inhabit it. Few leave disappointed. The most common reports involve an ever-present, low-hanging fog that seems to follow visitors around as they explore the cemetery grounds. Also common are reports that faint music can be heard coming from the far corners of the graveyard.

More specifically, a number of ghosts directly related to the activities of the good doctor of long ago seem to be hanging around. Most often seen are the wandering spirits of the unfortunate women who were dumped into the pond. Many people have reportedly found bones on the water's edge, particularly after heavy rains, which seem to unearth them. The spectral mothers are often seen wandering the wooded areas at the edges of the cemetery, and their babies play there at night. Even the doctor himself, clad in a white medical coat, has been seen walking through the graveyard. Others have seen him hanging from a tree in the cemetery, where he supposedly committed suicide. The apparition of the hanging doctor is said to appear on the first Friday of every month. It seems that all of the players in the dark affairs of long ago are still hanging around Goodleburg Cemetery.

Goodleburg's Lady in White

If you guys plan on checking out Goodleburg Cemetery, make sure you spend some time on the number of desolate roads that surround it too. This is often the best way to see the ghosts that come from the graveyard. I have seen orbs and strange lights a number of times, and even once saw the famous lady in white. She is supposed to be one of the abortion doctor's patients—she wanders the whole area in a white dress. My friends and I saw her late one night in 1997. She was off in the distance and hazy, but we definitely believe it to have been the famous specter.
–Dustin W.

Mind Your Manners, Ghost Hunters!

The hauntings of Goodleburg Cemetery are caused as much by dumb teenagers as they are by anything else. It is absolutely essential that people learn to be respectful while out trying to scare each other on their ghost hunts. The house behind the cemetery now has people living in it. Do not bother them. And for God's sake, be respectful of the graves. A couple years ago, some kids dug up a few for kicks. This is totally inappropriate, and I believe has as much to do with why so many pissed off spirits haunt Goodleburg as anything else!
–Cecelia Michele

Every Visit a Thrill

My friends and I have been to Goodleburg quite a few times within the past two years. Almost every experience was exciting. There are two nights that stick out in my mind. I do not have the dates that we were there, but I do know that it was about twelve thirty to two, both times on a Friday or Saturday night.

The first night was unbelievable. We went there to take some pictures and get a feel for the place. All of the pictures that we got had orbs in them; some had a weird fog/smokelike image. There is one picture in particular (I call it our ghost picture) that stands out. It looks like a human holding something in its hand. You can make out the outline almost perfectly of a human head, neck, torso, and arms. There were orbs of all different colors. The feeling of that place became too much to bear for one of us, and we thought we should leave.

The second night was more feelings than photos. As soon as we walked into the cemetery, the wind started to blow very strong. Then, as we were walking through the cemetery, we were taking some pictures, and while the flash from the camera went off, a friend and I both saw a black image of a man wearing a top hat standing in front of us. We both saw the same image and described it to a tee to each other. As we looked at that picture, there was only a blue orb . . . no man and no fog/smoke.

About fifteen minutes later, we were walking back farther into the cemetery, and three of the five of us felt a force stopping us from going any farther. I know my hair stood up all over my body and it seemed very cold. The force was not physical, but more like an energy wall. It is very hard to explain—similar to taking two magnets and trying to put two positive sides together. Then a scream was heard; I am not sure where it came from or who it came from. We left right then and there. We knew once that happened that it was time to go. I have never heard babies or dogs or seen the woman in white. One of my friends said that every time we go, she feels as though she is being watched. I feel this also, but I think it is just because we already know something is there. I do ask that if anyone goes there, be careful. It is a dangerous area. And please be respectful, for it is a place of rest, not a place to hang out.*–Jennifer*

Gurnsey Hollow

Most cemeteries are eerie by nature. After all, there are all those dead people lying around. But Gurnsey Hollow Cemetery, located outside Frewsburg, is a more likely candidate for paranormal activity than most. Not only is it well hidden and extremely old (the oldest stones date back to the very early 1800s), but it is also the site of a brutal tragedy that has spooked the area ever since.

A casual visit to the cemetery reveals that many children are buried here. Stories say that one of these is not only interred here but actually met her demise in the cemetery as well. And her death was truly shocking.

The child in question was a seven-year-old mentally retarded girl. She was killed by a gang of local townsfolk who chased her into Gurnsey Hollow late one night. It has been lost to the ages whether the girl was killed because of some specific infraction or whether she was simply feared and hated because of her condition. Regardless of the exact circumstances, the end results were the same. The poor girl was stoned to death by the angry mob. Her body was buried in the same cemetery in which she was killed, and since the day of her death her ghost and a number of others have terrorized late-night visitors to Gurnsey Hollow.

Besides the ghost of the girl, people have also seen a lady in white and a little boy patrolling the cemetery grounds. The little boy follows visitors out to the main entrance, then disappears. He is not the only guardian of the cemetery. An elderly woman also stands on the outskirts of the graveyard glaring at trespassers.

People often hear unearthly moans, see apparitions and orbs, and experience electronic equipment failures once they step into the graveyard. And the forces are powerful. Some people even say their cars shut off when approaching Gurnsey Hollow.

Frewsburg Is a Weird Place!

I have to admit that few places have intimidated your *Weird New York* author as much as the Gurnsey Hollow Cemetery. My trip there was easily one of the more chilling experiences I have had in my life, and I have visited literally hundreds of purportedly haunted sites.

My trepidation started when I rolled into the very quiet town of Frewsburg. Since I didn't know the exact location of the cemetery, I headed to a local gas station to see if I could track it down. A young girl was at the counter. She seemed to be in her late teens or early twenties, and I figured that she would have heard of the place.

"Excuse me," I started, "but I have a weird question. Have you ever heard of the Gurnsey Hollow Cemetery?"

"Yeah, I've heard of it." She smiled back. "Everybody's heard of it."

"Oh, well do you have any idea what road it's on?" She shook her head that she did not. "Or at least what direction it's in?"

Again she didn't know. "Maybe it's on the local map," she offered up, and pointed toward a hand-drawn piece of paper hanging on the back of a door. I walked over and

immediately saw "Gurnsey Road" listed clear as day. This, I assumed, would be a logical place to search for Gurnsey Hollow. Looking at the map, I saw that I would just need to find Frew Run Road and it was then a matter of a few turns.

"Do you know which way Frew Run Road is?" I asked the girl. Again she didn't know. I was flummoxed, as this was FREWsburg and FREW Run Road was clearly one of the main roads in town, according to the map.

I didn't know the name of the road I was on now, since I had just pulled into town, but figured that it at least would give me a starting point. Back to my informative friend at the counter.

"Well, what road are we on now?" I asked her.

"I don't know."

"You don't know the name of the road that you are on, the one you work on?"

"Uh-uh."

I was flabbergasted. How could this girl not know the name of the street she was standing on? If I asked her, "Where are you right now?" her answer would probably be, "I have no idea." My bewilderment only got worse when I went outside and looked at a street sign. We were on Main Street.

I tell this story to illustrate that things in Frewsburg struck me as a little bit off. You can only imagine what the cemetery, which stands out above the rest of the local weirdness, is like.

Gurnsey Road starts off as a very desolate but still relatively normal street. It's paved, there are homes on it, and it seems like nothing more than an out-of-the-way country road. After just a few miles, though, it turns into a single-lane dirt road that would rival any featured in the "Roads Less Traveled" chapter of this book. It's bumpy and potholed, and twists and

turns through a thick forest. There are very few homes on this section of the road, and the ones that are there are all peppered with large NO TRESPASSING signs. There are also burned-out old school buses in the woods, as well as dark trails into the deep forest. At each curve, it seems that the road cannot go on for much longer, but around that curve is an even skinnier and more poorly maintained section.

After traveling down this path a number of miles, any adventurer would be a bit intimidated. So it only makes it worse when, nearly at the end of the road, you look off to the left, where there is a tiny gravel trail leading into the woods. This trail is blocked by a rusty gate and two large granite stones: It is the entrance to the Gurnsey Hollow Cemetery.

Okay, then, this is the place. I grabbed my camera, got out, and sprinted up to the hill to the tiny cemetery. When I got to it, I saw that it was surrounded by a black iron fence. There was exactly one entrance/exit to the cemetery. As I stood there alone in the woods, I realized that if anyone came up that trail behind me, I would be completely trapped inside the Gurnsey Hollow Cemetery.

Inside it turns out that a large majority of the graves have been vandalized. Centuries-old obelisks are tipped over everywhere. Only the smaller, harder-to-destroy graves have been left unscathed. I began to frantically snap pictures, wanting to get out of there as fast as I could. There was the sound of a stream or small waterfall coming from the woods beyond the iron bars off to my right. I also heard a distinct low-pitched, guttural moaning.

With that, I picked up the pace as I made my way through the graves. At the top of the hill, overlooking the entire burial ground, was a large cross. I approached it, figuring that it was a necessary photograph. When I got closer, I saw the charred remains of some sort of bonfire sitting directly in front of the cross.

That was the last straw! Maybe it was just the remains of some high school kids' weekend of drinking at the cemetery. But, alone in those circumstances, I would have no trouble believing this fire was the remains of a pagan sacrifice. I turned and literally ran.

It may have been just because I was alone or because the sun was quickly falling as I took these pictures at the end of a very long day. But in that moment, running down that trail at the end of that long dirt road, Gurnsey Hollow was completely terrifying. If you decide to visit for yourself, take caution.

Long Island's Most Legendary Final Resting Place

To say "Mary's Grave" on Long Island is to bring forth an array of tales about tragedy, death—usually a violent one—and loss. Over the years, dozens of variations on the story of Mary's Grave have been told. The truth has been lost to time; now only the stories remain.

Even the location of this legendary grave is uncertain. We'd like to tell you just where to find it, if it exists at all, but we're afraid we cannot. There seem to be as many possible locations for the grave as there are versions of its story. But with folks from all over Long Island eager to claim the legend as their own, we're sure that this is one grave site that will live on in local lore for a long time.

Here, Rob Levine, of Long Island Paranormal Investigations, describes the many tales of Mary's Grave he has heard over the years:

The story of Mary's Grave has too many different variations to list them all. Some people say that it is in Head of the Harbor, but others insist it is to be found in Saint James, Huntington, Port Jefferson, Sayville, Amityville, and Stony Brook.

One story says that Mary was tried as a witch for killing local children. She was convicted and hanged in front of her home, then buried nearby. (No word as to where "nearby" is.) The legend also says that if children go to her grave at night, Mary will appear and kill them, so maybe it's just as well the site is uncertain.

Another story says that Mary's husband was a sailor. While he was away, Mary would light a candle in the upstairs window of their home to guide him back to her. At some point, her husband died while at sea. Mary never got over the loss and committed suicide. Legend says that on some nights if you look to the house where she lived, you will see a light in the upstairs window.

Another tale has a more modern twist. This one says that Mary had broken up with her controlling boyfriend. She started seeing a new guy, but the ex didn't like it and wanted her back. He had Mary get in his car and started driving. They got into an argument, and he pushed her out of the moving car. Mary, though injured, was still alive after the tumble. As she lay in the street trying to get up, another car came down the road. The driver didn't see her until it was too late and ran her over. Not surprisingly, Mary died at the scene. However, she is said to haunt the area. She appears in front of cars driving down the road and then disappears.

At the Head of the Harbor site, there are a couple of additional legends. One says that if you go to the concrete-bunker-like object off Shep Jones Road, make the sign of the cross, and say the "magic words," you can wake the dead. The other tale is that if you pass another car while driving down the dark, tree-shadowed road and then stop and turn off your engine, your car will not start when you turn it on again.

My group hasn't really found anything there. One day we spoke to two residents of the area, a father and his daughter. When we asked if they had heard any stories about the place, they got fearful expressions on their faces and the girl ran inside. The father said there was nothing there, and that was it.

Mary Makes the News

The legend of Mary's elusive grave was featured in a 2005 article of *Newsday* in which a reader asked the following question of Staff Writer George DeWan:

Question: I grew up in Centereach during the '50s and '60s. Many people my age at the time used to look for "Mary's Grave." I have since met others from surrounding towns, i.e., Saint James, Smithtown, who also remember people talking about Mary's Grave. None of us can recall why anyone was looking for this grave. Have you ever come across any information that might shed light on this?–*Lynn Baglio, Mount Sinai*

Answer: This story has been around for a couple of generations. It was given new life in the 1970s when students at a few high schools in the Smithtown area spread a rumor that the ghost of a Mary Smith occasionally surfaced in a private cemetery in the area. This led students to congregate at the cemetery for late-night parties that led to vandalism and damage to the gravestones. Richard Hawkins, who is in charge of the Long Island collection at the Smithtown Public Library, says that a few years ago several students came into the library looking to corroborate various versions of the story they had heard. He asked them to write them down. Here are some of them:

> More than a hundred years ago, Mary went insane and hacked her parents to death with an ax, and even today her ghost roams around looking for young virgins to kill. . . . Mary's boyfriend caught her cheating on him and hanged her on a tree, and on certain nights, if you look closely, you can still see her swinging back and forth. . . . When Mary's boyfriend returned from the Revolutionary War, he betrayed her, whereupon she murdered him and hanged herself. . . . Mary was a nurse, and when many of the children she was caring for died of small-pox, she was accused of being a witch and murdered. . . . Two boys murdered Mary in the woods, and after being found guilty, they died mysteriously; every year on the anniversary of her death, Mary rises from the dead and murders two more boys. . . . In 1952, a girl named Mary was harassed by women in Saint James for fooling around with their husbands; she hanged herself from a tree in the middle of a field and was then buried under the tree.

Hawkins said that many of these accounts used specific locations, streets, fields, barns, and homes in a relatively small area in Suffolk County's North Shore. He investigated. "I can attest that viewing several of these sites has not cast any light upon the legend for me," Hawkins wrote in a spring 1995 article in the *Long Island Forum.*

The Crypt Keeper Knocks BACK!

This is one creepy phenomenon I know to be true, because I heard it.

In a cemetery located on Route 8 between Unadilla and Bridgewater is a crypt belonging to Eunice Welsh. If you knock or pound on the door, you will hear a rustling sound from inside, and you will have your knock returned! I have done it, and I have heard it! I have tried this phenomenon twice, once alone and again six months later with a girlfriend, who swears she heard a voice hiss, "Leave me, leave me, go!" I didn't hear that, but I did hear the two knocks returned.

The cemetery has no name, but is visible on the left-hand side going north on Route 8 on a slow curve of road followed by a large cornfield.–*Red*

Three Strikes, Then They Were Outta There!

When I was a teenager we heard about the Vanderbilts' tomb in Staten Island. We tried several times to find it, each time being scared out of our wits. The story is that they were not buried, but propped up like statues in a tomb that resembled a large mansion. It's supposed to be in a cemetery in Staten Island off Todt Hill Road.

We went there three nights in a row after midnight. The first night, as we started in, we passed a hillside with all these small tombstones. They were all only a couple of years old. We had started to walk away, when we heard a baby's cry. We looked at each other and asked, "Did you hear that?" We panicked and ran out, scared stiff.

The next night we went a little farther, until a glowing light appeared, resembling a girl with long hair. We ran so fast that we jumped over the top of the fence in one leap.

On the third night, we approached a wrought-iron fence with what appeared to be a large mausoleum set in a hillside with rotunda on top. We turned around, and there was a man in a suit standing next to us. We looked at each other, and he vanished instantly. We then ran the hell out of there. Was it a case of mass hysteria or was it real? We will never know. We never went back.–*Joe Bruschetta*

Not All Voices Are from Beyond the Grave

Vanderbilt's is pretty sick. The tomb itself is at least three stories high. It's part of the Moravian Cemetery, but it's separate from the whole cemetery. There's a locked gate at the entrance to the cemetery, but the area also borders High Rock Park, so it's easier to get in from the woods. The tomb is actually built into the side of a hill, so you can walk up the back path onto the top of it.

There's also another smaller mausoleum called the Sloane tomb. The family buried there built some of the houses on Sloane Avenue, which is a block bordering the main entrance of High Rock. It used to be a hangout for people who knew about it, but security has gotten tight there at night. Recently they put a motion detector there, which has a recording over a loudspeaker telling you that you're trespassing. Every four years or so, the tomb is opened for the family to go inside. I don't know how many people are buried there. Overall, it is a really freaky place to be at night. There are plenty of unexplained noises. It's definitely worth seeing in person.–*RekSumAss*

The Legend of the Tomb

Legend has it that if you take a picture of the Vanderbilt tomb, either the person in the picture will not be in it when you develop it, or there will be another person in the picture that was not there originally. I plan on getting some more pictures sometime in the future (it's kind of risky since it's on private property inside the cemetery).–*EchoBase1005*

Unusual Epitaphs and Curious Carvings

A Sensual Stump?

I wanted to tell you about an odd tombstone found in my hometown of Port Jervis. It is not a headstone, but the footstone of a man named Hiram Horn, who died in 1907. The grave marker is a sculpture of a tree stump with truncated limbs, but that is not the odd part, as this is a fairly common motif in cemetery statuary. The strange thing about the stone is that on one side of the tree stump, in a smooth area where the bark has fallen away, is a carving of a round bulge that looks more anatomically human than arboreal. It appears to be a protruding belly button or perhaps even a nipple. Of course, stones and trees are a lot like clouds in that what you see in them really depends on the kind of imagination you have—right? That's what I thought until I walked around to the other side of the stone and saw another carving in the tree trunk that is unmistakably in the form of a woman's private parts! I don't know if this was a little dirty joke perpetrated by the stone carver, or if it was the final wish of the late Mr. Horn (or perhaps we should call him Mr. Horny), but it sure is oddly erotic.

—Name withheld by request

Final Words

We found the following three noteworthy tombstones in a book called *Laughter and Tears* by Robert E. Pike (H-H Press, 1971).

He Asks a Good Question

The tombstone of Lee Neal Jr. (1927–1952) in the St. John's Lutheran Cemetery on Pine Ridge Road in the town of Cheektowaga reads WHY LIVE AND BE MISERABLE WHEN YOU CAN BE BURIED COMFORTABLY FOR A FEW BUCKS PLUS ERIE CO. SALES TAX?

Sweet Revenge

It's often said that revenge is a dish best served cold, and that certainly seems to be true in one particular Brooklyn man's case. His name was John, and he mistakenly blamed his wife's physician for killing his beloved Mamie. John waited a couple of years and then exacted his revenge by murdering the doctor. He was later executed for the crime but unrepentantly had this epitaph inscribed on his Cypress Hills Cemetery tombstone: REVENGE RENEWS OUR HAPPY LOVE IN HEAVEN FOREVER.

The Doctor Is Always In

The grave of Dr. Fred Roberts (1875–1931) reads OFFICE UP STAIRS. The marker can be found in the Maple Grove Cemetery in, appropriately enough, a town called Hoosick Falls.

Crib Clone

This grave with white iron fencing found in Ellenville/Wurtsboro looks very much like a baby's crib. *–Robin Groves*

Dead Lay Claim to Parking Spots

The Palisades Center Mall is in New York about ten minutes off the Garden State Parkway. If you go to the back end of the mall, you will find in the middle of the parking lot a graveyard with tombstones that look very old. It's odd that they would build a parking lot around this graveyard. I would say it is about fifty feet from the mall itself. *–Fixer*

Without question, death is the great equalizer. A tour through any of New York's cemeteries will confirm this, as you'll find renowned historical figures lying side by side with those who led much humbler existences. In the end, though, the great and the small all had but one life to live, and each of their monuments has a story to tell.

Harry Houdini Escapes from His Own Grave

The world's all-time most famous escape artist, Harry Houdini, managed in a sense to escape from even his own grave. The evidence of this is there (or more accurately, not there) at his very odd final resting place, located in the Machpelah Cemetery on Cypress Hill Street in Queens.

There are a number of fascinating circumstances surrounding Houdini's death and his tombstone. For one, he died on October 31 (Halloween), 1926. Nine days before his death, he was giving a lecture proclaiming Spiritualism, the belief that people can communicate with the souls of the dead, a fraud. During the lecture, a spectator unexpectedly punched Houdini in the stomach three times to test his legendary strength. Houdini didn't see the blows coming, and one of them ruptured his appendix. He survived for over a week before finally giving up the ghost on Halloween. The idea that he was speaking about death and then passed away on Halloween has helped Houdini's death become truly legendary.

This is what the Houdini Historical Center in Appleton, Wisconsin, has to say about the magician and his final passing.

Houdini was known as a debunker of fake mediums and spiritualists. His interest began during his bereavement after the death of his mother, Cecilia Weiss. Because of his background as an illusionist, he recognized the techniques of mediums who claimed to have contacted the spirit world. Houdini became a crusader against these charlatans who bilked grieving families of their money. He frequently attended séances in disguise in order to expose the mediums. . . .

The Official Houdini Séance, held each year since the magician's death in 1926, originated from Houdini's efforts to expose fraudulent mediums. He claimed that if there were truly a way to contact the living after one's death, he would do so. He set up a code with his wife Bess, who faithfully attended the annual séances and awaited his return for 10 years, after which time she gave up. The séance, currently organized by Sidney H. Radner, is held each year in a location with a significant connection to Houdini's life.

Whether he returns from the dead or not, the magician's grave site in Queens has become a popular destination for curiosity-seekers, who have found a number of noteworthy things about it. The strangest thing, though, is what is not there. At one point, a bust of Houdini sat on top of his grave. It disappeared years ago, and there have been no clues to its whereabouts since. Only Harry Houdini could pull off a disappearing act from his own grave.

Professional magicians circle a chair containing a picture of Houdini, a pair of handcuffs he used, a book he wrote, and candles. They attempted to contact Houdini, asking him to move one of the objects if he could. None of the objects moved

Uncle Sam's Grave

If you ask most people who Uncle Sam is, the first thing they think about is the scowling, red-white-and-blue-clad guy pointing his finger out from those military recruitment posters saying, "I want YOU!" That image was created by artist James Montgomery Flagg during World War I. Long before that, though, Uncle Sam was a real person who lived and died in Troy.

His name was Samuel Wilson, and he was born in Arlington, MA, in 1766, but he spent most of his life here in New York, where he was in the meatpacking business. During the War of 1812, Sam supplied meat to the U.S. Army and would stamp his shipping barrels with a U.S., earning himself the nickname Uncle Sam. Before long the moniker came to symbolize not only the man, but also the U.S. government. The Uncle Sam character was soon being featured in political cartoons of the time, especially those of Thomas Nast.

While Uncle Sam may be immortal, this was not the case for his earthly namesake. Samuel Wilson died in 1854 and was buried in Oakwood Cemetery in Troy, where his tombstone bears a plaque commemorating him and the patriotic character he inspired. His final resting place is maintained by the local Boy Scouts, who raise and lower the American flag over it each day.

One Comedian Who Loves to Die

No comedian has enjoyed dying more than Adam Allyn. Any stand-up comic knows the terrible feeling of dying on stage. And New York City has long been a place where comedians come from far and wide to meet their fate in front of large crowds. Sometimes they go out with glory; sometimes they just die.

One comedian loved the idea of dying in New York so much that he noted it for all eternity. Located in the graveyard of Manhattan's Trinity Church, the headstone of Adam Allyn, who died in the eighteenth century, makes a point to mention that he was a comedian. This strange grave has attracted many visitors over the years. Over time, it has been noticed that an unusual haunting seems to be attached to the peculiar stone. Many report that at night the unmistakable sound of a high-pitched cackle can be heard in the vicinity of this funnyman's tombstone.

The inscription reads: "Sacred to the Memory of Adam Allyn, Comedian. Who Departed this Life February 16, 1768. This Stone Was Erected by the American Company as a Testimony of their unfeignd regard. He Posesed many good Qualitys. But as he was a Man He had the frailties Common to Mans Nature."

John Burroughs Grave Site

John Burroughs was a celebrity in his time, a famous naturalist who came from the picturesque Catskills. He grew up north of Roxbury and spent much time sitting on a rock that overlooked a nearby valley, which he referred to as his meditation rock. Upon his death, he was buried in this remote area. His grave is now a New York State historical site. The meditation rock sits right next to his burial plot. Curiously, many report that when they sit on the rock in the same spot Burroughs frequented, the rock is ice cold!

Be forewarned, though. The John Burroughs grave site was easily the most remote of all the spots *Weird New York* visited in researching this book. We drove for hours through the picturesque Catskills just to get to the town, a beautiful, but long, ride. After arriving in Roxbury, we asked around and found the grave site. It was high up on a ridge positioned on a mountain overlooking the town.

When we got to the ridge, it seemed like a simple enough task to find the grave. After all, there was a sign and a picnic area marking this as the location of the site. But we didn't see the grave itself. We were, however, at the foot of a steep incline in the mountain. Since Burroughs was a naturalist, it made sense that his grave would involve literally climbing a mountain.

What followed this realization was close to two hours of pure stupidity. Step by agonizing step we made our way

up the mountain, sinking knee-deep into snow time after time. (I forgot to mention that two days previous to our visit there was a full-on blizzard.) We never found that grave up on top of the mountain, and after over an hour of searching, we called off the hunt. It was a painful choice, as we had driven so long to get there, but it was starting to feel physically dangerous to continue. We were cold and wet. It was time to admit defeat.

The journey back down the mountain was even more treacherous than the one up, as we slid and tumbled down, gathering long streaks of muddy snow and wet leaves along the way. Your author grew up in the suburbs of northern New Jersey, leading a "front lawn and asphalt" kind of existence, which left him unprepared for impromptu mountain climbing in the Catskills. Finally we came out about one hundred yards down the road from where we had parked the car directly at the entrance to the John Burroughs grave site. And there we encountered the final indignity. In front of us, at the same altitude as the street itself, was the grave.

So learn from this cautionary tale, dear reader. If you find yourself in a similar situation at the John Burroughs grave, don't rush headlong up the mountain. Simply turn to your right and walk between fifty and one hundred steps. It will save you much time and much embarrassment, and you won't need to buy a new pair of jeans later in the day.

Remembering the Amiable Child

Manhattan is fast-paced and constantly changing. From one generation to the next, buildings come and go, streets are rearranged, and land goes through a variety of uses. The Manhattan of one hundred years ago would in many ways be unrecognizable to the city's inhabitants today. Perhaps this is what's so remarkable about the grave of the Amiable Child. For over two hundred years, this monument has stood quietly, firm and undisturbed, in one of the most quickly changing areas of the world. And it all centers around a five-year-old boy.

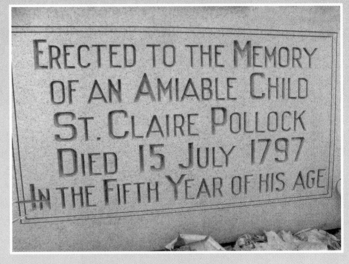

The so-called Amiable Child, whose grave has become locally famous, was St. Claire Pollock. As a child growing up near what is now Manhattan's Riverside Drive, Pollock was a member of a local family of linen merchants of Scots-Irish descent. The Pollock family mansion stood near the river in this exclusive area, then known as Strawberry Hill. One day, young St. Claire was playing near the family's home when he slipped and fell off the cliffs high above the Hudson River. Tragically, he died from the fall, and was buried on his family's property.

When the land was sold to Mrs. Cornelia Verplanck in 1800, the family made a request of the new owner. George Pollock, who was either St. Claire's father or uncle, wrote Mrs. Verplanck personally, noting that "there is a small enclosure near your boundary fence within which lie the remains of a favorite child, covered by a marble monument. You will confer a peculiar and interesting favor upon me by allowing me to convey the enclosure to you so that you will consider it a part of your own estate, keeping it, however, always enclosed and sacred." Mrs. Verplanck honored George Pollock's request to maintain St. Claire's final resting place, and miraculously, so has every subsequent owner of the land.

St. Claire Pollock's grave is enclosed by a black wrought-iron fence now and is barely noticeable in the crowded area along Riverside Park. It is especially obscured due to the fact that the imposing Grant's Tomb has been erected just across the street from it. The grave simply reads ERECTED TO THE MEMORY OF AN AMIABLE CHILD, ST. CLAIRE POLLOCK and lists the date of the boy's death in 1797.

The Amiable Child grave stands in an area that was once farmland and is now a local park. It's somehow touching that in such a fast-paced, constantly morphing environment, respect for the life of one little boy has left a tiny piece of New York forever untouched.

America's Oldest Pet Burial Ground

Hartsdale, located in Westchester County just a half hour outside Manhattan, is the home of the world-famous Hartsdale Pet Cemetery. This former apple orchard is the final resting place of over seventy thousand animals. The cemetery bills itself as "America's First and Most Prestigious Pet Burial Grounds." After seeing the celebrity status of some of the animals and/or their owners buried there, as well as the elaborate lengths to which some have gone in an effort to commemorate their pets, it's hard to argue with this billing.

The Hartsdale Pet Cemetery was founded by a veterinarian named Samuel Johnson in 1896. Johnson practiced pet medicine in Manhattan and spent most of his time there, but kept land in rural Westchester County as a retreat. The apple orchard on the grounds of this retreat became a world-famous pet cemetery purely by accident.

A distraught female client of Dr. Johnson's contacted him with an odd request. Her dog had just passed away, and she wanted to give the pooch a proper funeral and final resting place. Unfortunately, she found that Manhattan had strict laws prohibiting this practice. She had considered finding a patch of land and creating a memorial herself, but she knew that the constant construction in New York City's busiest borough would eventually lead to her dog's grave being plowed over and forgotten. She turned to Johnson for help, wondering if her vet knew of any options for the burial.

Johnson did not. But he did offer his own land to the saddened woman. He told her that if she was willing to make the trek out to Hartsdale, he would allow her to bury her dog in his serene apple orchard. So she did.

Johnson didn't think the beastie burial was much more than a good story. A few days later he related the tale to a reporter friend. Much to Johnson's shock the reporter thought the story was interesting enough to print, which he did in the local paper. Within weeks, Dr. Johnson was inundated with requests from grief-stricken pet owners wanting to

HARTSDALE
PET CEMETERY

Established 1896
America's First Pet Burial Grounds

CEMETERY HOURS

MON THRU SAT   8:00 AM TO 4:30 PM
SUNDAY   9:30 AM TO 4:00 PM
HOLIDAYS   9:30 AM TO 3:00 PM
NEW YEARS DAY   CLOSED

JUMPER TAYLOR
(DINKY DOO)
FEB. 28, 1990 – AUG. 5, 1997

YOU TOUCHED OUR LIVES
WITH SUCH JOY AND HAPPINESS
THAT A LIFETIME OF LOVING
MEMORIES WILL FOREVER REMAIN

The
BEAR

THE BEST DOG EVER

REISMAN

memorialize Fido or Fifi. The Hartsdale Pet Cemetery was born.

There are the obvious animals represented in the cemetery—dogs, cats, birds, and so forth. But there are also some unusual creatures, including a lion cub. Some of the animals' grave sites are elaborate, expensive memorials that put most humans' graves to shame. The most lavish plot is the Walsh mausoleum, a structure built at a cost of over $25,000 to memorialize a dog.

Many famous people have had their pets interred at Hartsdale. Singer Mariah Carey, legendary millionaire Hetty Green, sports figure Joe Garagiola, and Pulitzer Prize–winning author MacKinlay Kantor are among the dozens of celebrities who have purchased plots here for their pets.

And a number of the pets themselves are famous. Westminster show dogs have come to Hartsdale to be buried. A police dog named Sirius is buried here. He lost his life searching for survivors in the rubble of the September 11, 2001, tragedy. There are dogs of war and police dogs whose loving memorials detail their deaths as sacrifices in the service of mankind.

Abandoned in New York

Abandoned places can be incredibly alluring and fascinating. They seem to carry with them the imprint of whatever happened in the years before they were shuttered and left dark. Many are littered with artifacts that speak of the people who once lived or worked in these places—photos of strangers who smile back at you, odd bits of clothing, things that seem to have been discarded with no more thought than a snake might give its molted skin. You can't help but wonder what brought this place to its present fate.

Just about any building, whether it's an institution, a castle, or simply a private home, can become the catalyst for weird stories if left abandoned long enough. Aside from any legitimate history, abandoned places just seem to inspire the imagination that way. And while it might seem like an odd hobby to some, there are many people who love going to these empty dark places. There's a creepy feeling that one can get only while stepping across the floorboards of some creaky old building on a foggy night. That is an experience that can be best described by those who have lived it. For this reason we will let our readers share with you the following stories of their own adventures beyond the no trespassing zone.

The Abandoned Monastery

History tells us that the St. Augustinian Academy, located in the Grymes Hill section of Staten Island, was once a boys' high school and later became a religious retreat, which was abandoned in 1985. Our readers, however, tell much different tales about what once went on at, and under, the deserted old building.

Better known in area lore simply as the Monastery, the school has been the inspiration for countless chilling tales and the chosen destination of a generation of late-night thrill-seeking adventurers. Now surrounded by suburban houses with manicured lawns, the all-but-forgotten fortress is shrouded in a tangle of overgrown weeds, vines, and gnarly trees. Turkey vultures circle lazily overhead, occasionally landing to roost on the building's crumbling bell tower, where they keep a watchful eye over the long-dead institution.

Spooky Staten Island Monastery

On Staten Island, there's an abandoned monastery in a dark forest. There are three floors, and the basement goes down at least ten floors underground. Rumors are there are dead bodies down there, which is probably true because there's the worst smell in the world down there. But no one dares to go down to the lower levels below the basement. While you're there, you hear footsteps behind you, people talking, and some people even see ghosts. It's really spooky!–*T.*

Ten Stories Beneath the Old Monastery

The story about the monastery goes like this: About sixty years ago, a bunch of monks lived there in solitude and silence. But there was one monk that went crazy and went on a killing spree, massacring all the other monks and dragging their bodies down to a secret sublevel (the monks slept in sublevels underground; people say they go down thirty floors). They say if you want to see the monks' ghosts, you have to go down to the last sublevel at night. So we wanted something to do on a summer night like any normal teenagers, but this night changed our lives forever.

We went down the road to the monastery and went around it, exploring the outside, too scared to go in just yet. There were a lot of satanic signs and gang graffiti. Finally we got the nerve to go in. The building consists of three floors, two wings, and whatever is below. It was dark and creepy, but there had to be at least thirty rooms on each floor. We went upstairs first. We saw that the roof had caved in and there were holes in the floor that dropped down two floors. There were also bloody animals wrapped in cloth hung from the ceiling. Every now and then we heard the sounds of chains dragging and a banging and the opening of a door behind us. No one was saying anything, but I knew I wasn't the only one that heard it.

Next we found stairs going down, so we proceeded that way. There was a kid with us that kept pushing us to go on farther. We followed him down three flights of stairs to the sublevels. At about the third sublevel, we found the monks' quarters. They were very small and cramped. The strange thing about the rooms was the walls had scratch marks down them that looked like fingernails were imbedded in them.

Then we came to a room blocked by wood. Behind the door were small stairs that looked like they went on forever. We followed the stairs down about ten floors, and they were really starting to shake now. We entered a room where there were what looked like jail cells. It was getting a little too scary, so we left.—*CP112*

Getting Subterranean at the Monastery

For years, kids have been going up to the monastery near Wagner College, scrawling graffiti and partying, but not too many have been to the sublevels.

A short walk around the building will reveal an out-of-commission fountain, which seems to be in the shape of a cross, but now is chipped and the home of dozens of weeds. Naturally, there's tons of graffiti on the higher levels, but as you travel lower and lower under the surface, signs of life become less and less evident. On one trip investigating a flooded seventh level, we found candles and something that made the hairs stand on the back of my neck: marks on one of the ancient wooden doors as if it were locked from the outside and someone had tried to claw their way out of the room.

What happened in the abandoned monastery? I have heard many stories but I only know one thing for sure. If you make your way to the last underground chamber, all your questions will be answered.–*Dale N.*

Sacrificed Cats and Axe Attacks

My friends and I once went in a room into the basement of the monastery and saw a sacrificed animal. There were bones, cups filled with blood, hanged cats, and crazy looking writing on the walls. We were all really scared, but it didn't stop us from going back every day. The last time I went I was with a couple of friends and it was at night. While walking up through the woods, we saw something move by the entrance. The next thing I remember is a man chasing us with an axe! It was the scariest moment of my life. That stopped me from going there for a long time.–*B. Hirsch*

The Monastic Life

I was a postulant at Augustinian Academy from fall of 1964 through spring 1965. This is the same building you know as the Staten Island Monastery. It was indeed a strange place. I felt I was being taken over by evil spirits before I ever heard the word "possession." I was fifteen years old at the time, and I kept requesting from the Father Prior that I leave, but he would not notify my family. In those days incoming and outgoing mail was censored, and there was little means to send a message home that was not intercepted.

I was well into a mental breakdown, which to this day I have not completely recovered from. Back in the '60s the popularity of minor seminaries was declining, although there were several seminaries in NY at the time. Somewhere close by was a Franciscan minor seminary. Augustinians were friendly with Franciscans; we despised Jesuits and nuns.–*Ted Bergeron*

Woodland Palace of Zog I

For years I would go hiking in this forgotten nature preserve in Muttontown, Long Island. When hiking in these woods, one often comes across ancient porcelain drainage gutters, dilapidated columns, and structures that seem very out of place in the middle of a forest.

One day my friend and I went off the trail and got a little lost. It was then that we discovered a fantastic site that we couldn't believe—an entire abandoned palace that seemed more appropriate for ancient Greece than in the middle of a nature preserve! As we walked around, we saw what appeared to be the remains of a gigantic gated garden, which must have been a sight to see in its day. As we continued, we witnessed a main building, now demolished, with two grand staircases leading to a magnificent set of columned gazebos, completely overgrown with vegetation. Remnants of statues and

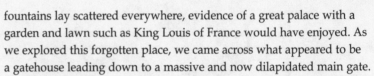

fountains lay scattered everywhere, evidence of a great palace with a garden and lawn such as King Louis of France would have enjoyed. As we explored this forgotten place, we came across what appeared to be a gatehouse leading down to a massive and now dilapidated main gate.

This six-hundred-acre preserve was originally four separate estates, belonging to Benjamin Moore, great-grandson of Clement Clarke Moore, author of *The Night Before Christmas;* the Hudsons; the Winthrops; and finally the Hammonds. Hudson built a large palace on his land. He named it Knollwood, and after his death in 1921 it was sold to the self-proclaimed King of Albania, Zog I. This monarch intended to establish a kingdom in the preserve for himself and his exiled countrymen! However, due to financial problems, the king was never able to live in the palace and his servants abandoned the estate after a few years. The grand home lay dormant for decades as the forest reclaimed the extravagance that was to be a kingdom within a nation. Before long, there were rumors of a buried treasure, and much of the palace has since been vandalized by looters.

—*John Alexander Genua*

Reliving the Past at Time Town

My family vacationed at Lake George every year from about 1975–1985. It was, and still is, home to many exciting family activities. There was a popular amusement park there called Time Town. My father remembers a story that the owners of the park created it for their ill son. The story goes that when the son died in the mid-1980s, the parents closed the park down.

In 1990, my brother and I made a trip to Lake George and decided to visit the old spot were Time Town once stood. Weeds had overtaken the entrance, which was guarded by a locked gate. We found a small hole in the gate and squeezed our way in. I knew we were trespassing, but I doubted the police patrolled the area too frequently. We found that the door to the main entrance area was unlocked. Inside were some old brochures and maps of the park. Unfortunately, I was too scared to take anything. We wandered through some other areas and decided that we had pushed our luck enough and headed back to the car.

The park was very unique, with many fun attractions, like a huge slide. To this day, I have never been on a larger slide than the one at Time Town. They also had a great laser light show and a ride where you stepped in an elevator to be transported "back in time" and you would then walk through the Space Caverns. This trip back in time has inspired me to create a website in order to help preserve the memories of this unique and unusual amusement park: http://mywebpages.comcast.net/rememberingtimetown/index.htm.–*Dustin Sullo*

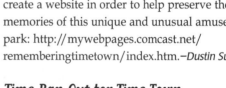

Time Ran Out for Time Town

This old amusement park is located on Coolidge Hill Road in Bolton Landing. In 1996, three teenagers used the desolate spot to practice firing handguns. Later in the winter of the same year, they shot a clerk at the Conoco station in Warrensburg, just ten miles away. When I first went up there in 1997, there were still old houses and a small train, with some papier-mâché characters here and there, all mottled with bullet holes.–*Clayton Gibbs*

Coney Island's Yellow Submarine

Called the *Quester 1*, this sub was built by a blue-collar man named Jerry Bianco, who grew up around Coney Island and worked as a shipyard laborer, repairing ships. His plan was to build a sub to help raise the Italian Line cruise ship *Andrea Doria*, which sank off the New England coast back in 1956. He had no prior submarine experience, but went ahead with his plan nevertheless. The sub, measuring approximately forty-five feet in length, was launched in Coney Island Creek, with much ballyhoo and local media attention, in 1971. Unfortunately, the crane operator lowered the sub into the water before allowing water ballast into the craft, causing it to turn over and sink. It was a PR fiasco. The sub remained docked in the creek until 1975, when a violent storm washed the boat ashore. It's still there, looking very much the worse for wear, just west of the new Home Depot on Cropsey Avenue. If you aren't careful, you'll probably miss it lying alongside some old wooden scow wrecks on the shoreline.

The inside of the conning tower is filled with fuel oil, probably a result of her tanks rusting through. A plywood inner hatch bespeaks of extreme cost-cutting measures taken in the sub's construction. The hatch is covered with flotsam and the bones of dead waterbirds. The outer hull is rusting through badly.–*Gerard Thornton*

Staten Island's Watery Graveyard

The Staten Island boatyard is like a collection of a thousand different stories all trying to be told at once. It seems like a group of ornery old men gathered at a retirement home, each yammering out his own unique life story, trying to outdo his neighbor. Each of the boats has its own tale to tell, each has had its own life, and now each is telling bits and pieces of its past.

The histories of these boats have been all but lost. The only clues are the ones they give now, sitting idle in the muck, watching the rhythm of the tides going up and down. Some were built in pairs, brother and sister ships which then went their own way, plying the rivers, harbors, and oceans as fireboats, tugs, merchant vessels, barges, or ferries.

The boats get more interesting as they age, revealing the complex layers of their construction and the textures of their materials. This is part of their language and their character. In my photographs I try to create portraits that capture their unique personality. *–Shaun O'Boyle*

Arsenal on the Hudson

Two hours north of New York City, in Beacon, the ruins of an old medieval-style castle can be found on an island just a thousand feet off the shores of the Hudson River. Emblazoned on the crumbling walls of the island fortress are the words BANNERMAN'S ISLAND ARSENAL.

The island on which the castle sits, officially known as Pollepel Island, has been the subject of legends dating back to the 1600s. Some local Indian tribes believed the island to be haunted, so it became a sort of safe haven for early Dutch settlers seeking refuge from the occasionally hostile natives.

The castle was built from 1901 to 1908 to warehouse the weapons of Francis Bannerman VI, an arms dealer. Francis, or Frank, was born in Dundee, Scotland, in 1857 and came to the United States at the age of three. He began collecting and selling scrap from the shores near his Brooklyn home at a young age and soon had developed a thriving business. Following the Spanish-American War, he purchased ninety percent of the army's decommissioned weapons and over thirty million rounds of ammunition. He was the first businessman to see the value in army surplus and is often referred to as the Father of the Army and Navy Store. He supposedly even sold a warship to a South American nation embroiled in revolution.

There came a point when the city of New York would no longer allow the weapons king to store his vast cache within the city's limits. Frank then moved his business up the Hudson and built his isolated fortress, which was reminiscent of a castle one might see in his Scottish homeland.

Bannerman was a bit of an oddball. He designed every building on the property himself, refusing to give any of them a single right angle. According to Jane Bannerman, his granddaughter-in-law, "Although Frank

An Unauthorized Visit to the Island Arsenal

We canoed out to Bannerman's island and what impressed me about the place was the incredibly thick vegetation. I had just gotten back from Costa Rica a few months before, and the island reminded me of the Central American rain forests, with the huge variety and quantity of plants. And it was really hot.

The island itself is quite beautiful. We hiked around a bit after shooting the ruins. The place had a peaceful quiet, like most ruins, broken only by the fan boats that were messing around on the Hudson in the afternoon. They were really loud, and we were worried they would attract the attention of the authorities, since we weren't supposed to be on the island.
–Shaun O'Boyle

Bannerman was a munitions dealer, he titled himself to be a man of peace. He wrote in his catalogues that he hoped that his collection of arms would someday be known as 'The Museum of the Lost Arts.'"

Due to suspicions that Bannerman was dealing with the enemy during World War I, troops were stationed on his island until 1918. This broke the patriotic man's heart, and he died shortly after the soldiers' exit at the end of the war. His family continued the business into the 1970s, but based it out of Long Island instead of the famous island arsenal. Eventually they sold the abandoned island complex to the state of New York for a small sum. On August 8, 1969, a fire ravaged the arsenal, leaving it in its present ruined state.

In 1962, seven years before the fire, Frank Bannerman's grandson Charles wrote prophetically of the fate of his family's island fortress:

"No one can tell what associations and incidents will involve the island in the future. Time, the elements, and maybe even the goblins of the island will take their toll of some of the turrets and towers, and perhaps eventually the castle itself, but the little island will always have its place in history and in legend and will be forever a jewel in its Hudson Highland setting."

The island is currently a no trespassing area, and is monitored by video surveillance. Swift currents around it can sweep small boats away easily. A nonprofit group called the Bannerman Castle Trust, Inc., is seeking to preserve and restore the site through its Friends organization, making the island safe for volunteers to work there and eventually for the public to enjoy. If you'd like to become a Friend of the Castle, you can join the preservation efforts by writing to the Bannerman Castle Trust, Inc., P.O. Box 843, Glenham, NY 12527-0843.

Asylums and Hospitals

In terms of eeriness, few experiences can compare to the exploration of an abandoned asylum or hospital. Not knowing what, or who, might lie in wait just around the next blind corner or down the next darkened corridor is enough to make any spine tingle.

New York has dozens of derelict institutions strewn about it. Asylums, tuberculosis centers, and various other medical facilities lie wasted and decaying all over the Empire State landscape. And the adventurous have found their way into all of these buildings. What is it that fascinates us so much about this particular type of abandoned structure? Hospitals remind us of our macabre medical past, of the horrid ways illnesses, especially mental illness, used to be dealt with. To see these reminders of mistreatments from decades ago rocks us to our core.

Wandering the vacant hallways of these spooky old buildings, one cannot help but imagine the suffering once endured by the unfortunate souls whose fate it was to spend their lives imprisoned within those walls. These feelings are made all the more tangible by the artifacts left behind when these institutions finally closed their doors for good. In some, patient records, fingerprints, and mug shots spill forth from overflowing file cabinets. In others, antiquated surgical tools litter the floors of operating rooms. Where fragile minds were once tinkered with, there are padded cells, electroshock tables, draconian restraint devices, and human cages.

These massive, sprawling monuments are often comprised of dozens of buildings, expansive grounds, and networks of underground tunnels to connect the complexes. Though they may be long dead, the power these magnificent monuments possess over those who visit them has not diminished. In fact, in their abandoned incarnations these ancient asylums seem to be even more potent as places of inspiration and personal reflection. They radiate a weird, almost supernatural aura, dark and somber, melancholy and mournful, not found anywhere else.

Asylums of Long Island

Long Island is home to some of the largest and most magnificent abandoned hospitals in the entire state of New York. John and Laura of www.lioddities.com checked in with *Weird New York* to tell us about two of these legendary abandoned facilities—Kings Park and Central Islip.

Kings Park

On the North Shore of Long Island lies a large community of abandoned buildings. Almost like a small city unto itself, Kings Park Psychiatric Center harbored mental patients for over a century. Now most of it lies quiet, bearing silent witness to its own history.

Back in the late 1800s, when Long Island was still mostly farming communities, there was a nationwide movement for better public services. This included publicly funded schools, jails, poorhouses, and asylums for the insane. People were feeling charitable and wanted to make sure the less fortunate and the helpless were cared for. Of course there had been places set aside for the insane in some counties before this. Treatment was hardly humane in these asylums, to say the least, and over-crowding made the situation much worse. Such was the case at Kings Park Lunatic Asylum, the parent hospital of Kings Park Psychiatric Center.

In the asylum, patients were shut up in crowded rooms and earned attention only if they caused a problem. In that case, they were often restrained in crude wooden chairs and leather straps. Due to the lack of space, many wards were located in damp and unventilated basements. In the 1860s, Thomas S. Kirkbride published his enlightened theories on the care of mentally ill patients. One of the requirements of his method was that patients live in a beautiful rural setting. This helped to pressure Kings County into purchasing a large area of land in what is now Kings Park, Long Island, and building an asylum there. It was first operated by the county, but graft and abuses led to its being taken over by the state and renamed Kings Park State Hospital. Many, many patients were treated there until its closing in 1996.

After over a century of caring for the mentally ill, the country seemed to change its mind. Instead of being isolated and cared for, patients were given medication and sent out into the world to try and cope. Often this led hopelessly ill people to the streets; you can still find former patients wandering the sidewalks and roads of many Long Island towns. Currently there are only a few small houses open at Kings Park, and they are used as group homes. Another two buildings are used for the director's house and the park office. The rest of the six-hundred-acre campus is abandoned.

Kings Park was meant to be almost completely self-sufficient; it had its own piggery, farm, power plant, shoe shops, and most other necessary industries. Part of the patient's care was to work at one of these occupations, which not only gave patients a sense of purpose but also helped the asylum survive on a shoestring budget. This all changed in the 1950s, when farming technology made it more profitable to buy mass-produced food and labor laws held that patient labor without salary was indentured servitude. The productive work and hands-on therapy was changed to television and Thorazine. Patients sat idle in dayrooms, which contributed little to their health. This is probably one of the key changes that led to the closing of the asylum.

Part of the grounds of the psychiatric center became Nissequogue Park in 2000 and were opened to the public. Nature trails and a bike path were put in place, and there is a soccer field as well as bird-watching opportunities. Of course entry into the boarded buildings of the psych center is illegal, and the park would prefer you paid more attention to the beautiful river, but some people do venture

During its operation, nearby town residents reported hearing screaming and moaning coming from the asylum.

into the former asylum. From them we get some eerie tales.

Within these halls are horrors, and within these halls are wonders one just needs to know what to look for. In one of the largest buildings, building 93, there is a recreation room on the first floor and all four walls are painted with a touching mural of patient life. The artist captured the room exactly as it was, perhaps back in the 1950s. There is one panel depicting patients using a loom, and the broken loom is just across the room. No one knows for sure who painted the murals, but it is believed that a patient was the artist.

During its operation, nearby town residents reported hearing screaming and moaning coming from the asylum. While things were much improved under the care of the state, abuse happened, as it does in every system. It is doubtful, though, that abuse explains all the screams heard nightly. More likely they were the torments of patients whose minds had betrayed them.

Some patients have been known to return to the asylum after its closing. For them it is the only home they have ever known and the only place where they feel comfortable. But is it possible that some former patients remain even after death?

There are a few ghost stories surrounding the buildings. In the medical/surgical building, a park employee was once going into the basement to do some work. Because he knew patients often return, he yelled out, "Hello," as he went so as not to frighten anyone. Once he entered the basement, a voice called out, "Hello," back to him, but no one could be found. That park employee made a very brief stay in the building.

There have also been numerous sightings of a white apparition, shaped vaguely like a person, floating around the place. A group of explorers in building 93 saw a white being with black eyes and mouth walking down the hall, and all of their cameras failed to turn on when they tried to snap a photo. Supposedly, it walked through one of the explorers, and he reports having felt the most horrible feelings he ever experienced. Kings Park also had a few cemeteries for patients. One of them was up on a hill. The tombstones are inscribed only with numbers. A group of young people reported heading back from the cemetery down a long and hilly road when a white humanoid form chased after them. When it got close, they say it issued a growling noise, but this was no animal they had ever seen before.

There have also been accounts of slamming noises in building 93. One group had just entered the building when a loud banging began. It was described as sounding like the building being shaken, and it continued to bang loudly and rapidly for about thirty seconds. It then suddenly stopped. This is not the only account of odd banging in the building. While it is understandable that old buildings settle, these noises are louder than what is usually heard, and people who repeatedly visit abandoned buildings quickly learn the difference.

The former Kings Park Psychiatric Center still lies abandoned and has managed to shrug off at least three potential developers, but some say demolition is just a matter of time.

Central Islip

The asylum at Central Islip was an offshoot of the larger ones in New York City, such as the Hart and Blackwells Island asylums. The first patients arrived there in 1889, sent for the therapeutic benefits of a more rural way of life. Central Islip had many of the same problems that the nearby Kings County asylum was having, such as overcrowding, and eventually the state took it over as well. At 1,000 acres, it was the largest state hospital in the area. (Pilgrim State was the largest in population.)

One of our favorite things about Central Islip is the

shape of the buildings. Two sets of buildings, which are now gone, were connected with short corridors, making them seem like two long buildings. They stretched over a mile and were known as the String of Pearls, because of their length and the workmanship put into them. They were so large that they had their own power plant, railroad spur, and utility buildings.

Another unique structure, which is still standing, is the Sunburst Building, once used for the care of patients with tuberculosis. It was built with a very long corridor that stretches into a half circle. Intersecting the arced hallway are twelve wards and a center section with dining halls and offices. These wards, unlike those in most other buildings, didn't have dayrooms. Instead, the patients would spend their waking hours in a caged-in porch. Since tuberculosis is a lung ailment, it was thought that the fresh air was good for the patients, who would be outside on those porches even in the dead of winter.

In 1984, when deinstitutionalization was happening at a rapid rate, most of Central Islip was closed and the New York Institute of Technology moved in. The school's campus and what was left of the old psychiatric center coexisted until 1996, when the last of the asylum vacated. N.Y.I.T. is still there, though, and that campus has always seemed very unusual, since mixed in with academic buildings are abandoned in-patient buildings, a power plant, and a laundry building. Many of the psychiatric buildings still have their old furniture and patients' belongings in them, left behind and forgotten by most.

Many of the patient buildings have survived relatively untouched, even though they have been abandoned for

between eight and twenty years. This is most likely because the campus feeds electricity to them and keeps on the lights, which in some of the larger abandoned buildings is a really eerie effect.

According to a campus facility manager, some parts of the center are haunted. He claims that in one building people constantly hear children that aren't there. After doing some checking, he found that building was once used to house disturbed children. He also went on to say that in other places people have reported to him that they heard screams and moans.

But the population that seems most represented here is not the haunted, but the homeless, who have taken to a couple of buildings as a refuge. One building, which was once a bakery, is littered with garbage, mattresses, and a handwritten sign that says something along the lines of, "Leave my stuff alone or I will get you!"

Rumor has it that N.Y.I.T. wants to close its Central Islip campus, leaving the future of this weird and wondrous place hanging in the balance. Only time will tell the fate of this abandoned place.

More Mad Asylums

Long Island isn't the only part of the state to harbor abandoned hospitals. New York is literally covered with them! Here are some stories from a number of other great abandoned institutions found across the Empire State.

Buffalo

For most of the twentieth century, America's mentally ill were institutionalized in asylums built according to the Kirkbride plan, a system of treatment that at its inception was thought to be revolutionary. Previously, mentally ill members of society were imprisoned or locked away in their homes and cared for by their families, so the concept of hospitalization as opposed to outright imprisonment for the mentally ill was seen as humanitarian.

But very quickly in the experience of the Kirkbride plan, things took a turn for the worse. Hospitals became overcrowded, resources became scarce, and patient abuses became increasingly more frequent. Mental hospitals went from being considered refuges of compassion and hope to dark places of despair and torment.

One such place was the Buffalo Psychiatric Center. Here the abuses were even more severe than at most hospitals, and the remains of this cursed place still stand as a reminder of how terribly things went wrong.

The facility built in Buffalo was unique even among Kirkbride hospitals. Instead of being located in a rural area, it was only a few miles from downtown. When the hospital opened in 1871, it held three hundred patients, the number it was designed for, but by the 1930s it was home to over three thousand patients. With this number, there was simply no time to treat every patient properly and no room to adequately house them. Patients were left to sleep on top of each other in filthy, dank hallways. Some even slept outdoors during cold Buffalo winters.

By the middle of the century, the asylum system was becoming obsolete. There were new drugs for mental illness and new theories on how best to treat these

by one subway line and, more prominently, via cable car. The entire island has an air of mystery about it, right down to the shops that line its main street. Instead of having names, they seem to be labeled only with such signs as CHINESE RESTAURANT and THRIFT STORE, like some faceless catalogue of places. Most strange of all is the huge gothic complex of abandoned buildings that stands on the island's southern tip.

unfortunates. This, coupled with patient abuse and the inadequacy of the hospital facilities, led to its closure in the early 1970s. It still stands today, a testament to a great idea gone awry. Not surprisingly, rumors abound that the castlelike structure is haunted by the ghosts of former patients who died there. They are said to roam the grounds frequently and to love most of all the tunnels that lay beneath the buildings, connecting them.

Roosevelt Island

Many residents of the five boroughs of New York City will tell you that they consider Roosevelt Island, a small strip of land in the middle of the East River between Manhattan and Queens, to be the strangest area of that sometimes strange city. The island, located beneath the Queensboro Bridge, is accessible from the Manhattan side

Anyone who has driven along Manhattan's FDR Drive has probably wondered about these massive structures, which are illuminated by spotlights at night. (Residents of apartments on the Manhattan shore opposite the island have paid to have the buildings lighted to add to their view.) One of the crumbling structures, known as the Smallpox Hospital, housed New York's sufferers of that disease for many years. Another building on Roosevelt Island, the New York City Home for the Insane, helped alleviate crowding at Manhattan's Bellevue Hospital. It has lain completely abandoned since 1955.

Today, the hospital's remains serve as both scenery and a focal point for storytellers and adventurers. Access is restricted, though, and fences abound, so we can't recommend that you try to visit these haunting ruins. Looking at them from Manhattan can be scary enough.

Utica

The New York State Lunatic Asylum at Utica was first opened in 1843. This massive structure, considered to be one of the nation's finest examples of Greek revival architecture, still stands today, although it has not been used for many, many years. Instead, its ruins remain, hinting at a storied history.

Utica started out with idealistic goals, but like many other asylums built in the nineteenth century it quickly fell into chaos. Overcrowding plagued the hospital for its entire existence. It has been closed for many decades and today hosts only the ghosts of the past and the curious of the present. Besides stunning architecture, explorers have stumbled upon murals patients left behind, painted on these empty halls by unknown and forgotten hands.

Coolidge Hill Tuberculosis Clinic

On Coolidge Hill Road in Bolton Landing, there are several dirt pull-offs along the winding road; one has a bright orange, spray-painted chain across it with a posted sign on it, warning not to hunt. After a quarter-mile, well-defined trail, I saw an old hospital cart. Following the trail, I soon discovered an old paddy wagon–style truck that was rusted beyond belief. Not far from there was the old tuberculosis clinic.

Since it was originally made of stone and wood, not much was left, other than a beautifully crafted archway and a very eerie barred-up cellar. I was told that at night, the screams of patients could still be heard. I didn't hear any screams, but I did hear a flute playing—from where, I have no idea. The woods surrounding that area are pretty thick and full of lots of old rusty relics of a time nearly forgotten.—*Clayton Gibbs*

Glued to an Asylum Floor

There are a lot of haunted places in New York, but one that really sticks out is Letchworth in Rockland County, an old run-down asylum that was shut down and is now state property. There are stories of how patients were tortured there, and some say they still haunt the numerous buildings. My cousin

and his friends once roamed these buildings, and some of the stories were really scary. There were noises of a little girl giggling at the end of the hallway. They said they heard desks dragging across the floors above them. Certain rooms would be freezing cold in the middle of the summer almost as if something was there with you.

As they were on their way down one of the hallways, one friend just collapsed and couldn't get up, as if she was glued to

A Chilling Place

In Rockland County, there is a small village called Letchworth. It is the home of an abandoned mental institution. Of course many rumors have surfaced about the old mental hospital. I know that my friends have experienced many things there, including hearing noises and seeing ghosts. The old hospital still contains some leftover patient files, writing on the wall, and old beds. Walk into the hospital, and you can feel nothing but chills going through your body.–*Anonymous*

the floor. When she finally got up, she said it felt like something ran through her. My cousin had experienced something similar, and his friends said it was like he saw a ghost. They tried taking pictures, but some didn't come out and others had little white orbs floating by. You have to be careful, because there is no trespassing. The cops actually came in and kicked us out one time. They said, "You guys are sick. We didn't even want to come in here after you." So that's gotta say a lot.–*Matty J.*

Haunted and Horrible

There is a place in Thiells, off Exit 14 of the Palisades Parkway, called Letchworth Village. It housed the mentally ill, mentally retarded, and people of lower intelligence. The abuse these people suffered there was horrible. The grounds are expansive, and the boys' side (where the haunted hospital is) is still intact but abandoned. The girls' side, however, is being partially used and developed. It is perfectly legal to be on the grounds during the day, as I was told by a cop who was parked near the girls' side during one of my travels there. People go there to jog, walk dogs, etc. However, before you get to the girls' side there is a research building, which I am assuming is the one next to a big smokestack. I know the hospital is haunted, and I'm sure the research building is also, because the research they did was horrible. —*Lostindelirium*

No Sunny Days at Old Rockland Psychiatric

One of the places I love to go to scare myself and others is the old Rockland Psychiatric Hospital, between Stony Point and Bear Mountain. The place has been abandoned for years, ever since the newer structure went up. When you drive through the main entrance, the first thing that hits you is how cold it is. I've been up there in the middle of July in the middle of the day, and it is still bone-chilling cold. When you enter, the sun always seems to disappear behind clouds and never comes out until you leave, no matter how long you stay there. I have gotten out of the car a few times there but have always hastily gotten back in. When you step outside, you feel your mind slipping and it's almost like someone is trying to drag you toward the buildings. My friends have said that their cars, never prone to breaking down or stalling, have coughed a few times and tried to die before exiting the compound. The last time I went there was almost a year ago. The cops don't look too highly on people stopping and gawking. —*DvlKitty2004*

Snuck a Peek into the Rockland Psycho Ward

My mother, knowing that I'm a morbidly curious "historian" took me to the Rockland County Psychiatric Hospital in Orangeburg. Half the property is new and operational, but there is another half that has been abandoned for what looks like many years. The decay and neglect of the hospital were evident. I was able to crawl up and peer into one of the windows that wasn't boarded up. It was creepy, to say the least, with smiling animals painted on the wall and an empty blackboard that looked down at what seemed to once have been a school for mentally disturbed children. To add to the ambiance, we came across a rib cage down the road from the hospital that was probably that of a deer picked clean by scavengers. —*Linda Mayer*

Harlem Valley

If you are ever in the area of southern New York on route 22, look for the Harlem Valley State Hospital in the town of Wingdale. There are nearly twenty large buildings for the mentally insane, both housing and a hospital. Some of the buildings are from as far back as the 1890s. In the late 1970s the hospital was closed due to major internal corruption and malpractice. There are many accounts of mistreatment and deaths. In the 1930s, a fire was deliberately set in a section in the housing facility. It killed thirteen people while injuring twenty-nine more.

In the 1950s, a modern twelve-story high medical facility was built adjacent to the original one. I'm not a believer or follower of ghosts, but there is major activity in the first and second floor of the basement. Basement floor one contains the morgue and a fallout shelter from the cold war. An animal cage is also present. I believe it held monkeys or primates of some sort, due to the presence of large swinging ropes and large feeding bowls and branches. Even two stories below the ground, one can hear the sounds of a pack of wild dogs. This is the scariest part of the whole adventure.

Once above ground, on the eleventh floor, there is a breaker room, and every wire is ripped out. There's absolutely no electricity in the place. But on the sixth floor, a light is on. The light switch is ripped from the wall. The tenth floor has an operating room. Here they did lobotomies and other treatments that are now outdated. On the fourth floor, there are isolation rooms one after another. Inside, there are blood stains and carvings of inmates' names. *–Mike Barrett XXX*

Asylum Is Fun for the Whole Family

My family had way too much time on its hands, so we snooped around an abandoned mental hospital in the area that my stepdad told us about. It's known as the Harlem Valley mental institute. It is in Wingdale.

My entire family wanted to see it. They brought a video camera with them to record every bit of it. Bad news: No flashlights, so we had to leave. Good news: Mom got some digital photos of the morgue; then her camera suddenly stopped working. Our family friend Joe claims he heard a dog growling in a staircase, but nothing was there. Later on he heard deep breathing somewhere else by the exit.

They returned without me (and with flashlights and a camera). It was nighttime, and the cops were on patrol. They went in and got pretty deep. They found a room with a cage in it. Around it, graffiti said DON'T FEED THE ANIMALS.

There is a legend that says in 1991, a man went exploring in the hospital, and in one of the over eighty buildings on the property, he was pronounced missing, never to be found. And the caretaker told me that he constantly has to go up to the seventh floor, in the operating room, and shut the lights off. There is supposedly a ghost that runs along the halls, and if you happen to get in its way, it shoves you to the side.—*Michael Krukiel*

Flying to the Moon at Wingdale

During the 1970s, I was a mental health worker at Wingdale and lived in one of the fairly Gothic but really beautiful staff residences on the property. One day while I was out, my husband was upstairs, playing Frank Sinatra on the record player. Suddenly one of the residents of the facility appeared in the doorway. We don't know where he came from or how he got in. He didn't seem threatening, but he did seem mesmerized by the music, which happened to be Sinatra's "Fly Me to the Moon." Slowly, in his baggy institutional garb, not exactly the picture of cool, the man started to move to the music, swaying, then bopping a little. My husband, not really knowing what to do, sensed that the song was having some kind of calming effect on the man. So he got up and started dancing with him! And so the two of them were there, bopping to Frank Sinatra's "Fly Me to the Moon" when the aides came to take the man away. It was pretty weird!—*JackieandJohn*

Seaview Hospital and the Farm Colony

Seaview Hospital and the Farm Colony were collectively named the first historic district on Staten Island, in 1985. Though Seaview Hospital is still in operation, a group of abandoned buildings lie within its confines. Eight buildings were erected between 1909 and 1911, as men's and women's wards for tuberculosis patients. Until the 1920s, these buildings, plus outlying powerhouses and nurses' quarters, made up the extensive hospital complex.

The buildings of Seaview are famous for their exterior terra-cotta murals depicting doctors, nurses, and children, meant to cheer up the patients of the clinic. In 1972, four of the original eight ward buildings were destroyed to make way for more modern facilities. The gorgeous murals of the remaining four are now suffering from decay and neglect. Pieces of the pastel-tinted façades have cracked due to water permeation and freezing, and some of the stone has broken loose. Major efforts have been made by grassroots preservation organizations to save the buildings and the murals, which seem to be in a race against time and the elements.

The hospital lies right across Brielle Avenue from the Farm Colony, which has a distinctly different origin, although the two facilities were run by the same administration at certain points. The colony was founded not as a tuberculosis clinic but as a poor farm, a place where New York City's downtrodden could help themselves and society.

In 1902 the Richmond County Poor Farm was renamed the New York City Farm Colony. Its purpose was described as follows: "While the inmates at other institutions under the Department of Public Charities look around and have nothing whatever to do, here they pay for their board twofold by their labor, working on the farm raising vegetables, not only for themselves, but for other unfortunates. No healthier spot within miles of Greater New York can be found . . . a beautiful site with its fertile fields, where any kind of vegetable thrives. All it needs is cultivation. . . ."

The recent history of the Farm Colony is pretty dismal. The last residents were removed in 1975. The city has since tried to sell off the land, but local activists have been successful in blocking its development. In 1983 and 1984, major strides toward the complex's preservation were made when twenty-two acres were designated as an untouchable greenbelt. Currently, the abandoned portions of Seaview and the Farm Colony have uncertain futures. While historians, developers, and environmentalists battle over how the site will be used, many teenagers and adventure-seekers have figured out their own uses for it.

Mental Mayhem at the Farm Colony

The old mental homes on Staten Island are on Brielle Avenue off Rockland Avenue. The story there goes like any other—these were mental homes, with many nut cases who were tortured, mutilated, raped, and murdered by the staff and others.

Many kids and adults began to be fascinated with the whole story and decided to check it out. Most go in once and do not go back again. I know I won't. The most common things people encounter are the moaning and groaning, the scratching on the ground, and the coldness. My friend still swears to this day that he felt a constant tugging of a little hand at his pants the whole time in there. Other common things are finding dolls hung from trees, the occasional carcass of an animal, and leftover medical equipment.—*Anthony*

Still Haunted by Visit to Seaview

At first I was afraid to go, so I gave my video camera to a brave few to check out the place. Upon viewing the tape, I noticed really strange things that cannot be explained. One was a face—a guy turned off the light, and a face appeared in the darkness. Then strange sounds occur in the background while my friends are walking through the buildings. I got up enough courage to go to the asylum, this time with ten friends and a video camera. I saw things that freaked me out. There definitely was a strange presence surrounding one building. We left there at four a.m., and all went to my house to watch the video—the loud growls that were in the recordings were not heard while we were there. I know because I would have run the hell out of there if I had heard them. While exploring the buildings' basements, we saw a dead, dismembered dog lying on a rusty bed. I noticed a painting of a man with scissors holding what looked like a baby—it was weird. The visit to the sanatorium has haunted my thoughts.—*Musiccrazy22*

Tunneling Beneath Seaview

My cousin used to work the graveyard shift over at Seaview as a security guard back in the late '70s. It is true that there were tunnels underneath the complex (which was huge). My cousin used to tell me about the few patients who would escape into these tunnels (and most of the time attack anyone who came down there (which is understandable, since they were so horribly abused). After it was closed down, they eventually built a college campus over it. —*Rolf Celones*

Gone but Not Forgotten

For one hundred and three years, Saint Elizabeth's orphanage stood on Mount Loretto on the windswept southwestern shore of Staten Island, overlooking the vast expanse of Raritan Bay. At any given point up until its closing in 1988 the Catholic institution was home to up to three hundred and fifty girls whose parents were lost or unable to care for them properly. The immense building sat on over two hundred acres of land that was decorated with ornate statuary and small cottages.

After it closed, the dark and foreboding abandoned orphanage became a hangout for adventure-seekers and local kids. The intimidating statuary and the looming empty buildings became a popular attraction for nighttime revelers. Tales of hauntings and strange sounds emanating from the massive vacant building spread rapidly.

Sadly, in March 2000, St. Elizabeth's burned down in a spectacular fire that raged for three days. Over one hundred and fifty firefighters fought the inferno, unable to put it out. The fire left Saint Elizabeth's standing as a burnt-out husk of its former elegant and imposing self. The only undamaged remnant was a copper cross that was mounted on the top of the building. The structure was deemed irreparably damaged and was demolished that April.

Two local boys, age sixteen and fifteen, were found to be the arsonists who had started the blaze. It seems ironic that the orphanage, which had provided help and home to thousands of children over the course of its existence, was ultimately taken down by two wayward youths.

The Most Evil Place on Staten Island

The most evil place in Staten Island is the old Mount Loretto, located on Hylan Boulevard in the Tottenville/Princes Bay area. One time I was there with six friends of mine, and we decided to go into the old building. It was supposed to be haunted by several hundred ghosts of small children who were beaten and killed by the nuns and priests who used to run the place.

Anyway, one of my friends decided to go in. The only way in is through a window, and this might sound a bit far-fetched, but she put about one third of her body in, and by the time she turned toward us to get her other leg in, she had been thrown about three feet out of the window and onto the ground outside the building. She swears that something pushed her, and I have heard several stories after that of people experiencing extreme violence upon entering the building. I believe whatever is in there wants no part of the outside world coming in.–X

The Haunted Shack in the Woods

Back in 1985, my parents came up with the most brilliant idea of purchasing a trailer, which was located on a campsite in Roscoe. As a fourteen-year-old, I was less than amused. Being crammed in a small trailer in the middle of nowhere with your ultra un-hip parents was no way a kid wanted to spend their weekends and vacation time. In retrospect, that trailer wasn't the most horrible place to spend some time. It was situated right on the Beaverkill River, where we would fish, swim, and go tubing. Plus there was always the Haunted Shack.

The story was relayed to us by our trailer neighbors, who were not inbred, toothless, moonshine-makin', bloodhound-ownin' yokels, but fine upstanding members of their respective weekday communities. They said that there was a house across the road and a mile or so into the woods that was deserted, dilapidated, and demonic. The place was haunted by the spirits of deceased drifters, miscreants, and vagabonds who used the dwelling as a safe haven throughout the years. Many of them died right there in the house. Upon hearing this, my apathetic teenage ears pricked up with interest. I wanted to go there!

To my complete and utter surprise, both my parents had the same yearning I did. Before I knew it, the three of us, led by two of our trailer neighbors, were marching out of the trailer park and traipsing up a barely recognizable path through the woods.

We seemed to be walking for a long time toward nothing, when one of my neighbors suddenly cried out, "There it is!" A dark, foreboding structure started to appear in the thick woods. But unlike the haunted houses I was accustomed to seeing in the movies, this one was rather tiny. The place was made of shoddy wood that looked like it was once painted white but was now dark gray, weathered, and covered in ivy.

The windows had been broken years ago. The door was peeling and warped from decades of wind, snow, and rain. I remember thinking that it definitely looked haunted, but should be known as the Haunted Shack. Thus it was newly christened.

No matter how small this place was, it still gave off an ominous vibe. So much so that even my parents looked a bit frightened. That scared me even more, and when my neighbors suggested we go inside, I was extremely hesitant. But I was sure as hell not staying outside in the dark creepy forest . . . alone!

With the twist of the rusty doorknob and a push from my neighbor's shoulder, the door swung open. What lay inside made my heart instantly jump into my throat. The entire place, which consisted of one big room, was covered from top to bottom in black soot. It smelled of mildew, oil, and decay. As we crept inside, I noticed the cardboardlike walls, the torn curtains, the decrepit but perfectly made bed with the soiled blue blanket, the table piled high with dinnerware, and the numerous rusty coffee cans. The cans covered every inch of the dirty counters. I inched closer and peered inside one, half expecting it to be filled with human bones or rotting flesh. Instead it contained an assortment of nails. An assortment of rusty nails! I looked in the next rusty can, which was filled with rusty screws. The next had rusty bolts in it.

I looked over and saw my father opening up one of the drawers in the broken dresser near the bed. He grimaced for a moment, stuck his hand in, and started to pull something out. I surmised it would be a decapitated raccoon head or a mummified human foot. Instead it was a rusty can opener. He plunged in with his other hand and pulled out another rusty can opener. "The entire drawer is filled with can openers," he said, laughing.

Apparently, the last occupant of this shack was an

From all the haunted house movies I had seen, I half expected a sorrowful voice to bellow forth as we left, "Come back with my can openers!!!" But all we were met with when we walked out was the loud thud of the door slamming behind us.

All the way back, we chuckled about the so-called Haunted Shack in the middle of the woods. Sure it was creepy, ominous, and extremely weird, but haunted? Come on now.

The last time I saw the shack was around 1994. My parents sold their trailer soon after, and there was no more reason to go up to Roscoe. But I still think about it a lot. I can close my eyes and picture myself slowly creeping up to the dwelling, cautiously pushing open the door and instantly being engulfed in the glorious musty smell. I can see the bed, always perfectly made with its dirty blanket and the rows of rusty coffee cans filled to their brims with nonsense. And when I go visit my parents' house, there is no escaping the Haunted Shack—especially if you need a can opened. Dad still has those two can openers and proudly uses them whenever he can. Ten years after the fact, and that shack can still creep into my present thoughts. You know, maybe in some regard that shack was haunted after all, because it has really done a number on me.—*Qraig De Groot*

anal retentive collector of useless junk. It made us all feel a bit relieved. But just for a moment.

Suddenly, the shack was flooded with light. We all jumped ten feet out of our socks. All of us that is, except for my mother. She spun in a fit of laughter, pointing up to the light chain she had pulled on the dangling light fixture. The Haunted Shack in the middle of the woods filled with rusty kitchen gadgets was still wired with electricity. Now that was just plain weird.

We picked through more drawers, discovering a collection of rusty knives and some other rusty utensils. The bare bulb lighting the dingy room added to the eeriness of the place. We unanimously decided to leave, but not before my father pocketed two of the can openers he found.

INDEX
Page numbers in bold refer to photos and illustrations.

WEIRD NEW YORK

By
CHRIS GETHARD
Executive Editors
Mark Moran and Mark Sceurman

ACKNOWLEDGMENTS

First and foremost, this book would not exist (nor would my life have turned out half as strange as it has) without the influence of Mark Moran and Mark Sceurman. Thank you both for giving me the opportunities you have and blazing the trail that I have willingly followed you both down for the past five years. I was your biggest fan before you guys ever hired me, and I remain so to this day.

I must also thank the like-minded individuals who graciously submitted materials to this book. To every single person who contributed words or photos, whether they were ultimately featured in this book or not, thank you. Thank you for your help, your interest, and your guidance in the completion of this project. John and Laura Leita of www.LIOddities.com and Clayton Gibbs were particularly inspiring in their vast knowledge of Long Island and Warren County, respectively, as well as their willingness to work with me in documenting this strange state we all live in.

I must also thank my parents, for not blinking twice when my professional interest turned toward traipsing through the woods looking for ghosts, and who have been ridiculously supportive of every cockamamy idea I've pursued in life.

I'd also like to thank everyone at the UCB Theater in Manhattan for being the funniest, oddest gang of people I know.

Publisher:	Barbara J. Morgan
Assoc. Managing Editor:	Emily Seese
Editor:	Marjorie Palmer
Production:	Della R. Mancuso
	Mancuso Associates, Inc.
	North Salem, N.Y.

PICTURE CREDITS